IONIAN TRADE AND COLONIZATION

BY

CARL ROEBUCK

I. The Eastern Mediterranean

IONIAN TRADE AND COLONIZATION

BY

CARL ROEBUCK

ARES PUBLISHERS INC.
CHICAGO MCMLXXXIIII

Exact Reprint of the:
New York, 1959 edition
ARES PUBLISHERS INC.
7020 NORTH WESTERN AVE.
CHICAGO, ILLINOIS 60645
Printed in the United States of America
International Standard Book Number:
0-89005-528-9

Preface

This study of the economic development of Ionia before the Persian Wars has grown out of several articles on Greek trade. In them I found myself grappling with two problems of early Greek history which have been the subject of recent controversy, how to assess the economic factor and how to define the role of Ionia. It seemed that some clarification might be made by studying their interrelation. Although Ionia was a colonial area of post-Mycenean Greece, it rapidly became the scene of significant achievement, the epic poetry of Homer and the literature, art and speculation of the sixth century. By that time this cultural accomplishment rested on a substantial economic basis and Ionian luxury was becoming a term of reproach. I have tried to reconstruct the growth and character of this prosperity, to describe how such difficulties as the lack of metals and of land and food to care for an increasing population were met. The Ionians found a solution to them in an extensive network of trade and colonization from Spain to the Black Sea. In so doing they (and perhaps Corinth also) enabled Classical Greece to tap the resources of the Mediterranean as a whole and to expand the organization of its limited agrarian economy. Since we are just beginning to acquire more precise archaeological information of western Asia Minor and of many of the Greek colonial regions, some of the conclusions drawn will necessarily be modified. Specialist knowledge could amplify or correct some of them at the present time, but perhaps a synthesis is the best means of obtaining a new perspective. If it stimulates further work, at least one purpose will have been achieved.

Since the study has been a long time in preparation, it is difficult to notice specifically the assistance and suggestions made in conversation and by letter from all those who have been interested. In particular, thanks are due to John M. Cook of the University of Bristol, who not only made his knowledge of western Asia Minor and of Old Smyrna available but read the manuscript in its first draft. Chapters I and II owe much to his assistance—and to the excavation of Old Smyrna. Acknowledgement is also due to R. M. Cook of Cambridge University, Professor Max Cary, Rodney Young of the University of Pennsylvania Museum, Machteld Mellink of Bryn Mawr College, Professor J. A. O. Larsen, and Professor Homer Thompson of the Institute for Advanced Study. Travel and work in Turkey in 1954 were made more profitable by the courteous assistance of the officials of the Museums at Izmir and Istanbul. I am appreciative of the stimulating articles on early Ionia by G. M. A. Hanfmann of Harvard University, if not always in agreement with them. Finally thanks are due to the members of the Monograph Committee of the Archaeological Institute of America for their constructive reception of the manuscript. The work was facilitated greatly by the award of a Fellowship from the Guggenheim Foundation coupled with a year's leave of absence in 1953–54 from Northwestern University. This was spent in the hospitable quarters of the Institute for Advanced Study at Princeton and of the American School of Classical Studies at Athens, Greece.

Northwestern University, Carl Roebuck
Evanston, Illinois.

Table of Contents

Maps

IONIA
AEGEAN SEA
LESBOS
CHIOS
SAMOS
IKAROS
KORSEAI
OENUSSAE IS.
AEOLIS
LYDIA
CARIA
Tmolus
Messogis
Latmus
Mykale
Sipylos
Mimas
Korykos
Gulf of Elaia
Gulf of Smyrna
Gulf of Erythrae
Gulf of Ephesus
Gulf of Miletus
Hermus River
Hyllos River
Lykos River
Caystér River
Maeander River
Gygean Lake
Sardis
Elaia
Pitone
Myrina
Kyme
Larissa
Neon Teichos
Phocaea
Magnesia
Nymphaeum
Bel Kave
Old Smyrna
Smyrna
Klazomenai
Teos
Lebedus
Colophon
Notion
Larisa
Belevi
Ephesus
Pygela
Kusch Adassi
Marathesion
Anaea
Panionion
Tschangly
Priene
Magnesia
Tralles
Myus
Miletus
Lade
Erythrae
Çeşme
Chios
Emporion
Kato Phana
Vathi
Samos
Heraion
KILOMETER
0 5 10 15 20 25 30

II. Ionia

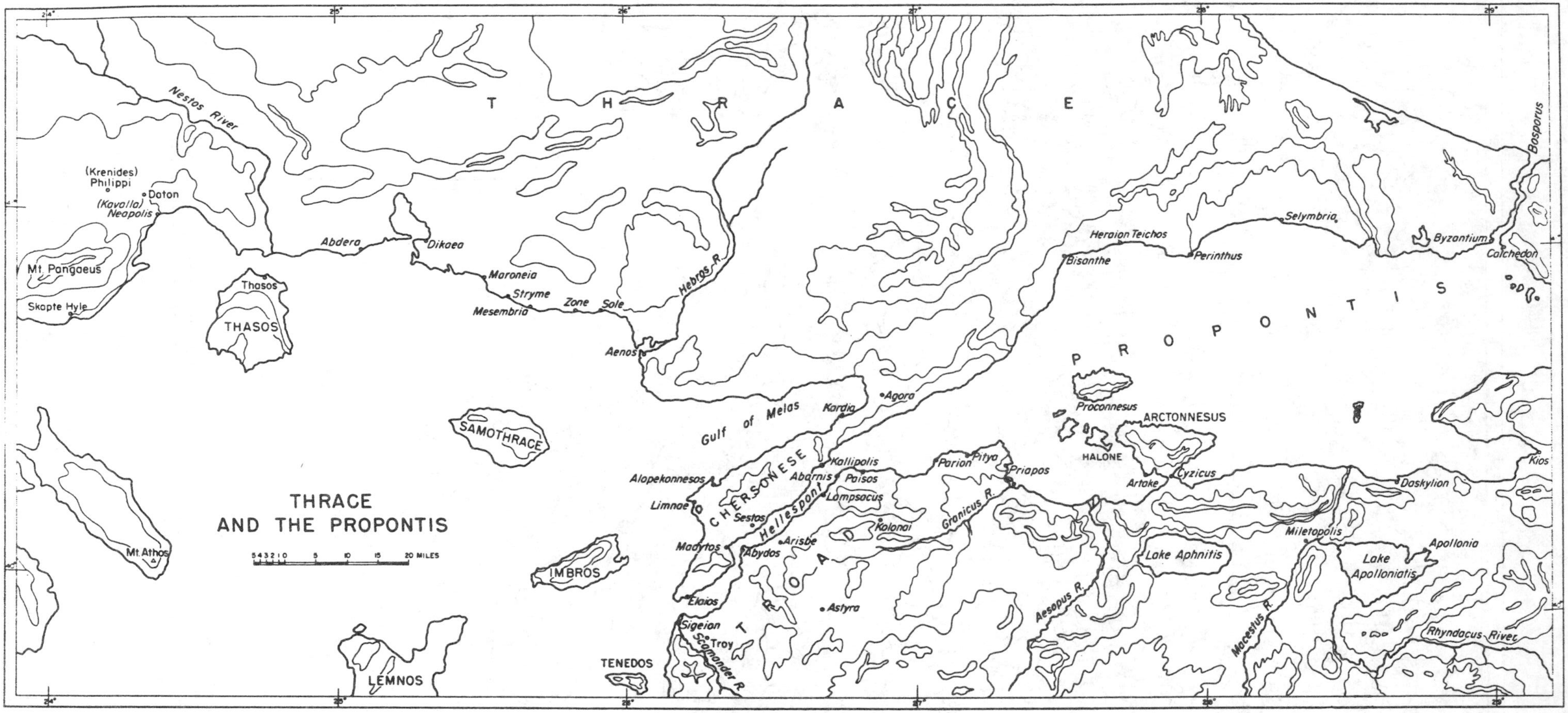

III. Thrace and the Propontis

INTRODUCTION

The Failure of Ionia

The first decisive political test of Greece was in the great war against Darius and Xerxes of Persia in the early fifth century. From that struggle Athens, Sparta and their allies emerged victorious to secure the future development of Hellenism. They had entered it with a failure before their eyes, for the preliminary contest had been fought and lost in western Asia Minor. There, the Ionians had long resisted the raids of successive Lydian kings against their cities only to be ultimately made the subject allies of Croesus in the middle of the sixth century. With Lydia they had been taken over into the fast growing Persian Empire. In 499, despite the seeming hopelessness of the attempt, the Ionian League had led a revolt against Persia, which spread from the Hellespont to Cyprus and lasted five years. This was crushed, and the cities of Ionia were restored to the Empire. The Ionians had failed to retain their freedom and failed to regain it. But Ionia had been a very important and powerful part of the archaic Greek world, and it was natural for its failure, where Athens and Sparta succeeded, to be discussed and a judgment rendered. To the Greeks the paradox of the situation seemed to lie in the contrast between the natural advantages of the Ionian land and the political failure of its inhabitants. A tradition arose in which the Ionians were depicted as weak, luxurious and effeminate.

The writers of the fifth century disparaged Ionian military ability. Herodotus (1.142) praised the land as a place more favored by skies and seasons than any other country and more productive than either the colder and damper regions to the north or the hotter and drier countries to the south. While this observation is not directly coupled with the charge of weakness, only a few lines farther on (1.143.2) he accused the Ionians of being the weakest of the Greek peoples. Hippocrates (*Airs, Waters, Places* 12), however, developed a cause and effect: the middle region of Asia Minor (of which Ionia is obviously a part) was very fruitful, well wooded, very mild and had ample water; its harvests were plentiful, and the offspring of its herds healthy; but this very favoritism of nature denied to its people, both native and Greek, the moral qualities of courage, perseverance, industry and spirit. Hippocrates admitted that institutions might ameliorate the effects of the climate, for those peoples, Greek or non-Greek, not ruled by despots were most warlike. Ionia, however, was ruled by the Great King. Perhaps we should recognize in Herodotus in embryo and in Hippocrates in developed form the rationale advanced by Ionian "natural science" for the defeat of Ionia at the hands of Persia. Ionia was a favored land, but its people had failed, and this failure was accounted for in accordance with the theory of ethnic diversity as the result of environment, both institutional and physical.

Akin to this disparagement on scientific grounds is that of the Ionians in popular opinion. The Athenians faced the rather difficult problem of both blaming Ionia for losing a war with Persia and dragging them into one and, at the same time, stressing their own role as the motherland of Ionia. During the Persian War the Athenians both reproached and coaxed Ionians in Persian service.[1] Later in the fifth century the dramatists developed the tradition of Athens as the mother-city of the Ionians in Asia and established it as the canonical view of antiquity.[2] The Spartans, who were not faced with this problem, could lump both Athenians and Asiatic Ionians together as examples of poor fighting men whom Dorian soldiers need not fear.[3] Apparently this climate of opinion also affected the historical estimates made of the Ionians of earlier generations.

We have already noticed Herodotus' general dictum on Ionian weakness after the fall of Sardis. He did not correct it explicitly elsewhere, but did notice the importance of Miletus in the latter part of the sixth century: the city was at its highest point of prosperity just before the Ionian revolt (5.28), when Aristagoras offered a bribe of fifty talents to Cleomenes of Sparta (5.51) and Hecataeus advocated building a great war fleet to seize control of the seas by using the dedications of Croesus at Branchidae (5.36). Even without such an expenditure Miletus is said have provided eighty ships at the battle of Lade in 494 (6.8). As I have argued elsewhere, Herodotus' history carries in such small details the refutation of his own verdict on the weakness of Ionia.[4] Thucydides' general view that Ionia was at its apogee, but no very high one, in the first part of the sixth century before the Persian conquest seems to have been colored by his own analysis of early Greek history in terms of naval power in war.[5]

Writers of the latter part of the sixth century offered a more naive explanation of Ionia's downfall. They did not have to explain the failure of the Ionian Revolt but did try to account for the Lydian and Persian conquest of Ionia. Explanation was found in the luxurious habits of the Ionian aristocracy who, it was charged, had been debauched by

[1] Her. 8.22.1–2; see also Aesch. *Persians* 176 ff. Herodotus reveals the popular attitude of the fifth century in such passages as 4.142; 5.69.1; 6.12–13.1. See A. W. Gomme, *Commentary on Thucydides* (Oxford, 1945) I 127.

[2] Busolt collects the references in *Gr. Ges.*, I² 285, n. 1; for discussion see C. A. Roebuck, *CP* 50 (1955) 39–40, notes 62,63.

[3] Thuc. 1.124.1; 5.9.1; 7.5.4; 8.25.3: in the speeches by Dorian commanders made in the course of the Peloponnesian War.

[4] Roebuck, *CP* 48 (1953) 9–16.

[5] *Ibid.*, p. 15, n. 7.

their contact with the Lydians. The best example is the well known passage of Xenophanes, which Phylarchus utilized to support his own exposition of the same theme (*FGrHist* 2A, No. 66): Xenophanes' townsmen in Colophon had learned profitless luxury from the Lydians before their conquest by the Persians; clad in varicolored cloaks and with perfumed hair they went arrogantly to the agora.[6] Phylarchus embellished the charge by contrasting this behaviour with their former austerity and adding the indictment of special legislation to facilitate long, drunken parties. Another Hellenistic historian, Douris of Samos, found some material in the poetry of his earlier compatriot Asios (*FGrHist* 2A, No. 60) to develop a similar theme. Asios' lines, if not merely descriptive and the product of the seventh century rather than of the latter part of the sixth, give a similar picture of luxurious habits:[7] the Samians attended festivals at the Heraion in all their holiday finery of fine chitons, with gold fastenings on their flowing hair and bracelets on their arms. It is a charming picture, despite the unfortunate use to which Douris has put it. While we may accept the details of these descriptions, it is important to realize that they are expressions of the moralizing which sought an explanation for Ionia's defeats and found it, as frequently, in the contrast with an earlier and more austere age. Thucydides put such habits in their proper perspective by the simple observation that the members of the old Athenian, as well as of the Ionian nobility, had formerly observed such sumptuous modes of dress (1.6). Sappho took a frank and winning delight in them, regretting that she could not get a Lydian mitra for her daughter, since the law-giver of Lesbos, Pittacus, had forbidden the importation of such luxuries.[8] Another link between Ionian morality and Lydian luxury is the notice given in the sources to the use of *bakkaris*, an unguent, which was a widely exported product of Lydia in the sixth century.[9] Its use was criticized by Hipponax (frag. 19). Thucydides' comment and Alcman's notice of the Lydian mitras worn by his Spartan maidens (1.67–68) indicate that luxury of dress was common to other parts of the Greek world, but, by the time of Bacchylides, Ionia had failed as a political power, and his reference (*Carm.* 17.2) to demoralizing Ionian luxury is routine practice.

Ionia was regarded as a land especially favored by a fine climate and fertility of soil, providing a high standard of living for its upper classes. Some of them, like Sappho,

[6] For this interpretation of the passage see Santo Mazzarino, *Fra Oriente e Occidente* (Firenze, 1947) 193; cf. also Theognis, lines 603–04 and 1103–04; on the passage of Xenophanes see C. Bowra, *CQ* 35 (1941) 119–26; below, p. 11, n. 19.

[7] It is uncertain whether Asios lived in the seventh or sixth century. If the latter, his lines are representative of this reaction against luxury discernible in Xenophanes and in the sumptuary legislation of the sixth century (Mazzarino, *loc. cit.*). Bowra argues that Asios wrote in the fifth century, romanticizing the past (*Hermes* 85 [1957] 391–401).

[8] Mazzarino, *Athenaeum* 21 (1943) 57–58; see also Sappho frag. 99 in which the import of a head ornament (χερρόμακτρα) from Phocaea is mentioned. The passage is very difficult, but at least that much is certain (C. Theander, *Eranos* 41 [1943] 150 ff.). Mazzarino (*Fra Oriente e Occidente* 279) attempts to connect the passage with Phocaean activity in southeastern Spain, but his emendation of the text is too drastic. Phocaean traders hardly exported such manufactured articles from Spain (below, pp. 98–101).

[9] Presumably *bakkaris* was exported from Lydia in the pots known as *lydions* (below, p. 56). Semonides of Amorgos also mentioned *bakkaris* (frag. 14). It was probably a specific Lydian product of the sixth century, while in the seventh *myron* was used for the same purpose (Archilochus frag. 27).

exulted in its wealth, while other poets and philosophers deplored it. Ionia's close relations with Lydia provided some of the luxuries, but probably that country received particular notice because it was associated with the impairment of Ionian independence. However valuable these traditions are as reflecting the thought of both Ionians and other Greeks on the political failure of Ionia, they represent the perspective of only two generations of Ionian experience. To explain how Ionia achieved the state of grace from which it fell we must turn to other evidence and an earlier period.

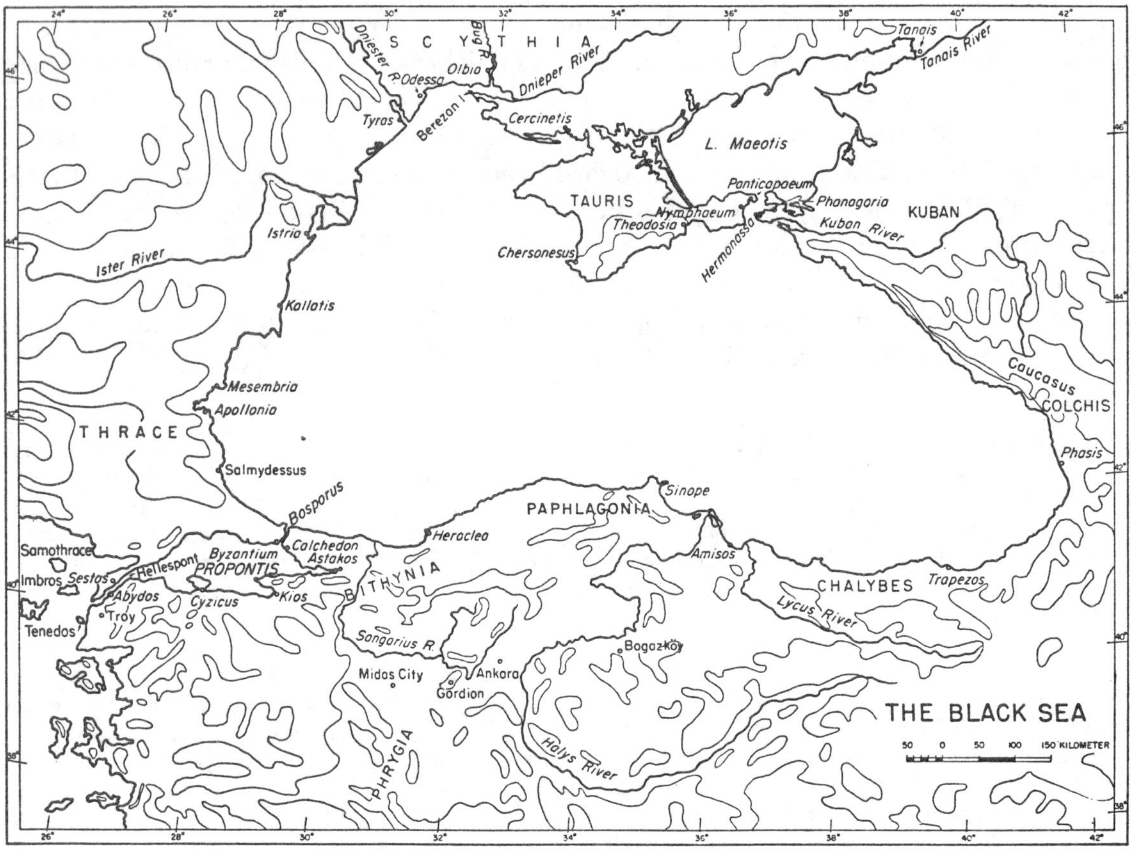

IV. The Black Sea

CHAPTER I

Ionia—The Land

This brief account of that part of the coast of western Asia Minor inhabited by the Ionian Greeks is designed to clarify the chapters which follow rather than to provide any detailed topographical or ecological study. Both would be very desirable, but they should be written by scholars thoroughly familiar with the area by residence and excavation. My own impressions have been formed by only two brief visits at widely separated intervals.[1] Moreover, it is rather arbitrary to describe only Ionia and omit its neighbors, but in antiquity the area (Map II) was considered a geographical as well as a political entity, the territory of the twelve members of the Ionian League. As we have noticed, Herodotus and Hippocrates singled out the central part of the coast as particularly favored in climate and productivity in distinction to the regions to the north and to the south. Strabo limited his Ionia to the traditional frontiers, from Phocaea and the Hermus River on the north to the Posidoneion of Miletus and Caria (13.1.2; 14.1.2). This territory of Ionia was obviously established by the League's political activity and a cherished tradition as to the ethnic unity of its members, but there is some justification for a purely geographical Ionia as well. South of Miletus are Mt. Latmus and the mountainous area of Caria with its forbidding coast line where Greek settlers could only find a hold on the peninsulas of Halicarnassus and Cnidus. Caria's important towns lay inland, and their history, from the Greek point of view, is one of Hellenization of the native inhabitants rather than of the foundation and maintenance of Greek colonies. North of Phocaea and the Hermus[2] Aeolis is drier,

[1] In September, 1939 and April and May, 1954. An easily accessible and useful map of Ionia and western Lydia is Sheet 3 of A. Philippson's series, *Topographische Karte des westlichen Kleinasien*, 1 : 300,000 (6 sheets, Gotha, 1910–13). It is reproduced with geological coloring in *Petermanns Mitteilungen, Ergänzungsheft* No. 172 (1911). For convenience of reference I have followed the spelling of modern Turkish names used by Philippson rather than modern official Turkish usage.

[2] The plain of Smyrna and the land up to the Hermus River were originally Aeolian, but taken by the Ionians before 800; below, pp. 28–29.

and its plains surrounded by lower and barer hills than in Ionia, thus affording a contrast to the traveler. Aeolis, too, had the reputation of being even more productive than Ionia (Her. 1.149). Ionia itself (Map II) was confined to the coastal plains along the Gulfs of Smyrna, of Ephesus and of Miletus and to the peninsulas which enclose them. While the Greek settlers succeeded in imposing their control over this coastal area and its native population, they were unable to expand inland. For a time the control points for access to the long river valleys were held: Larisa (by Aeolians) for the Hermus; the pass by Bel Kave and Nymphaeum from Smyrna to the river plain of the Hermus and to Sardis; the corridor by Belevi from the plain of Ephesus into the river plain of the Cayster; Magnesia, the key to the Maeander valley. Since these outposts marked the farthest points of Greek penetration inland, Ionian territory was oriented to the Aegean rather than to the great river valleys and the central plateau of Anatolia.

The way to Ionia from European Greece led across the Aegean Sea (Map I). At present the goal of cross-Aegean traffic is the large port of Izmir (Smyrna). In antiquity, however, Old Smyrna was not an important trading city and, after its destruction by Alyattes, *ca.* 610, became a village.[3] The termini of the cross-Aegean routes were then Samos and, to a less degree, Chios. This is apparent from the activity of the Ionian and Persian fleets at the time of the Ionian Revolt and during the Persian Wars, for their mustering points in Ionia were Myus, Lade and Samos.[4] The route to Samos from the Saronic Gulf literally may be seen all the way across, from landfall to landfall. Normally, of course, Greek sailors preferred to take advantage of the islands and creep along the coasts. At Samos traffic might split north or south to make its way up to the Hellespont or down to Rhodes.[5] From Samos, too, it could run straight into the Gulf of Ephesus or, with a slight divergence round Mykale, to Priene, Miletus and Myus. Samos was thus the pivot of navigation for western Asia Minor. The other cross-Aegean route, to Chios, led through the Cyclades as far as Mykonos where it turned northeast across the open sea to the south tip of Chios and thence up the strait between that island and the mainland. This, however, seems to have been used more rarely, since it served for a feint in the Persian attack on Naxos in 499.[6] For these journeys across the Aegean a trireme probably took 2 to 3 days under favorable conditions, since Herodotus indicates the traveling speed of a trireme as 700 stades (about 87 miles) by day and 600 stades (75 miles) by night (4.86).

In general, the wind and current system in the Aegean[7] facilitated the use of the southerly route through the islands and helped to develop trade across and in the southern

[3] Below, p. 27.

[4] Her. 3.47–48; 6.95; 5.36 (Myus); 8.132 (Samos); 6.7 (Lade); Xerxes' fleet assembled at Samos in 479 (Her. 8.130). Mardonius is said to have conceived the idea of a line of beacons across the Aegean islands to Sardis to announce his victory (Her. 9.3). This is literally possible by way of the Cyclades to Ikaros, Samos and the mainland.

[5] Samians sailed to Egypt by way of Karpathos (Her. 3.45); Darius' expedition sailed from Cilicia to Samos, then by way of the Cyclades (Naxos, Delos) to Euboea (Her. 6.95).

[6] Megabates set out from Miletus as if to the Hellespont, sailing north to Chios. There, he put in at Caucasa whence he sailed southwest to Naxos (Her. 5.33–34).

[7] *Mediterranean Pilot* IV 10 ff.

Aegean earlier than in its northern waters. In the summer, the proper season for navigation, the winds are steadily from the north from mid-June to early September (the Etesians and Meltemi) with variable and heavy blows for a few weeks before they become established. In the winter the winds in the northern Aegean are cold northeasterly blasts, while in the south they blow from the south and the southwest. Certain local conditions also contributed to this development of the trade in the southern ports. At Rhodes and Samos, for example, sailing conditions were favored by the regular Etesians from the northwest, but hampered at Lesbos and Chios, since the winds blow directly down from the north. Cross-Aegean traffic was drawn to the former ports, while the growth of the latter waited on the settlement of eastern Thrace and the Propontis. After that, shipping south from the Hellespont was aided by the winds, but that north had to creep along the coast using lee shores and headlands. Such ports as Miletus, Samos, Chios and Phocaea were well chosen to provide the needed shelter. The failure of Ephesus and Smyrna and the towns inside the gulfs to develop into important trading cities in this early period may in part be ascribed to the land and sea breezes which are strong enough to set up a heavy chop. They blow in strongly from the sea in the daytime, bringing ships in easily but making it very difficult to get out before midnight. The flow of the currents was, apart from local sets created by the islands and headlands, strongly affected by the winds, so that they, too, contributed to the use of the southerly routes. For example, in the summer the current from the Hellespont runs on each side of Lemnos across the Aegean to the west and then sets south through the channels between Euboea and Andros, between Andros and Tenos, and Ikaros and Mykonos. Since natural conditions made the island of Samos and its adjacent region the key to the Ionian coast, it is convenient to begin a detailed description with that area.

This region (Map II) was the site of the most intensive and earliest Ionian settlement. At the head of the Gulf of Ephesus on the estuary of the Cayster River was Ephesus, and at the base of the Mykale peninsula in the plain of modern Tschangly the Panionion, the federal sanctuary of the Ionian League. Its chief kingship seems to have been established at Ephesus. Between the two were other smaller sites in the fertile plain of which Pygela, Marathesion and Anaea eventually belonged to Ephesus, while Melia, perhaps to be identified with the Carian fort near Tschangly,[8] was probably a Carian town until its destruction early in the League's history. Fom Tschangly to the tip of Mykale the terrain was too rocky to permit settlement, and the only ancient remains are those of small towers probably erected by Samos in the Hellenistic Period. On the north side of the gulf across from Ephesus lay Notion, the harbor town of Colophon, and the important sanctuary of Claros. Colophon was founded inland behind a steep ridge at the southern edge of the large plain which occupies the base of the peninsula forming the north side of the gulf. Midway along the north shore was the small town of Lebedos and nearer the entrance Teos. Samos itself is separated from Mykale by a strait only two and a half kilometers in width. We might envisage the line of migration from Greece coming through the

[8] Below, p. 10.

Cyclades, disdaining the bare spine of Ikaros as unsuitable for settlement, pausing at Samos and then running into the Gulf of Ephesus to the fertile plains at its head or thrusting off a branch around the tip of Mykale to Miletus, Priene and Myus.

SAMOS

The island of Samos was happily situated (Map I) to provide that meeting ground of Orientalizing influences from Cyprus and North Syria, Anatolian from Ephesus and Greek from the Cyclades which have been noticed in the archaeological material from the Heraion. The site of the city (Tigani) was well chosen to control the largest plains on the island and the traffic converging to it by the sea routes (Map II). The archaic city has been investigated only incidentally, since the main effort of the excavators has been directed to the Heraion[9] at the west end of the plain which stretches from Tigani for about seven kilometers along the shore of the strait. Probably the earliest settlement was made on the small promontory where the remains of a Byzantine and Italian *kastro* are now located, but in the archaic period the town grew to include the slopes of a fortified acropolis and of the high ridge through which Polycrates cut his famous water channel. It was walled in that period, but only extensive excavation might clarify its topography in detail. The eastern part of the island, which supported the city of Samos, is much more productive than its rocky western part. In addition to the plain between the Heraion and Tigani another lies between the city and the modern port of Vathi situated on the northeast tip of the island. The latter's harbor is better than that of Tigani, which is exposed to southerly winds, but there is little room for settlement and access to the plain is difficult from the harbor level. Presumably the initial choice at Tigani was made for agricultural reasons, but its advantages for shipping speedily became apparent.

EPHESUS

The site of the town of archaic Ephesus (Map II) has not been definitely identified, and, as in the case of Samos, most of our archaeological material for this period comes from its sanctuary, the Artemision. The locality for the archaic city favored by Keil[10] is the large hill (Panajir-Dagh), the Pion (?), against which the sea once lapped. This long ridge has high defensible points at the north and south ends, but is heavily cut into on the sea side (west) by the construction of the stadium, the gymnasium of Vedius and the great theater of the Hellenistic and Roman city. Keil found some archaic pottery in pockets in the area of the stadium, and I have picked up fifth century black-glazed sherds near the Church of the Seven Sleepers on the northeast corner and on the slope above the Magnesian Gate

[9] For a recent discussion of the chronology of the Heraion and bibliography see G. M. A. Hanfmann, *HSCP* 61 (1953) 4–5, 9–10; below, p. 29, n. 23.

[10] J. Keil, *JOAI* 23 (1926) *Beibl.* 250–56; Hanfmann (*op. cit.*, p. 8) suggests, following Wilamowitz, that the settlement was made from Samos and that the Greeks first occupied the southeast end of the Koressos ridge (Bülbül-Dag).

at the southeast end. The advantages of this site considered with the pottery finds, slight as they are, make it a better candidate for the archaic city than the hill at Ajasoluk near the Artemision.[11] The latter has produced only medieval pottery, but is badly eroded as, for that matter, is the Pion. It might be diffidently suggested that the north end of the Pion was the site of the archaic city and that Ajasoluk was the area of the native settlement whose influences on the cult of Artemis are so apparent. Greek Protogeometric pottery has been found[12] on a site to the south of Koressos (Bülbül-Dag), between Ephesus and Kusch-Adassi but it can hardly mark the place of the earliest settlement of Ephesus itself. Throughout most of its early history Ephesus controlled the Cayster estuary and presumably the narrow river valley to the corridor by Belevi out of which the broad river plain opens. In addition, the city at least disputed and held part of the river plain for a time, since a tradition tells of the capture by Ephesians of a native town, Larisa, under Mt. Tmolus (Strabo 13.3.2). This must have been lost when the kingdom of Lydia was formed under Gyges. Ephesus probably controlled the passage to Magnesian territory also, although it did not take over Magnesia (Muradli) until after the Trerian invasion of *ca.* 650.[13] Its land may have stretched south along the shore of the gulf to the plain of Tschangly, for Pygela, Marathesion and Anaea in that area are eventually known as Ephesian dependencies.[14] Since Ephesus controlled this relatively large amount of fertile land, the city's economy remained largely agricultural and its contacts with the natives close.

PANIONION

The site of the Panionion is still unknown, but reasonably conjectured to be in the southeast corner of the gulf in the plain of Tschangly (Map II).[15] It was not a town site, but a sanctuary administered by the Prienians for the League, which hints that Priene held land in the plain. Samos, too, had claims in this area, which it asserted with varying success,

[11] For Keil's investigations near the Magnesian Gate, unfortunately without result for the location of the archaic city, see *JOAI* 21–22 (1925) *Beibl.* 107ff.; 25 (1928) 33. Ajasoluk: A. Philippson, *Milet* III, 5, p. 29. In antiquity, since the gulf penetrated inland almost to Ajasoluk, the estuary plain was much smaller than at present, which helps to explain Ephesian interest in the territory south of Koressos.

[12] It is reported by J. M. Cook, University of Bristol.

[13] Strabo 14.1.40 (Meineke); I have preferred the emendation, Ἐφεσίους, in the text of Strabo to the reading, Μιλησίους (see the edition of Strabo by Kramer, 1852). The emendation has some palaeographical foundation, accords better with our knowledge of early Ephesus than of Miletus and receives some support from Athenaeus 525c. See also Archilochus frag. 19 and Theognis 1103 for the destruction of Magnesia.

[14] Their affiliations in the early period of Ionian history are obscure. In the division of the land of Melia after the Melian War, as reported by the Hellenistic historian, Maeandrius of Miletus, who is quoted as evidence in a boundary dispute between Samos and Priene (*Ins. v. Priene* No. 37, lines 53–59), it is stated that Miletus lost some territory, the name of which began with AI..., but gained Thebai and Marathesion; the Colophonians lost Anaea; the Samians got Karyon and Dryoussa. According to other historians, however, Samos received Pygela (line 118). While it is hardly possible to accept this evidence of Maeandrius in detail, since it was suspect even in antiquity, it is apparent that several of the important Ionian towns were awarded land in the gulf plain; presumably this had been Carian for the most part, belonging to Melia (Roebuck, *CP* 50 [1955] 32–33). Perhaps Ephesus was the state to which Anaea, lost by Colophon, was given.

[15] *Priene* 24–26.

as the evidence of a long boundary dispute with Priene reveals.[16] It is tempting to see in this plain the first landing place of the Ionian migration to Anatolia—not merely because of the religious significance of the Panionion, but because the broad, level plain stretching back from a sandy beach is the first sight to greet the eyes of a traveler sailing down from Samos along the rocky shore of Mykale. It is likely that the plain had to be wrested from the Carian natives, for we hear of a Carian fort (Melia) in the boundary dispute. The fort is identified with some remains near Tschangly at the outlet of the pass from Priene over Mykale. Although some Protogeometric pottery has been found nearby in graves,[17] this can scarcely have been the site of the sanctuary. Possibly search should be made midway between Tschangly and Daourtla near the road which skirts the south edge of the plain. In a peasant's yard there I examined a door-sill of blue marble which, I was told, came from a nearby field; another such slab from the same place was reported in Daourtla. This, of course, may merely prove that blocks stray from their original position, but the provenance of these was located significantly in relation to a landfall for a ship sailing into the corner of the bay from the north (Ephesus). Projecting prominently from Mykale ridge is a bare conical spur, which may be lined up with the modern surveyor's block in the center of the beach. On this line at the inner edge of the plain was the marble door sill. It seems probable that the sanctuary should be sought at the inner edge of the plain rather than near the beach, despite the fact that an inscription, which fixes the Panionion in this general area, was found in a chapel at the water's edge.[18] Aside from the natural reluctance of the Greeks to spoil good agricultural land with a sanctuary or town site, in the area of the former chapel I have seen only some Roman and modern tile fragments and pottery. It may have been a small landing place. Thorough investigation of the sites in this corner of the gulf would probably be very useful for early Ionian history, perhaps more so than in the heavily overbuilt quarters of the great Hellenistic and Roman cities of Miletus and Ephesus.

[16] The disputes between Samos and Priene over land in the Tschangly plain may be traced from the very early period of Ionian history into the second century B.C. Most important are the documents, C.B. Welles, *Royal Correspondence* No. 7 and *Ins. v. Priene* No. 37. Apparently two tracts of land were involved, one called Batinetis and the other, an area containing two forts, Karyon and Dryoussa (Welles, *op. cit.*, p. 48, n. 4). The latter area was awarded to Priene by a Rhodian arbitration of the second century B.C. (*Ins. v. Priene* No. 37, lines 25–27) on the basis of its historical claims. Presumably Priene had received it in the division of land in this area made after the Melian War (above, n. 14). The Batinetis, however, was confirmed to the Samians by Lysimachus in 283/2 (Welles, *op. cit.*, No. 7, lines 4–6). The Prienian argument preserved in the inscription, and not credited by Lysimachus, indicates that in the archaic period Priene was normally in control, but that both Samians and Prienians were settled on the land before Lygdamis captured and occupied it in the mid-seventh century; Samos took it over again after Lygdamis' withdrawal, but it reverted to Priene by the settlement of Bias in the sixth century, only to be lost again to the Samians. Evidently Priene, by virtue of its guardianship of the Panionion (below, p. 31), held a large part of the Tschangly plain, but Samos, from its own holdings on the rocky tip of Mykale, made successive attempts to seize land in the plain by force or by the infiltration of individual settlers.

[17] V. Desborough, *Protogeometric Pottery* 221, 304.

[18] *Priene* 24–25. For recent investigation see *AJA* 62 (1958) 103–04; it would locate the Panionion near Tschangly village.

COLOPHON

Archaic Colophon (Deïrmendere) is not precisely located (Map II), although a part of the Geometric cemetery has been excavated and the "old" city is mentioned in a fourth century inscription, which provided for it to be enclosed in the walls of that period.[19] The site is strikingly like those of the major Mycenean cities of Old Greece, if not those of the colonial area of the Mycenean *koine*. It is set inland about thirteen kilometers from the sea (by road to the harbor) where a very steep acropolis overlooks a large, fertile plain. The acropolis falls off into ravines on each side and is detached from the ridge at its rear, which blocks off Colophon from the sea. It is easily defensible, and projecting tongues of land provide level ground for an *asty* or lower town. Probably this acropolis served the archaic city. There are a few remains of "Cyclopean" terrace walls on its slopes which have a different orientation than the walls used to terrace the buildings of the city of the fourth century. Probably at that time the old city was so drastically remodelled and reoriented that its buildings were largely destroyed. The acropolis by itself, however, is not large enough for a substantial city, so that probably a lower town formed on the tongues of land projecting along the stream Deïrmendere. Colophon livelihood, like that of Ephesus, was based primarily on agriculture, and it had sufficient land to become one of the major states of Ionia. Its own large plain opens at the east into the great river plain of the Cayster and the passage to Smyrna, which enabled Colophon to lay claims to them. On its own peninsula the city controlled the road to Lebedos and Teos to the west and founded a colony, Klazomenai, on the south shore of the Gulf of Smyrna. In view of the extent of its territory it is hardly surprising that Colophon is the only Ionian city for which a cavalry force is attested and that it played little part in overseas trade and colonization.[20]

LEBEDOS

There is little evidence for the archaeological history of Lebedos (Xingi),[21] but, to judge from its siting (Map II) and small place in tradition, it was evidently one of the

[19] L. B. Holland, *Hesperia* 13 (1944) 91–171; Hanfmann, *op. cit.*, p. 8. Holland located the "old" city on a ridge north of the acropolis (*op. cit.*, p. 92, figs. 1, 3 [8]; p. 171); on the acropolis an early house wall and late geometric and archaic sherds were found (pp. 139–42). For the cemetery see H. Goldman, *AJA* 27 (1923) 67–68 and Lorimer, *Homer and the Monuments* 106, 348–49. The wall inscription is published by B. Merritt, *AJP* 56 (1935) 358–72 and interpreted by Holland, *op. cit.*, pp. 169–71. A pillaged Mycenean tholos tomb with some remaining L. H. III pottery was also found (Lorimer, *op. cit.*, p. 106, n. 4). The chief defect in Holland's reconstruction of the history of Colophon is the thesis that it was captured by Gyges and reduced to dire poverty in the seventh and early sixth centuries. Gyges is said by Herodotus (1.14.4) to have captured the *asty* only, and Xenophanes' reference to Colophonian wealth and luxury probably dates from this period of "poverty." C. Bowra (*CQ* 35 [1941] 119–26), in a discussion of the fragment of Xenophanes (3), argues that the period of Colophonian luxury is after the time of Alyattes, when Colophon and Lydia had made an alliance (Polyaenus 7.2.2).

[20] For the cavalry force see Strabo 14.1.28 and Polyaenus 7.2.2. The colonization is discussed by Bilabel, *Philologus, Supp.* 14 (1920) 206–09; Colophon probably sent a colony to Siris in Italy after the capture of its *asty* by Gyges (Strabo 6.1.14; Dunbabin, *The Western Greeks* 34); it perhaps colonized Myrleia in the Propontis and *limen Kolophonion* in Thrace, but the evidence is obscure (Myrleia: Pomp. Mela 1.99; Steph. Byz. *s.v.*; *limen*: Thuc. 5.2, but the reading is doubtful).

[21] G. Weber, *AM* 29 (1904) 228–31.

minor Ionian towns. There seem to have been two areas of settlement—a small, fortified town on a peninsula, presumably the earlier, and an open town on the hillside which rises behind it. Lebedos had only a small agricultural area and, since it lay well inside the gulf, engaged in little shipping, thus remaining an establishment of secondary importance.

TEOS

Teos (south of Sigadjik),[22] on a promontory near the entrance to the Gulf of Ephesus (Map II), was of greater importance. Something is known of its Hellenistic and Roman levels, but little of the archaic town. Its acropolis was near the tip of the peninsula, which provided a good sheltered harbor on the east side, but the archaic town probably extended at least as far as the theater of the later city, where I have picked up some archaic and fifth century sherds. The site has easy access to the hinterland of low hills and small plains which characterizes the crossing to Klazomenai on the Gulf of Smyrna. The land on Teos' side is marked off sharply by a divide and is drier and less productive than that of Klazomenai, but there was sufficient for tillage and grazing to support a moderate sized community. From its position near the entrance to the gulf the city enjoyed some of the coastal shipping but was mainly agricultural.

MYKALE

The high ridge of Mykale (Map II) made communication between the Gulf of Ephesus and the cities of the Maeander estuary, Priene, Miletus and Myus, difficult. There was a mountain track from Tschangly to Priene[23] but the main roads skirted the east end of Mykale. One followed the line of the modern railway from Ephesus to Magnesia (Muradli), the other probably that of the modern road from Kusch-Adassi to Söke, which crosses the ridge rimming the coastal plain. Priene was most conveniently situated for communication with the rest of Ionia, but Magnesia was the important junction for the Maeander valley. The topography of the estuary has changed considerably since the archaic period, when the harbor of Myus could accomodate a fleet of two hundred triremes. Before the Persian Wars the Maeander seems to have run along the south flank of Mykale. Miletus and Myus were ports on the rocky south shore of the gulf, and there was no wide, flat, alluvial plain around and beyond Lade. It was then an island protecting the harbor of Miletus. At some time between the fifth century and the Roman period the course of the river turned south across the plain toward Miletus, silting up the harbor of Myus and eventually, by late medieval times, "alluviating" Miletus out of existence.

PRIENE

The site of archaic Priene is unknown and perhaps undiscoverable. It is likely that the town was set on a tongue of land projecting from Mykale (Map II) and washed by the

[22] W. Ruge, "Teos," *RE* 5A (1934) 539ff. For the preliminary report of the French excavations see *BCH* 46 (1922) 307-55 and 49 (1925) 281 ff.

[23] *Priene* 14–23.

waters of the gulf which eventually silted it in and covered it over. The Hellenistic city is set well up on the slopes of Mykale and probably farther inland. Presumably Priene controlled the north bank of the Maeander and the slopes of Mykale as far inland as Magnesia. Also, as suggested above,[24] it probably had a share in the rich Tschangly plain. With these resources Priene seems to have been a moderate sized town, mainly agricultural, but with a little trade.

MILETUS

Miletus (Balat) bulks large in Ionian tradition as one of the great cities of the archaic period and earlier. This is true of the late seventh and sixth centuries, but may be doubted for the earlier period, when agricultural resources were more important and Miletus less favored than Ephesus and Colophon on that score. The precise location of the early and archaic city,[25] obscured by the impressive remains of Hellenistic and Roman date as at Ephesus, is not known. Its general location, however, was on the northern end of the peninsula projecting from Mt. Latmus into what was then the sea (Map II). It was on the entrance to a deep gulf, commanding the exit to the sea and the coastal shipping. As a typical Ionian peninsular site, Miletus' development depended on the amount of fertile land in its possession and on its relation to the main trade routes. Exploitation of the shipping lane along the coast had to wait until the development of trade in the seventh century. The land route through the Maeander valley to the interior was probably little used until after the Persian conquest, for earlier the center of gravity and the chief markets of native Asia Minor were at Sardis and in the Hermus valley. Accordingly, Miletus' relations were primarily with the Carian mountaineers in its own neighborhood. Its share of the rich plain of the Maeander was much less than the present situation suggests. Throughout most of the archaic period the city's territory was largely confined to its own rocky promontory and the adjacent heights (Her. 6.20). It may have held an enclave of territory across the Maeander and to the west of Priene, since the little town of Thebai, which belonged to Miletus in the fourth century, was in existence in the archaic period.[26] Evidently the city began to feel the pinch of an expanding population in the early seventh century when it started to colonize and take to the sea. To secure their approaches the Milesians occupied Ikaros and the small chain of islands down the Carian coast, known as the Milesian islands.[27] Although this expansion added little tillable land, it facilitated the city's hold on the trading routes. Thus, Milesian prosperity in the archaic period was based on trade and colonization rather than on its local resources.

[24] Above, n. 16. On the limits of Prienian territory see *Priene* 28–31; for other views concerning the location of the archaic town, *ibid.*, p. 4.

[25] See Hanfmann, *op. cit.*, pp. 4, 7ff., for discussion; A. von Gerkan (*Bericht über den VI Internationalen Kongress für Archäologie*, 1939, 323–25) considers that the site of the archaic city has not yet been found; see also Philippson, *Milet* III, 5, pp. 19–20; for the results of current investigation, *AJA* 60 (1956) 379–81.

[26] *Priene* 29–30, 469–74; according to Maeandrius of Miletus, Thebai had been awarded to Miletus after the Melian War; he adds Marathesion also, which lay on the north side of Mykale, but Maeandrius' evidence is suspect (above, n. 14).

[27] Philippson, *Milet* III, 5, pp. 19–20; Bilabel, *op. cit.*, pp. 54–55.

MYUS

Myus (north of Afschar Kalessi) was investigated to some degree at the time of the main excavations at Miletus, and the site of the archaic town discovered.[28] It, too, occupied a promontory with a large and good harbor (Map II), but opportunity for trade was curtailed by Miletus' position farther to the west and its agricultural hinterland was small, so that, like Lebedos, the town never became of more than local importance.

GULF OF SMYRNA

Although the northern Ionian towns around the Gulf of Smyrna (Map II) were secondary foundations,[29] two of them, Chios and Phocaea, grew to considerable importance through their advantageous position for the coastal shipping route. The island of Chios lay off the entrance to the gulf, and Phocaea on its northern headland. The topography of the Hermus estuary, like that of the Maeander, has changed considerably since the archaic period. The site of Old Smyrna was in the northeast corner of the gulf, and there was no town on the site of the modern port until the Hellenistic city was founded by Lysimachus. Old Smyrna controlled the coastal plain at the head of the gulf, but the land lying to its west was made later by the alluviation of the Hermus. In antiquity the river emptied into the gulf closer to Phocaea, which made that town the terminus for communications with Sardis and Lydia.

KLAZOMENAI

Klazomenai was probably founded as an agricultural colony by Colophon rather than to provide that city with a harbor on the Gulf of Smyrna. The archaic city was slightly inland from the shore (Map II), where J. M. Cook has discovered archaic sherds. In the late archaic period the citizens moved to the modern quarantine island, which was fortified and ultimately linked to the coast by a causeway as at present.[30] None of the pottery picked up on the island seems earlier than the very late archaic period. The city of the seventh century was strong enough, probably with Colophonian aid, to inflict a heavy defeat on Alyattes when he raided it.[31] Supported by the adjacent coastal plains and the rolling hills behind it Klazomenai seems to have been a town of moderate size like Priene.

ERYTHRAE

Erythrae was situated on the west coast of the Mimas peninsula across from Chios (Map II), although the precise location of the archaic city is not certain. It is usually identified with Ildir, which was the site of the city in the fourth century and later, but nothing earlier than that period is reported from there.[32] Cook, however, proposes another

[28] W. Ruge, "Myus," *RE* 16 (1935) 1435–37; the results were not published.

[29] Below, pp. 29–30.

[30] *ATL* I, pp. 503–04; *Klio, Beih.* 14 (1923) 132–33, n. 4; J. M. Cook, *EphArch* 1957, 149–57.

[31] Her. 1.16.2.

[32] *ATL* I, pp. 485–87; Bürchner, "Erythrai," *RE* 6 (1909) 575–90; Weber, *AM* 26 (1901) 103–18; J. Keil, *JOAI* 13 (1910) 5–74 (topography of the Mimas peninsula).

site, Ilica, which has archaic material; it is about two kilometers west of the spa of Cesme on the south side of the Gulf of Erythrae. Probably Erythrae was originally a small peninsular site, like so many of the Ionian foundations, which shifted to larger quarters in the fourth century. Its communications across the peninsula by road are difficult, so that Erythrae's relations with Chios were closer than with Klazomenai or Teos. Since the Mimas peninsula does have considerable fertile agricultural land and small villages, Erythrae, its largest town, was a city of some wealth.

SMYRNA

The site of Old Smyrna (Bayrakly) has been definitely identified (Map II) and carefully excavated by a joint Anglo-Turkish expedition.[33] The original foundation was on a promontory with a small harbor on each side of its base. It was readily defensible and controlled the fertile plain of Smyrna as well as the road leading from Ionia to the Hermus estuary and into Aeolis. Since the land to the west of Bayrakly is formed from alluvial deposit, it is likely that this road led over the ridge behind Old Smyrna rather than around its end as at the present time. A more direct road to Sardis was across the plain of Smyrna, through the pass by Bel Kave and the territory of the town of Nymphaeum into the great river plain of the Hermus. Yet Smyrna's location was unfavorable for the Lydian trade. This road to Sardis crossed hilly terrain, and Smyrna itself suffered the disadvantages of a position at the head of its gulf.

PHOCAEA

The site of Phocaea (Eskidje-Fotscha) is definitely identified and excavation has been resumed there.[34] Its position on the north headland of the Gulf of Smyrna and to the north of the Hermus (Map II) was very favorable both for the coastal shipping and for trade with Lydia along the river valley. In the estuary the main road from Lydia was apparently on the north side of the river, to judge from the location of the Aeolian towns of Larisa and Neon Teichos. At the corridor through the hills where the river breaks from the valley is a ford, so that traffic from Sardis, far up on the south side of the great river plain, probably crossed at that point. Near Larisa this road met that from Smyrna into Aeolis. From Larisa to Phocaea the road ran over flat plains and easy hill slopes. Its terminus at Phocaea provided an admirably protected harbor. The town is guarded on the land side by a steep ridge and lies on a promontory projecting into a small bay which

[33] The excavation by Miltner is published in *JOAI* 27 (1932) *Beibl.* 127–88. The recent excavations have been published only in preliminary form: E. Akurgal, *Ztsch. d. phil. Fak. Univ. Ankara* 8 (1950) 52–97; *ILN*, Feb. 28, 1953, pp. 328–29; reports in *JHS* 67–73 (1947–53) and in *Anatolian Studies* 1–2 (1949–50).

[34] J. Keil, "Phokaia," *RE* 20 (1950) 444–48. Herodotus located the mouth of the Hermus with reference to Phocaea (1.80), and the Lacedaemonian envoys sent to Cyrus in 546 landed at Phocaea and presumably went up the Hermus valley to Sardis (1.152.3). Excavation on a trial scale was started at Phocaea in 1953, *Türk Arkeoloji Dergisi* 7.1 (1957) 39; much fine black-figured pottery was found as well as house walls of the sixth and late seventh century (*AJA* 59 [1955] 236; 60 [1956] 382–83). Pottery from Sartiaux's excavation is published, P. Jacobsthal, *Gallia Graeca* 13 ff.

is sheltered from the sea by spits and a small island. While the tillable area on the shore is very small, probably Phocaea cultivated the coastal plain to the south as well as land east of its ridge. There is, however, little good land, and Phocaea's prosperity and place in tradition were owed to the initiative of its citizens in taking to the sea.

CHIOS

Chios lay off the Gulf of Smyrna (Map II) much as Samos did off the Gulf of Ephesus.[35] Unlike Samos, Chios was not the terminus of a regular route across the Aegean by an easy island run, but its city was very favorably situated for trade along the coast of Asia Minor from the Hellespont. It was founded on the east side midway along the island, looking directly across to Erythrae and the peninsula of Mimas. Its topography is unknown, for the modern town is apparently built directly over the medieval and ancient city. Probably the early foundation was made on the several low hills near the sea.[36] As well as enjoying this favorable position for trade, Chios was at the northern end of the large fertile plain known as the *Kampos*, which is the center of inhabitation and of the road system of the island. The northern part of Chios is rocky and infertile, but the *Kampos* and the southern half of the island are capable of supporting a large population. This area was suitable for that development of specialized crops, vines and olives, which began in Chios at an early date. Potentially the island was much wealthier than Samos and ranked with the major Ionian states of the archaic period, Ephesus, Colophon and Miletus. In addition to the main city there were in antiquity several small towns and ports on the island, like the recently excavated Emporion,[37] but they seem to have been completely organized into the city state of Chios as a single political unit and member of the Ionian League.

The Ionian cities were thus perched rather precariously on the shore line of Asia Minor. The settlers showed a marked preference for easily defended promontory sites and defensible hills near the shore, which gave them access to the fertile plains. Only Colophon, perhaps a Mycenean city with an enduring tradition, was situated inland. Priene is completely unknown. In addition to these major cities, which were members of the Ionian League or, like Smyrna, aspired to become such, there were small towns and villages on their territory; a few are identified satisfactorily, others known by name or remains only. Some perhaps represent the trial and error of settlement and were given up for the archaic cities which, in their turn, chose better sites in the Hellenistic Period. Only adequate surface exploration and excavation can work out such a process. The evidence offered by the major sites shows that the colonists moved into a hostile land which had to be won from its native inhabitants by force or compromise, for the sites are little more than beachheads. The primary aim of the Ionian colonists was land to till and graze, but they selected some places with a good eye to the sea trade, which gradually developed. Such were Samos,

[35] For a topographical survey of the island see D. W. S. Hunt, *BSA* 41 (1940–45) 29–52.

[36] Some excavation has been carried out on the outskirts of the ancient city of Chios (J. Boardman, *BSA* 49 [1954] 123–28), and graves with subgeometric and archaic pottery were excavated in 1952 at Rizari by Kondoleon (*ibid.*, p. 128).

[37] *JHS* 74 (1954) 163–64; J. Boardman, *Archaeology* 8 (1955) 245–51.

Miletus, Chios and Phocaea. Other cities, like Colophon and Ephesus, controlled sufficient land to become large and wealthy without any special development of trade by sea, and, to judge from the sequel, the land could assure a rising standard of living and growth of population for all.

COMMUNICATIONS

Within Ionia the comparative ease and shortness of communications contributed greatly to the high degree of cultural unity which the Ionian cities achieved and to the close ties with Lydia which ultimately developed. Travel by water was short and direct, and probably the sea served Phocaea, Erythrae, Miletus and Myus almost as much as the islands of Samos and Chios. While paths were difficult over the ridges of Mykale and Mimas, conditions for land travel in Ionia were no harder than within Attica and considerably easier than between many of the separate states of Greece.

The main land route (Map II) was a north-south axial road linking the Maeander and the Hermus valleys and tieing the three clusters of towns together.[38] The terminus in the Maeander valley was Magnesia, probably a native city and hostile, at least to Ephesus, until its land was taken over after the Trerian raid of *ca.* 650. Perhaps before that the track over Mykale from Priene received considerable traffic. From Magnesia the road ran northward through Ephesian territory, entering the plain of the Cayster by the narrow corridor at Belevi, so important in Byzantine times. Sardis might be reached by crossing the plain of the Cayster and a spur of Mt. Tmolus, as the Athenian and Eretrian raiding party did from Ephesus in 497 (Her. 5.54, 100). A track to Colophon might be taken over the low hills or a better road from the northern part of the plain into which that of Colophon opens. From the Cayster plain a comparatively easy pass led to the plain of Smyrna and across it to the city in the northeast corner of the gulf. As we have described, routes led from Smyrna northwards into Aeolis and through the territory of Nymphaeum to Sardis. For Lydian access to Ionia the key points were Smyrna and Ephesus. Alyattes destroyed the former, no doubt retaining possession of Nymphaeum, and cultivated the Ephesian nobility by a policy of marital alliance.[39]

There is a little information about the use of this road system in the sources, which indicates that by the fifth century recognized itineraries had been made up. The standard of measurement was the day's journey of the "well-girded man," which seems to have varied between 20 and 25 miles. For example, in one passage of Herodotus it is equivalent to 200 stades or about 25 miles (4.101), in another to 150 stades or about 19 miles (5.53) and in another we are told that a 3 days march was 540 stades, an average of about 22½ miles per day (5.54). The journey from Ephesus to Sardis over Tmolus took 3 days, from Ephesus to Smyrna, 2 days (Strabo 14.1.2); from Sardis to Smyrna and Sardis to Phocaea would have taken 2 and 3 days and from Miletus to Sardis or to Smyrna 5 and 4 days respectively. An alternative, but longer and harder, route from Miletus to Sardis was to

[38] On the road system of Asia Minor in general see T. R. S. Broughton, *Economic Survey of Rome* IV 860–68; D. Magie, *Roman Asia Minor* I 39–42, II 786–802; E. Gren, "Kleinasien und der Ostbalken," *Årsskrift, Uppsala Univ.*, 1941, No. 9, 39–59; H. H. von der Osten, *Eranos* 49 (1951) 68–84.

[39] Below, p. 31, n. 31.

travel up the Maeander to Tralles, thence north across the ridges; from Tralles, too, ran the main route into the heart of Caria as at the present time. While the junction at Tralles was scarcely used by travelers from Ionia to Sardis, it was important for those going to the main Carian towns and was the regular point of departure north and south for traffic coming down the Maeander from the plateau (Her. 7.26ff.).

It is unlikely that the route to the interior through the Maeander valley (Map I) was much used until Persia had established provinces in western Asia Minor. In the eighth century, Gordion in Phrygia and in the seventh, Sardis drew traffic through the Hermus valley. The route up the Maeander followed the north bank of the stream to Hierapolis where it turned up the Lycus, then ran to Apamea and Ipsus to join a branch of the road coming south from the Hermus route. That road remained easy along the course of the Hermus itself but became difficult as it crossed the *Katakaumene*, the "Burned Land," and the mountains to Phrygia on the central plateau, which it reached at Afyon Karahissar. One branch, that of an old Hittite military road, led east to Gordion and Ankara, while the other turned south to Ipsus. From Ipsus led the great roads east into Cappadocia and south through Lycaonia to North Syria and Cilicia (Map I). Even in the period of Persian control the importance of Sardis made the Hermus route the first leg of the famous "Royal Road" (Her. 5.52f.). In contrast to this, the Maeander road passed through the territory of Carian and Lydian mountaineers who would have been more disposed to prey on its traffic than guarantee safe passage.

It is obvious that only goods of a certain type could move along these routes because of the difficulties and distances involved in transportation, small goods of a luxury nature, precious metals in ingot or manufactured form, textiles and wool which baled easily. Animals or slaves might be traded, since they furnished their own motive power. Conditions of travel had to be reasonably secure, whether the security was obtained by orderly government or purchased from local tribal chieftains. A market with considerable wealth had to exist for trade under such conditions. Also, the climate tended to make travel seasonal, for the passes up to the plateau might be blocked with snow or made extremely difficult by flooding and mud. While stretches of road for cart traffic could exist in certain areas, goods would normally have been carried by pack animals. It is salutary to remember that, even in the period of the Roman Empire when Asia Minor was organized under an efficient administration, urbanized to a considerable degree and provided with a network of good Roman roads, bulk goods, like grain, were not moved very much from the interior to the coast, or even by land at all, except for military purposes.[40] Thus, any trade between the western coast and the interior of Asia Minor or from North Syria by land into the interior was on a very small scale and in luxury articles. Its effects might be potent in the sphere of artistic influences, but have no effect whatsoever on the social and political organization of the participants. The only basic commodity which could have been transported was metals. They have been frequently carried over long and difficult routes, as in Spanish exploitation of Central America and Mexico, where ingots were packed down from the mines in the mountains.

[40] Broughton, *op. cit.*, pp. 867–68.

RESOURCES

Ionia was regarded in the fifth century as a country unusually favored by nature with productive land and herds, with trees, water and a good climate. In contrast to the small Aegean islands and to much of Greece, the Ionian cities were well off for pasture land and tillage. The hill slopes and the marshy estuaries provided pasture for sheep, goats, cattle and, at least in Colophon, for horses as well.[41] Cereal, vegetable and fruit cultivation could be carried out on the plains and the gentler hill slopes. It was a lusher and larger Greece. The benefits to be derived from this, however, were relative to the degree of specialization in the farming and to the population. We are poorly informed on both topics, but it is apparent that in Chios and Miletus, at least, the conversion to specialized farming was made early.[42] To judge from the record of colonization, the balance between food supply and population was reached *ca.* 700. Certainly the land could not support the population of the late archaic period for which it is possible to suggest a figure.

In general, in Ionia as elsewhere in the Aegean area, the diet was relatively simple for most people, although it may have contained a larger proportion of meat and fish than in Greece. The literary sources allow some comparison to be made. Hesiod described the fare of a Greek peasant, a substantial freeholder, in Boeotia which is a good parallel to Ionia. The staple was bread, probably of barley at that time, and variety largely seasonal (*Works and Days* 442, 588–92). In summer the farm owner could avail himself of meat, and a good meal consisted of meal cake (*maza*), goat's milk, young beef or lamb and a local vintage watered three to one. For the urban poor and slaves in sixth-century Ephesus the fare was scantier, figs and barley bread (Hipponax 39.6; 42.3). The Ionian farmer, however, probably ate as well as Hesiod's peasant. This diet would have been staple also for the wealthy but diversified by the luxuries which wealth and the opportunities for hunting allowed. Hipponax adds honey paste and tunny fish, probably imported from the Propontis, some game such as hare and partridge (39), while Ananius (5) enlarges considerably on the variety of meat and fish at particular seasons, favoring a sort of shrimp dolmada made with fig leaves. If Alcman's distaste for raw local Laconian vintages (53) may be taken as valid for that of the Ionian aristocracy, the latter was developing a taste for good wine. Omitted from the literary sources, but to be taken for granted, was the other staple of Greek diet, olive oil.

The sole agricultural product of which Ionia, or perhaps only Miletus, had a surplus was wool, for there is some evidence for its export in the archaic period.[43] The products of specialized agriculture, oil and wine, were exported, but their cultivation made less land available for grain. To judge by our evidence of the wooded condition of Ionia and of the export of furniture in the fifth century,[44] the land was probably self-sufficient in timber and pitch for ship building. It also possessed the clays necessary for pottery. Many products were imported which might be classed as necessities for the urbanized states of

[41] Above, p. 11.
[42] Below, p. 41.
[43] *Carmen Pop.* 35; Athenaeus 540d (sheep to Samos); 519b (to Sybaris).
[44] Critias 1.5–6 (Chios and Miletus).

the seventh and sixth centuries, even if an earlier age could do without them: papyrus, which replaced the earlier parchment; ropes and cables, such as Xerxes used for his bridging activities; linen for padded corslets and clothing; perhaps hemp as a substitute for linen; luxury foods, brought for the wealthy to eat, and various costly articles for their pleasure; exotic dedications for the shrines, which should be regarded as a necessity in this age. Slaves, too, were evidently an important import, not only for domestic use but for agriculture, as in Chios. They were sought beyond the boundaries of Ionia.[45]

The scarcity of metals of all kinds in the Ionian states was of equal importance to that of grain and was felt at an earlier period. There is no indication in the literary sources or from geological reconaissance of any substantial deposits of gold, silver or electrum. Small deposits of silver are reported at Gümüldur in the territory of Lebedos and at Zestor in Samos, but in neither case do we have evidence of their exploitation.[46] Iron, too, was scarce or lacking, except perhaps to Miletus. There are deposits on Mt. Latmus, which are said to have been worked in ancient times, but they receive no notice in the literary sources. Iron is said to be found on Samos, but again there is no evidence of its exploitation.[47] Copper, too, was probably in short supply. Deposits are reported in the mountains between Ephesus and Smyrna, but they do not seem to have been worked and were possibly in Lydia rather than in Ionia. Also, there is no literary notice nor traces of working of the deposits on Mykale. Samos was a center of bronze-working, but could have obtained its copper from Cyprus with which it had close trading connections.[48] Tin was a necessary import for Ionia as well as for the rest of Greece and perhaps the whole of Asia Minor, as discussed below.

On the other hand, the Ionian states either had ample supplies of the less important metals and stone in their own territories, exchangeable in local trade, or easy access to them. Building stone of good quality was common along the whole coast, and imports of special stones were made only for particular purposes.[49] Minor stones are mentioned only in late sources, but were probably known in the archaic period, mill-stones from Erythrae, agates from Lesbos, carbuncles from Chios and Miletus.[50] In addition, there was a copious supply of the colored earths from which pigments were made. The most valuable, however, Sinopic miltos (cinnabar) was found in Cappadocia and exported from Sinope[51]. It was

[45] Papyrus: Her. 5.58.3; cables: Her. 7.25, 34; linen: Her. 2.105 (Colchian and Egyptian); hemp: Her. 4.74; amber: Her. 3.115.1 (from the *eschate*); *libanotos* (frankincense): Xenophanes 1.7, Her. 3.107; myrrh: below, p. 56; styrax (a gum): Her. 3.107.2; cinnamon: Her. 3.111.2, 107.2; *ledanos* (gum): Her.3. 107.2, 112; for the trade in these exotics see below, p. 69, and for the slave trade, p. 108.

[46] Forbes, *Metallurgy in Antiquity* 150–51; Gümüldur: *ibid.*, p. 192, No. 21; Zestor: *ibid.*, p. 192, No. 24.

[47] Forbes (*ibid.*, p. 386) mentions ore deposits on Samos; the deposits on Mt. Latmus have been examined by Paton and Myres (*Geog. Journal* 9 [1897] 50 ff.). The deposits near modern Corançez (Forbes, *op. cit.*, p. 386) are considered to have supplied the iron-working industry of Cibyra about which we hear in Strabo (13.4.17), but could hardly have supplied the coast because of the very great difficulties of transport in this mountainous area.

[48] Forbes, *op. cit.*, p. 303. For Samian bronze-working see Paus. 8.14.8; 10.38.6; below, pp. 67–68.

[49] Magie, *op. cit.*, I, c. ii, *passim*.

[50] Broughton, *op. cit.*, p. 625.

[51] For the various types of colored earths and their origins see Broughton, *op. cit.*, p. 623; for Sinopic miltos, Strabo 12.2.10. It was mined in Cappadocia but given the trade name, Sinopic, since Sinope was

widely distributed until Spanish cinnabar cut into its market. The value of these earths, used for painting ships and the like, is evident from the Athenian attempt to monopolize the miltos of Ceos in the fifth century. Presumably, throughout the archaic period, that from Sinope and those found in the territories of the Ionian states, Erythrae, Ephesus and Samos, were distributed by Ionian traders. For the manufacture of brass, which may have been carried on in the archaic period, there was a supply of zinc at Andeira in the Troad.[52] Antimony, used sometimes in bronze alloy, was found in Lydia in the upper Cayster valley on Mt. Messogis.[53] More useful than either of these was lead, but, since it was a by-product of silver production, the supply came from those areas which exported silver to Ionia.

Since Ionia had to find supplies of both precious and basic metals from the outset and could not feed its population adequately from the early seventh century, it is apparent that any picture of Ionian economy based on its local resources is illusory. The Ionians used colonization and mercenary service abroad as a cure for excess population, but, even so, the land did not produce enough food for those who remained. From the latter part of the seventh century,[54] they began to found trading factories in the grain-producing lands of Egypt and the north coast of the Black Sea. The trade which sprang up cannot be interpreted simply as an enterprise to satisfy the taste for luxury of a landed aristocracy. Grain was imported on an increasingly large scale as the population grew, and a system of trade was organized, which covered the Mediterranean. The prosperity of the land in the sixth century rested on this basis of trade and colonization, which enabled it to support a population of over a quarter of a million free inhabitants.

POPULATION

The figures given by Herodotus (6.8) for the Ionian fleet at the battle of Lade afford some basis for an estimate of the Greek population of Ionia *ca.* 500. From the examination of the various sites it seems possible to supplement this and to suggest a conjectural figure for the whole of Ionia, exclusive of slaves. Probably there were no independent native communities left in Ionia by that time. It is likely that the estimate is valid for the period from *ca.* 550 to the time of the Ionian Revolt, for Ionia as a whole suffered little loss of population under the early years of the Persian regime. Phocaea and Teos lost some citizens by migration *ca.* 540, but Miletus seems to have prospered.

The estimates already made[55] were based on the conclusions that triremes were used at Lade, that the complement of a trireme was 200 men, that this effort represented the fullest possible mobilization of Ionian men and warships and that those who served were

the center of shipment (W. Leaf, *JHS* 36 [1916] 11–15). Its exploitation by Sinope was apparently curtailed *ca.* 315 when Ephesus cut into the market by bringing the earth directly down from mines near Sizma in Lycaonia—a rather striking example of the fact that direct Greek trade on any scale with the interior of Asia Minor was late and that the earlier trade moved primarily by sea.

[52] Strabo 13.1.56; Magie, *op. cit.*, II, p. 804, n. 29.

[53] Magie, *op. cit.*, II, p. 807, n. 47.

[54] Roebuck, *CP* 48 (1953) 13.

[55] *Ibid.*, pp. 10–12.

Ionian citizens and metics. Thus, by multiplying the number of warships of each state by 200 a figure was obtained for its military force. The usual ratio, 1:4, for men of military age in the population was used with the following results:

State	Ships × Men	Force × 4	Population	
Miletus	— 80 × 200 =	16,000 × 4 =	64,000.	
Priene	— 12 × 200 =	2,400 × 4 =	9,600.	
Myus	— 3 × 200 =	600 × 4 =	2,400.	
Teos	— 17 × 200 =	3,400 × 4 =	13,600.	
Chios	— 100 × 200 =	20,000 × 4 =	80,000.	(sailors)
	— 100 × 40 =	4,000 × 4 =	16,000.	(marines)
Erythrae	— 8 × 200 =	1,600 × 4 =	6,400.	
Phocaea	— 3 × 200 =	600 × 4 =	2,400.	
Lesbos	— 70 × 200 =	14,000 × 4 =	56,000.	
	*— 8 × 200 =	1,600 × 4 =	6,400.	
	* (with Histiaeus at the Hellespont).			
Samos	— 60 × 200 =	12,000 × 4 =	48,000.	

Klazomenai, Colophon, Ephesus and Lebedos were not represented, for their lands were occupied by the Persians. Probably, however, some of their citizens were serving with the other Ionians. To comment on some of these figures.

Miletus was hardly in a position to man its fleet fully, for it had suffered losses in battle with the Persians in Caria shortly before (Her. 5.120) and was threatened by a land attack which would require the manning of the walls (Her. 6.6). Possibly, 80 was not the full number of ships in its war fleet; probably, some of the ships were manned by refugees from the captured Ionian cities or by men from agricultural states which had only a small fleet. In any case, the Milesians had a fleet of 80 ships which they had presumably built in the expectation of manning fully. The figure does not seem too large when the aggregate of Milesian land and trade in the sixth century is considered.

The figure for *Priene* is well above the 4,000 usually estimated for the Hellenistic city. The latter, however, was on a different site, and archaic Priene held land in the Tschangly plain.

In the fifth century *Myus* was a fishing town, providing *opson* for Themistocles;[56] evidently it was small.

Teos may have had more inhabitants than the indicated 13,600. Since, however, some citizens had migrated to Abdera *ca.* 540 (Her. 1.168), it seems reasonable to use that figure.

The population of *Chios* is a difficult problem, but, before discussion it is useful to remember that the present population of the island is *ca.* 75,000 and that many Chiots serve abroad in the Greek merchant marine. It is unreasonable to assume that only the marines mentioned by Herodotus were Chiots, for that yields too low a figure. The Chiots evidently manned their ships at Lade to the fullest extent, since they resisted as long as possible. Yet the figure of 96,000 based on the assumption that both marines and sailors were Chiots is very high. Several possibilities may explain it: some slaves were used or,

[56] Thuc. 1.138.5; Diod. 11.57.7.

more plausibly, men from Erythrae, for which the figure is too low, served along with the Chiots; in any case, the island evidently had a population well in excess of the capacity of its cereal production,[57] and, as at present, many of the citizens found their living at sea.

The figure for *Erythrae* is too low in relation to the amount of arable land and the number of villages on the Mimas peninsula. Its population should have been between that of Teos and of Colophon, and the small number of warships explained by its agricultural character.

Phocaea is probably a special case. The area of its town and land was small, on a par with Myus, but its trade was extensive, so that the population, like that of Chios, was larger than the land area indicates. More than half of the citizens had remained behind *ca.* 540 when the others sailed off to Corsica. Perhaps we may assume that its population had been about 5,000 and accept the figure of 2,400 for the latter part of the century.

The population of *Samos* may have been greater in the mid-sixth century, for the Persians had put many citizens to death at the time the city was restored to Syloson (Her. 3. 149; Douris, *FGr Hist* 2A, No. 66).

Lesbos was not in Ionia and should be omitted from the totals. The figure of 62,400 is probably rather low, for the island is very fertile and has a large amount of tillable land in relation to its size. It also had some trade.

For the other Ionian states we can only conjecture from analogy. Since *Lebedos* was one of the minor Ionian cities, probably on a par with Myus or Phocaea, *ca.* 2,400 is a fair estimate. *Klazomenai* was of moderate size, like Priene, and *ca.* 9,000 may be conjectured. *Colophon*, however, was one of the major states with large, fertile plains and a predominantly agricultural economy. Its villages and harbor town should be included. The only figure which we have for it is the "1,000" who resorted to the agora in their finery (Xenophanes 3), but that may be a conventional name for those with full citizen rights or a round number. Perhaps an estimate of twice the population of Teos would be satisfactory, *ca.* 30,000. Ephesus, too, was a very important city of Ionia, perhaps less so in relation to Chios and Miletus in the sixth century than earlier, but it controlled a large land area with small towns: thus, *ca.* 30,000.

The total Greek population of Ionia based on these estimates was about 313,800 men, women and children. Probably in the military crisis which provoked the mobilization for Lade, every man and youth able to bear arms was called up, not only those of formal military age. Some, too, were absent on the merchant ships which brought provisions to Ionia during the revolt. Perhaps the ratio to use is 1:3 rather than 1:4. If so, the total figure is 235,800 rather than 313,800. The figures are more than double those which may be conjectured for contemporary Athens, but the Ionian fleet at Lade was proportionately larger than the Athenian element in the Greek fleet at Salamis.[58]

[57] Roebuck, *op. cit.*, p. 15, n. 36.

[58] There are no reliable figures for the Athenian population in the early fifth century, but Herodotus gives an estimate of 30,000 for the number of citizens and states that 8,000 Athenian hoplites served at Plataea (9.28). A. W. Gomme (*Population of Athens* 3) considers that Herodotus' 30,000 may have been based originally on an accurate estimate. If so, it indicates a total population of about 120,000 free men, women and children (metics excluded).

CHAPTER II

Early Ionia

In the present state of our knowledge of early Ionia it is scarcely possible to discuss its development in concrete historical terms or to present a continuous narrative. Accordingly, I have centered this treatment on two problems which seem of particular importance: first, on the political development of Ionia as exemplified in the ethnic and political association of the Ionian League;[1] second, on the economic and social character of the communities which made up its membership. In the several hundred years between the time of the settlement of the Greeks on the western coast of Asia Minor and the career of Gyges in the first half of the seventh century, the small Greek colonies evidently developed into city-states, *poleis*, in the proper sense of the word. At the same time the colonists fostered a strong sense of ethnic unity, which, despite fusion with the natives and internecine strife, endured throughout their history. About these processes we can do little more than conjecture. The literary evidence consists of the legends of migration and the local traditions of the separate communities preserved in later authors such as Herodotus, Pausanias and Strabo. While the working out of the traditions is an interesting exercise in historiography, it is no guarantee of their validity. The archaeological investigation of the Greek and native sites on the western coast is proceeding rapidly, and that of Old Smyrna allows the literary tradition to be supplemented and checked, but a generation of excavation and study is needed to produce an adequate commentary. During this period and in this locale, epic poetry was developed to its crowning achievements of the *Iliad* and the *Odyssey*. To use their evidence for the institutions of the early Ionian towns

[1] Herodotus distinguished among the Ionian cities by dialect. His criterion was the type of native influence on the various groups of cities and their proximity to one another (1.142). He grouped Miletus, Myus and Priene (in Caria); Ephesus, Colophon, Lebedos, Teos, Klazomenai and Phocaea (in Lydia); Chios and Erythrae (proximity); Samos (isolated). These divisions accord in general with the process of expansion of the Ionian League as developed in the text.

is to raise the question how to separate out the traditional elements of the Late Bronze Age and the material of the Transitional and Geometric periods more contemporary with Homer. The poems picture a non-monetary, largely non-commercial society antecedent to that of the late seventh and sixth centuries when the forms of Classical Greece were taking shape. We can scarcely establish the strict historicity of its institutions, but they may be used to point the contrast with its successor, the enlarged world of archaic Greece. Into that world the Ionian towns seem to have emerged by 700 as strong, individual communities, in full possession of their coastal plains and on the threshold of that expansion by sea and inland which is our main theme.

THE DEVELOPMENT OF THE IONIAN LEAGUE[2]

In the legends of the migration from Old Greece to the west coast of Asia Minor, which were developed and preserved by writers of the archaic and later periods,[3] there is a strong insistence on a connection with Mycenean Greece. To some writers the connection seemed very close, for they reported traditions of direct colonization. The earliest literary notice, in Mimnermus of Colophon, the lyric poet of the seventh century, tells of settlers coming directly to Colophon from Pylos (frag. 12). In the fifth century Pherekydes of Athens apparently regarded Neleus, the founder of Miletus, as having come directly to that town from Pylos (Strabo 14.1.3). It is pertinent to point out that there is evidence of a small Mycenean settlement at Miletus and that the site of Colophon, of all the Ionian towns, most resembles the Mycenean sites of Old Greece. On the whole, however, there is little in the legends to indicate a firm tradition of a large-scale migration in the Mycenean period. The archaeological evidence, too, indicates only slight connections, which can hardly have resulted in more than small settlements like that at Miletus. As Hanfmann has pointed out, there is little possibility of a strong Mycenean tradition having been carried down through them.[4] Some memory of settlement and some Mycenean Greek families may well have survived at Miletus and Colophon, in particular, but, in general, the traditions of Mycenean Greece and the enduring wave of Ionian settlement seem to have come to Ionia after the collapse of the great centers in Old Greece. Had there not been a strong, new wave of colonization, it is probable that the Greek settlements on the west coast would have suffered the fate of those in Cilicia, as at Karatepe, where the house of Mopsus endured but with its Greek character obscured by native influences.[5] In Ionia the towns remained essentially Greek in culture, and the colonists sought to emphasize their affinities with Mycenean Greece.

[2] The discussion in this section is based on my article, "The Early Ionian League," *CP* 50 (1955) 26–40, from which I have repeated the essential documentation. Its present form is a revision of a paper read before the American Philological Association and the Archaeological Institute of America at Harvard University in December, 1954.

[3] Strabo 14.1.3ff., based mainly on Pherekydes, a fifth-century Athenian writer, but preserving local traditions also; Paus. 7.2.5 ff. For bibliography and discussion see Roebuck, *op. cit.*, pp. 34–35 and notes 61–63 on pp. 39–40.

[4] Hanfmann, *AJA* 49 (1945) 580–81; 52 (1948) 143–46; *HSCP* 61 (1953) 3–5.

[5] Mellink, *BibOr.* 7 (1950) 141–50; R. D. Barnett, *JHS* 73 (1953) 140–43.

Accordingly, the makers of the legends pictured the founders of Aeolis and Ionia as the refugee descendants of great Mycenean royal houses, attributing the Aeolian migration to the descendants of Agamemnon (Strabo 13.1.3–4) and the Ionian migration to the Neleids of Pylos. This legend of the Ionian migration developed greatly under the stimulus of Athenian patriotism in the fifth and fourth centuries, but parts of it are found also in local Ionian traditions and perhaps in Solon's poetry.[6] It was not entirely of Athenian imperial manufacture, however much the developed form celebrated Athens as the mother-city of Ionia. The canonical story of the migration told of a well organized, large-scale expedition from Athens, which had served as a concentration point for refugees after the collapse of the Mycenean kingdoms. It was led by the sons of King Codrus, who founded the twelve cities of Ionia which ultimately were included in the Ionian League of the sixth century. In command of the expedition was either the founder of Ionian Miletus, Neleus, or of Ephesus, Androclus, depending on the respective claims of each city to primacy in Ionia. Thus, an Ionian state organized under a supreme king was represented as being in existence from the outset. The towns of its cadet rulers became the member cities of the later League, but the original form of the Ionian League was a kingdom. The time ascribed to this migration in the traditional chronology is after the fall of Troy and the Dorian invasion, in the eleventh century.[7]

There is much to object to in the legends. The Athenian claim to be the mother-city of all Ionia is exaggerated; local traditions, as Herodotus invidiously pointed out, derived settlers from Boeotia, from Euboea, from elsewhere in central Greece and the Peloponnesus, a mixed lot (1.146.1). Elements in the traditions may be traced to local Ionian or to Athenian origin, to writers of archaic and classical Greece or to the antiquarians of the Hellenistic period. In this complex historians have chosen to stress one or other of the two strands and have presented us with two contrasting pictures of early Ionia: either a migration in the late eleventh century, which brought a selection of Mycenean refugees to Ionia with the memories of their past still strong or a straggling migration across the Aegean islands from various parts of Greece in the ninth century;[8] out of these disparate elements the new Ionia had to be formed.

Certain historical factors seem to attest a core of truth in the canonical legend. Herodotus acknowledged the existence of a proper Ionian element among the Asiatic Ionians, those who had come from Athens and still kept the feast of the Apaturia (1.146.2-147). Modern scholars point to the four old Ionian tribes in Athens and in some of the Ionian cities and their colonies.[9] The legends, unlike the accounts of the historical period of Greek colonization in the eighth and seventh centuries, derived the colonists from an earlier Greece

[6] Solon frag. 4.2; Roebuck, *op. cit.*, p. 40, n. 63.

[7] In 1086/85 or 1076/75 (Jacoby, *Mar. Par.* 27, pp. 151–52 and *FGrHist* 2D, No. 239, comm. on 27); in 1044/43 according to Eratosthenes who placed it four generations after the fall of Troy; 1045/44 for Ephesus and 1039/38 for the other cities according to Eusebius 1.187.36.

[8] For bibliography see Roebuck, *op. cit.*, p. 39, notes 61 and 62.

[9] See, in particular, Bolkestein, *Klio* 13 (1913) 429–30, 443–50; M. P. Nilsson, *Sk. ut. av Svenska Inst. i Athen*, 1951, pp. 143–49; 1953, pp. 4–6. This original composition was modified by the incorporation of non-Ionian Greeks and of natives into the Greek communities. See below, pp. 32–34.

of territorial units and ethnic entities, not from city-states; the founders of the Ionian cities were related to the great families of Mycenean Greece, not to the aristocracies of the cities. While these and other factors indicate that this is a different process of colonization than that which spread the Greeks throughout the Mediterranean, they do not give any very precise indication of its time. Aside from the traditional chronology, the only evidence is that of archaeology.

At the present time that tends to support the traditional picture of a Greek migration to Asia Minor in the eleventh century, but, as we shall discuss later, requires an adjustment of early Ionian development.[10] The support comes from the excavation of Old Smyrna, published only in summary form as yet.[11] It has provided the first detailed picture of the growth of a Greek town during the Dark Ages—a stratified, if at times fragmentary, record of a town site as well as of its pottery. The settlement is traditionally Aeolian Greek and occupied an existing native site. Presumably a group of militant Greek colonists subjugated and to some degree mingled with the resident native population. The excavators recognize the start of Ionian influence there by the appearance of imported and locally made Protogeometric pottery along with the native bucchero ware. The date assigned is *ca.* 1000, and the town is considered to have become completely Ionian, in material culture at least, *ca.* 800. While this Protogeometric pottery is related in style to early Athenian Protogeometric, it is considered to have sufficient individuality to attest its development in a different locale, presumably that of Ionia itself. It still remains to excavate fully the early strata of a proper *Ionian* town site, but this evidence from Old Smyrna records the inhabitation of Greeks on the coast in the eleventh century and the spread northwards of Ionian influence into the Aeolian area from *ca.* 1000, evidently the result of local trade and infiltration. The dating of Protogeometric and of East Greek Geometric pottery does not have any basis in absolute chronology, but Old Smyrna is a stratified site on which a relative chronology may be reconstructed by intricate cross-connections. It has a firm lower limit in the destruction by Alyattes of Lydia *ca.* 610,[12] while the imported pottery from Corinth provides checks to about the middle of the eighth century. Thus, there is archaeological evidence to support the case for the actuality of the canonical Greek legend. Is there a more specifically historical basis? Can we find out who these Ionians of the eastern islands and coastal cities were?

There can be little doubt who they thought they were in the sixth and fifth centuries, for Herodotus tells of their pride in considering themselves as *The Ionians par excellence.* He refused to grant their exclusive appropriation of such a name, but admitted that some of them, those from Athens, were properly Ionian. The Athenians, too, considered themselves Ionians, if only proud of it when it suited their political convenience, and elsewhere we

[10] I have followed the implications of the evidence from Old Smyrna as published in preliminary form by the excavators and as the result of a visit to the site in 1954. For a much more cautious appraisal see Hanfmann, *HSCP* 61 (1953) 1 ff.; for criticism of Hanfmann's treatment, Mellink, *AJA* 59 (1955) 184 and R. M. Cook, *JHS* 75 (1955) 157–58.

[11] J. M. Cook, *JHS* 72 (1952) 104–06; Cook and Akurgal, *ILN*, Feb. 28, 1953, pp. 328–29.

[12] Her. 1.16; Strabo 14.1.37. The Early Corinthian pottery found on the site of the destroyed temple indicates a date early in Alyattes' reign (*Anatolian Studies* 1 [1951] 16).

learn that the Ionian ethnos was considered to include many of the Aegean islanders.[13] Yet, the Ionians of Asia Minor appropriated for themselves the name of *The Ionians* by which they designated the citizens of the twelve member states of the Ionian League. Through some historical process that organization had been established as an exclusive association prior to the sixth century B.C. Its members regarded themselves as distinct from their Aeolian neighbors to the north, the Aeolian League, from the Dorians to the south, the Dorian hexapolis, and also from the Ionian ethnos as a whole. For the Delian Amphictyony, which was wide enough to include Athens and the islanders, included the citizens of the Ionian towns of Asia Minor as individuals, but the Ionian League was distinct and separate from it.[14]

The members of the League celebrated their national festival, the *Panionia*, at the Panionion,[15] where the shrine of their national deity, Poseidon Helikonios, was situated. Unlike the other famous cult centers of Greek Asia Minor, Branchidae, Claros and the Ephesian Artemision, this cult was non-oracular and free from such native accretions as Ephesian bees and hawk-goddesses. It is usually considered to stem from the cult of Poseidon in Boeotia.[16]

The League of the sixth century also had a political function, for it organized Ionian and Aeolian resistance to the conquest of Ionia by Cyrus in 546–40 and directed at least the latter part of the Ionian revolt of 499 against Darius. It was not, however, simply a military alliance brought into existence by needs of defence against Persia. Rather, it began to aquire the politically cohesive character of a true federal alliance at that time, finding the bond of union in the ethnic and religious character which had survived from its original form.[17] That form seems to have been a quasi-feudal kingdom of Ionians, the political solidarity of which had been lost in the evolution of the independent city-states in Ionia. For when we meet the League in historical times, the members are twelve city-states, independent and autonomous.

The twelve members were: Miletus, Myus, Priene, Ephesus, Colophon, Lebedos, Teos, Klazomenai, Phocaea, Samos, Chios and Erythrae.[18] It is significant that Herodotus states that Smyrna was the only state which applied for admittance to the League and was refused, although it had become Ionian.[19] Since Old Smyrna was destroyed by Alyattes of Lydia *ca.* 610, at some time prior to that date it had applied for admittance to the League and had been refused. Can we determine this time more closely?

According to the literary evidence Smyrna became an Ionian city before 688. Pausanias, evidently using the Olympic Victor List, reports that a Smyrnaean won an Olympic victory

[13] Her. 1.142–48; Roebuck, *op. cit.*, p. 37, n. 7.

[14] On the Delian panegyris see, most recently, Wade-Gery, *The Poet of the Iliad*, 3, 16 ff.

[15] Above, pp. 9–10.

[16] Wade-Gery, *op. cit.*, pp. 4–5.

[17] For the sixth century league see Roebuck, *op. cit.*, pp. 26–31.

[18] Her. 1.142–48; the same list is found in *Mar. Par.* 27; Strabo 14.1.3; Paus. 7.2.5 ff.; Aelian *Var. Hist.* 8.5; Vitruvius (4.1.4) adds Melite, and Velleius Paterculus (1.4.3) omits Teos, an omission of no apparent significance. See the table in Lenschau, *Klio* 36 (1944) 217.

[19] Herod. 1.143.3; Roebuck, *op. cit.*, p. 38, n. 38.

in the 23rd Olympiad, 688, and adds that Smyrna was then Ionian (5.8.7; 4.21.5). He apparently had in mind the story of its capture from the Aeolians by Ionian refugees of Colophon, which is told in some detail by Mimnermus and Herodotus.[20] It seems reasonable to equate this capture of Smyrna, which made it politically Ionian, with the archaeological evidence, which indicates that Smyrna was culturally Ionian *ca.* 800.

It is likely that the request for admission to the League was made soon after the town became completely Ionian, and we may conclude that the League was in existence in the early eighth century. It is also probable that it had acquired its twelve cities by that time, so that there was a feeling that the number was fixed by tradition. Perhaps there is a reflection of this in the *Iliad*, where Neleus, the father of Nestor of Pylos, is said to have had twelve sons.[21] The same jealous feeling of a fixed traditional membership was strong in the Delphic Amphictyony. If the League was functioning in the eighth century, it is necessary to revise Wilamowitz's reconstruction of the circumstances of its foundation. He had considered that the League came into existence *ca.* 700 as the result of a war between the twelve members-to-be against a thirteenth powerful state of Ionia, Melia. I have argued elsewhere that most of the detail surrounding this Melian War is anachronistic and that it seems to have been an episode of the early struggles of Ionians against Carian natives.[22] Let us return, then, to this pursuit of the League into the Dark Ages.

Despite this apparent manifestation of the strength of Ionian exclusiveness in the case of Smyrna, it is evident from the local foundation legends of the League members that not all were regarded as primary Ionian foundations. Some had become Ionian, like Smyrna, by a process of cultural infiltration and colonization from the primary Ionian centers, but, by the end of the ninth century, had been incorporated into the League. That is, it had attained its full form by a process of growth in the tenth and ninth centuries.

The originally non-Ionian cities were Chios, Phocaea, Klazomenai, Erythrae and perhaps Samos. Samos, in tradition, was settled a generation before the main Ionian migration. Androclus, the founder and king of Ephesus, is said to have attacked the son of Procles, founder of Samos, driving him from the island. The alleged cause of the war was Samian co-operation with the Carians against the Ionians.[23] Perhaps Samos was brought into the League very early by conquest. The other four states are all on the northern fringe of Ionia proper, and their inclusion represents the fruits of northward expansion. Klazomenai was a Colophonian colony, not a primary Ionian settlement;[24] Phocaea, probably an

[20] Her. 1.150; Mimnermus frag. 12; Roebuck, *op. cit.*, p. 38, n. 37. My views there were based solely on the literary evidence, but have been amplified by discussion of the excavation with J. M. Cook.

[21] *Il.* 11.692; Momigliano, *StItal* 10 (1932) 277–78. My thanks are due to J. M. Cook for pointing out an error in my reference to this analogy in *CP* 50 (1955), p. 38, n. 40; there, it was stated that the Neleus referred to in *Iliad* 11.692 was the founder of Miletus; he was, of course, the father of Nestor and progenitor of the Neleid dynasty. The Neleus of Pherekydes, Strabo's source (14.1.3), was a descendant.

[22] Roebuck, *op. cit.*, pp. 32–33. J. M. Cook disagrees with the view that Melia was a Carian city.

[23] Paus. 7.4.2. Hanfmann is very skeptical about the presence of Mycenean Greeks on Samos and wishes to lower the date of the earliest Greek levels (*op. cit.*, pp. 4–5, 8–9). Desborough, however, notes the existence of more Mycenean material than was recorded, but leaves the question of a settlement open (review of Stubbings, *Mycenaean Pottery from the Levant*, *JHS* 73 [1953] 181).

[24] Paus. 7.3.8–9.

Aeolian foundation originally, is said to have received its Codrid kings from Erythrae and Teos.[25] The Ionian settlement of Erythrae itself is placed later than the migration settlements.[26] The entry of Chios into the League has, unlike the others, the ring of historical record. It is said to have been joined to the League by its king, Hektor, after he had consolidated the island on which there were earlier Greek colonists and natives. King Hektor has been dated *ca.* 800 by Wade-Gery in his book, *The Poet of the Iliad*.[27] While this study led Wade-Gery to the suggestion that the Ionian migration was to be placed *ca.* 900, perhaps that is rather the time when Ionian colonists began to enter Chios from the towns to the south. In any case, we are brought once more by another route to *ca.* 800 as the time when the League had attained its full form. Its northern expansion from a pre-existing group of states is to be set in the ninth century.

That nucleus consisted of Miletus, Myus, Priene, Ephesus, Colophon, Lebedos, Teos and probably Samos, all clustering around the Panionion. These towns must have been peopled by settlers who had a coherent organization of their own and a strong sense of identity as Ionians. This was maintained so effectively that it obscured the origin of other Greeks, who came in weaker bands at a later date, and outweighed the native influences from intermarriage and affiliation. Like the Greeks in Libya and Egypt the Ionians were able to maintain their Hellenic character.[28] The colonists of Libya and Egypt, however, had a developed Hellenic background in the cities from which they came and maintained their connections by a network of trading relations. What did these early Ionian settlers have? The traditions of Mycenean Greece in their epic poetry could have nourished their cultural ties with Old Greece, and the cult of Poseidon preserved the Ionian ethnic consciousness in religious form. Yet, the expansion of the League indicates that the group of old settlers around the Panionion also maintained political coherence and supremacy. It is perhaps reflected in the local traditions of Ephesus.

Strabo commented:[29] "The royal seat of the Ionians was established there and still now the descendants of Androclus' family are called Kings and they have certain honors." This Ephesian kingship had a more than local importance in early Ionia. A king of Ephesus is said to have waged war on the Greeks of Samos for aiding Carians against Ionians, to have aided Priene against the Carian natives, to have captured a town, Larisa under Mt. Tmolus, from the native Maeonians, to have fought against Magnesia on the Maeander, probably a native town.[30] These notices may be colored by an age conscious of the

[25] Paus. 7.3.10.

[26] Paus. 7.3.7.

[27] Paus. 7.4.9–10 (based on Ion of Chios); Wade-Gery, *op. cit.*, p. 7. On these northern Ionian towns see Wilamowitz, *SB*: *Berlin* 1906, 55–57, 62–63. The excavation of the very promising site of Aeolian Kyme was begun in 1953. Its early fill is deep and already has produced much geometric and archaic pottery and house walls. Careful and extensive excavation of this site should throw considerable light on the problem of Greek settlement on the coast.

[28] F. Chamoux, *Cyrène*, 387–88. For Naukratis see Roebuck, *CP* 46 (1951) 216. The position of the Greeks in Egypt was apparently regulated by Egyptian royal charter.

[29] Strabo 14.1.3; Roebuck, *CP* 50 (1955), p. 40, n. 66.

[30] Samos: Paus. 7.4.2; Priene: Paus. 7.2.9; Larisa: Strabo 13.3.2; Magnesia: Roebuck, *op. cit.*, p. 38 n. 41.

distinction between Greek and barbarian, but they can also reflect the position of the King of Ephesus as champion of the early Ionian settlers who met at the Panionion. This primitive league was not a league of city-states. Kings would rule its member-towns with the King of Ephesus as their chief. Perhaps in the *basileus* of the League known in Roman times we have the descendant of the early chief king of the Ionians. His duties had then become purely religious, and the office was no longer attached to a single family in a particular city.[31] When the towns of the primitive league developed into city-states in the eighth century, their kingships, too, became religious offices and the old quasi-feudal ties with the chief king lapsed. The religious celebration of the Panionic festival remained to reinforce the feeling of being a separate people. The feeling of political separateness from the other Ionians, whom those of Asia Minor joined as individuals in the Delian festival, indicates an earlier and stronger cohesiveness. Should we not see in this early League the transference from Greece of a post-Mycenean kingship to Ionia and, in the vivid pictures of the uneasy relationship between chief and subordinate kings in the *Iliad*, a reflection of the position of the rulers in the Ionian towns in their early political association? Perhaps, too, that poem's military emphasis reflects the bitter struggle to hold their place in Ionia against its native residents. In Athens we know that there was a cultural continuity from Mycenean times;[32] perhaps a Mycenean kingship survived to the time of the Ionian migration. As we have noticed, the sons of Codrus who fell in battle before Athens traditionally led that migration. Poseidon Helikonios was their god. The threads seem to lead to Attica and Boeotia.

SOCIAL AND ECONOMIC DEVELOPMENT

While these early Ionians were able to ensure the survival and expansion of their League they cannot have been very numerous. We know next to nothing of the resources and techniques of eleventh and tenth century Greece, but large-scale expeditions were surely beyond its powers. Since the penteconter was probably not invented until the late eighth

[31] *OGIS* II, No. 489; *SEG* I, No. 399; *Ins. v. Priene* No. 536; A. Momigliano, "Il re degli Ioni nella provincia romana di Asia," *Atti del III Congresso Nazionale di Studi Romani*, 1934, 1, pp. 429–34; H. Bengtson, *Philologus* 92 (1937) 130 and *Griechische Geschichte* 53. Aside from the notices of Codrid kings in connection with the migration, there seems ample evidence of kingship in the Ionian states to attest that it was the regular system of government in prehistoric Ionia. Herodotus states (1.147) that, in addition to the Codrid kings, some of the Greek settlers set up Lycian kings of the family of Glaukos, while others were ruled by both native and Greek houses. This remark should indicate intermarriage between the noble Greek families and their Anatolian counterparts such as we find in historical times. For example, one of the Melanidai of Ephesus married a daughter of Alyattes (Santo Mazzarino, *Fra Oriente e Occidente* 198); cf. also the intimate relations between the Milesian and a Carian royal family as told in Aristotle (*FHG* II, p. 164, frag. 199). Evidence of post-Codrid kingship is found in Chios: Wade-Gery, *The Poet of the Iliad* 6–7; in Erythrae (Basilidai): Aristotle *Pol.* 5 v. 4 (1305b); in Aeolian Kyme: Wade-Gery, *op. cit.*, p. 7; Herakl. Pont. (*FHG* II, p. 216, frag. 11); Plut. *Quaest. gr.* 2 (292a); in Ephesus (Basilidai): *FGrHist* III, pp. 77–78.3; in Lesbos (Basilidai): *IG* XII, 2, Nos. 6, 18; Santo Mazzarino, *Athenaeum* 21 (1943) 43; in Miletus: Nik. Dam. *FGrHist* 2A, No. 52; Konon *Phot. Cod.* 186, 139; in Samos: Her. 3.59.4. These kingships seem to have developed into aristocracies by the early seventh century.

[32] O. Broneer, *AJA* 52 (1948) 111–14.

century, smaller and more rudimentary boats were used before that time,[33] and colonists of the early expeditions were numbered in two and three figures. If an analogy may be used from the historical period, the colonization of Cyrene is instructive. The first expedition was made in two penteconters, carrying perhaps two hundred people; two generations later, *ca.* 580, after the colony had been firmly established, large numbers of colonists came there from Doric and Ionian states to make a proper city of it. They were associated with the original citizens by the creation of new tribes, but Cyrene remained essentially Doric in its traditions.[34] The Ionian towns must have grown by a similar process so far as their Greek element was concerned. Probably, when the initial settlement had proved successful, reinforcements came from Greece and the islands. Their tradition is left in the notices of mixed origin for which Herodotus reproached the Ionians. The newcomers became enthusiastic Ionians, but the latter were not all descended from the old settlers who came from the town hall of Athens. The opportunity for migration was offered by the more peaceful conditions in the tenth century which Desborough notes.[35] The evidence is presumably to be seen in the distribution of Protogeometric pottery and the affinities of its various groups. Since the material from Asia Minor is still being studied, we may turn to the growth of the towns.

The first holdings of the Greeks on the coast were precarious.[36] Many of the towns were on promontories where the sea sides were easily defensible and the connecting isthmus could be walled off. The adjacent plains were evidently worked under threat of attack from the natives, for there is an almost unanimous tradition of conflict, subjection of natives to serf status and intermarriage with their women. Yet, the Greeks did not have to resist the pressure of a strongly organized state. As Hanfmann has pointed out,[37] there is no evidence of highly developed native cultures on the coast nor of Late Hittite kingdoms on the western part of the Anatolian plateau. Phrygia was remote, and its main contacts were to the east and south, towards Urartu, Assyria and the states of North Syria rather than west to the Aegean.[38]

The Ionians in their walled towns survived the attacks of the relatively unorganized natives and eventually controlled the plains along the coast, but were greatly influenced by native contacts in their crafts, religious cults and social habits. These influences, in antiquity, worked characteristically along certain lines and at certain levels in the social structure more intensively than others, through slaves, intermarriage with the natives, trade contacts and the like. Over against them we should set the strong conservatism of

[33] For the development of the early Greek ship see Carpenter *AJA* 52 (1948) 7–8; Kirk, *BSA* 44 (1949) 134–44.

[34] Chamoux, *op. cit.*, pp. 139–42, 387.

[35] Desborough, *Protogeometric Pottery* 299–304.

[36] For the pattern of migration settlements in Aeolis and Ionia see J. M. Cook, *Historia* 4 (1955) 40–42; he has informed me that the earliest fortification found at Old Smyrna was of the Geometric period; "by inference there was an earlier fortification (? of the Bronze Age). We have no evidence for Protogeometric times."

[37] Hanfmann, *AJA* 52 (1948) 143–55.

[38] Below, pp. 43–44.

Greek political institutions and social organization. In early Ionia these seem to have been cherished by a vigorous and individualistic aristocracy which found an expression of its values in Homer and support in continuous intercourse among its own members and across the Aegean.

The process of fusion which set in was evidently very complex. There does not seem to have existed in this early period, or in the archaic period, any strong feeling of "racial" antipathy or contempt between Greek and barbarian. Apparently Greeks of both high and low social levels intermarried with their Anatolian counterparts, probably perforce by the shortage of women. The example of the Milesians and Carians noticed by Herodotus is well known, but there were many others as indicated by the evidence that native tribes became an integral part of the Greek communities.[39] This may have had a perceptible effect on the crafts. For example, the use of captured slave women and the presence of native wives in the households were a natural means of transmission for techniques and motifs in textile work, the particular province of the distaff side of the household. Perhaps to this is owed the tapestry-like effects made by much East Greek pottery.[40] The craftsmen of a community, potters and smiths, might contain a large percentage of natives of the lower-class, while their Greek counterparts would not be subject to the patriarchal discipline which characterized the aristocratic Greek households, and so freer to mingle with their native colleagues. Perhaps from these factors, as much as from trade, the Anatolian influences perceptible in pottery and metal work were derived.[41] The Greeks, however, seized the lands on which their livelihood rested from the native owners. They do not seem to have come to Anatolia to trade,[42] but as settlers looking for homes and fields to till or, better, that the conquered natives might till.

We have traditions of wars undertaken by communities and perhaps by the League itself against the natives. Evidence of a native serf class, the Gergithes, which was kept down by force, exists for Miletus.[43] Where conquest of land from natives failed, fellow Greeks might be attacked, as the efforts of Samos to acquire a *peraea* at the expense of

[39] Her. 1.146; below, p. 34.

[40] See, for example, the discussion in K. F. Kinch, *Vroulia* 233 ff.

[41] Hanfmann, *HSCP* 61 (1953) 16–17, 20–21; below, pp. 45–46.

[42] Hanfmann (*op. cit.*, pp. 11 ff.) has suggested that the initial Greek settlement in western Anatolia was made by small groups of traders in the native towns. The Greeks were of mixed origin and succeded in Hellenizing and eventually taking over the towns when an influx of regular colonists came in the period *ca.* 850–800. This argument rests on the archaeological considerations that the East Greek Protogeometric and Geometric pottery is found in small quantity and is of mainland inspiration, that the *koine* of East Greek Geometric appears only in the early eighth century with Rhodes as the center of its development. The hypothesis seems unsatisfactory for several reasons. What was the material of trade in the tenth and ninth centuries that would lure Greeks to settle generally along the coast of Asia Minor, when its native towns were as poor materially as those of Greece itself? The "Homeric" community was self-sufficient except for metals and had no special class of traders. Perhaps the west coast of Anatolia was the center of a metal- and utensil-exporting trade at this early time, but that seems unlikely from our knowledge of conditions in Anatolia between the thirteenth and eighth centuries (below pp. 87–88). Further, as the discussion in the text indicates, the emphasis of the literary sources is on the militant character of the colonization; there is great difficulty in transferring it to the latter part of the ninth century, which would be necessary if Hanfmann's argument is followed.

[43] Athenaeus 524a (from Herakl. Pont.).

Priene and of Chios from Erythrae indicate.[44] Where war and raiding were not successful, compromise might be achieved through marital alliances with the native dynasts. Consider the terms on which Glaukos was taken into the royal family of Lycia (*Il.* 6.191–95). Perhaps the record of such alliances and compromises may be seen in the *pyrgoi* list of the fourth century from Teos in which native and Greek names of the Heroic Age are found side by side. They are plausibly identified by Hunt[45] as the family names of estates from the foundation period of Teos. The personal names indicate that the native families there Hellenized, which was the usual direction of the process. The degree of native influence probably varied in different communities depending on the local circumstances of development. Ephesus is usually regarded as strongly affected by the Lydians, and Miletus by the Carians. There was a Carian tribe in Samos, and a strong native element is attested for Erythrae.[46] Whatever the local results, it seems apparent that no great change was made in the fundamentally agricultural life along the coast by the advent of the Greeks. Their economy continued to be based on cultivation of the land and on pasturage. Perhaps some changes were introduced into the system of land tenure, but as to that we can only conjecture.

Hunt has suggested that the old Anatolian system of large estates worked by serf labor continued to be employed.[47] While the Greek nobility might have gained large holdings by right of conquest or by their marital ties with the Anatolian landed rulers, all the settlers were not nobles, even if they were conquerors. Probably small free-holdings were allocated from captured land, and some retainers found work on the estates of their lords. We do not have any explicit evidence, but two considerations support this view. If the Homeric social system is a reflection in any part of the conditions in Ionia, there was such a system in operation.[48] Second, there is evidence for the emergence of a hoplite class in the Ionian cities in the seventh century, despite the stress sometimes put on Ionia as a land of cavalry supported by its large plains and landed nobility. Cavalry forces are attested only for Lydia and Colophon, where, from the extent of their plains, they might be expected. Other states would no doubt have small forces, but both Mimnermus and Callinus in the seventh century record the hoplite as the characteristic Ionian warrior.[49] Like his counterpart in Greece, he is presumably the free, middle class farmer with a moderate-sized holding. We do not have any record of a "middle class" revolution in the Ionian cities until the sixth century, so that the proper time for the allocation of such lands was in the period of conquest from the natives.

[44] Bürchner, "Erythrai," *RE* 6 (1909) 585; Samos: above, pp. 9–10.

[45] *JHS* 67 (1947) 71, 76.

[46] Samos: Wilamowitz, *SB: Berlin* 1906, p. 74; Erythrae: Paus. 7.3.7; in Ephesus the Ionian tribes seem to have been partly subordinated into smaller units, M. P. Nilsson, *Sk. ut. av Svenska Inst. i Athen* 1951, 143–45.

[47] Hunt, *JHS* 67 (1947) 74–75.

[48] M. Finley, *The World of Odysseus* 49 ff.; Finley gives a general treatment of Homeric society which he diffidently suggests as true of the tenth and ninth centuries (p. 44).

[49] Mimnermus frag. 13; Callinus frag. 1; Sappho mentions infantry, cavalry and ships (frag. 27a); a hoplite is represented in a silver figurine from Chios, which is dated in the first half of the seventh century (*BSA* 42 [1947] 110, 128).

We may discern in early Ionia a militant group of settlers, for even Mimnermus mixes warfare with his roses,[50] gradually extending their influence and possession over the coastal areas. Their life was predominantly agricultural but with walled towns a necessity for defense against natives and fellow Greeks. The early years of settlement were turbulent with wars and raids. Both circumstances, agriculture and warfare, contributed to the dominance of an aristocracy which was Greek and drew additional support from Greece by its relations in the Aegean and by the continuous arrival of new settlers.

The tangible evidence of this intercourse is as yet slight: in general, we may point to the pottery found in Old Smyrna from *ca.* 1000 B.C., but it is still unpublished. The emergence of a *koine* of East Greek art in the early eighth century, as pointed out by Hanfmann,[51] also presupposes a considerable degree of intercourse in the region, but its study, too, is in the early stages. Occasion for meeting was afforded by the panegyreis at Delos and Ephesus which Wade-Gery has stressed.[52] Yet, it is unlikely that any very detailed picture of these connections will emerge for the tenth and ninth centuries. Aside from the archaeological problems posed by the excavation of the major Ionian sites with their extensive overbuilding in Hellenistic and Roman times, there is the general consideration that the early Ionian towns were small and poor. As soon as it was safe the nobility may have lived outside the walls, as they seem to have done in Teos on the *pyrgoi* and in seventh-century Miletus (Her. 1.17). If Old Smyrna is typical, the towns of the tenth and ninth centuries counted their population in hundreds and housed them in one-room mud brick huts.[53] There was little margin of wealth for the development of crafts and the purchase of imported goods in these essentially agricultural towns. Any extensive development along such lines had to wait on the growth of population, of trade and of the process of urbanization which is hardly perceptible until the late eighth century. Perhaps the poems of Homer reflect the start of this transition, if our eyes are not dazzled by the gleam of gold from Mycenae.[54]

The significance of the poems from this point of view is their picture of an agrarian society, which, in the *Odyssey* at least, is depicted as beginning to take to the sea to engage

[50] Mimnermus frags. 1 and 13. The evidence of the lyric poets is, of course, for the seventh and early sixth centuries rather than for this earlier period. It is a useful antidote for the moralizing criticism of the latter part of the sixth century (above, pp. 2–3).

[51] Hanfmann, *op. cit.*, pp. 13–14.

[52] Wade-Gery, *op. cit.*, pp. 3, 16ff.; p. 62, n. 6 (Ephesus).

[53] *ILN*, Feb. 28, 1953, pp. 328–29. The oval hut illustrated is dated *ca.* 900. Remains of rectangular huts of the ninth century were also found, but not until the seventh century did the houses become substantial. This is a far cry from the palaces of Homeric description and of the Late Bronze Age.

[54] That is not to suggest that the poems give a historical picture of conditions in Ionia in the tenth, ninth and eighth centuries. Recent work on the archaeological background, as in Lorimer's *Homer and the Monuments* and Gray's article, "Metal-Working in Homer," *JHS* 74 (1954) 1–15, has shown that the material background is one of traditional Late Bronze Age, Transitional and Geometric elements, with a few from the seventh century, by which time the poems had ceased to be fluid. As the translation of the Mycenean inscriptions proceeds, perhaps it will be possible to separate out the elements of the institutional background with more assurance. My own viewpoint is that the institutions belong for the most part to the ninth and eighth centuries. In the picture of wealth and labor which I have drawn there is rather more fluidity than in that of Finley in the *World of Odysseus*, particularly with respect to trade and sea-faring.

in trade. Sea-faring does not have a place in the typical scenes of life pictured on Achilles' shield, but in the *Odyssey* Homer sketches the maritime state of the oar-loving Phaeacians. The picture may be contrasted to that of Hesiod whose farmers venture to sea only to sell their surplus by peddling it along the coasts in the autumn. Hesiod's father, however, came from Aeolian Kyme, which did not realize for three hundred years that it was set on the sea (Strabo 13.3.6), to settle inside Boeotia of equal maritime repute. In Ionian Smyrna and Chios, with which Homer's own life is traditionally associated most closely, conditions were changing in the latter part of the eighth century.

The basic occupation of the Homeric community was still agriculture. Its kings and nobles were landowners, while most of its people made their living by farming activity of some type, working either for themselves or for the noble landowners in the capacity of retainers or *thetes*. Other activities receive little notice: fishing, while mentioned,[55] was probably a diversion from the round of agricultural activity to eke out the food supply; although mining is not attested, the smelting of iron is well known;[56] lumbering seems to have been carried on for the immediate purpose of building a ship or home, rather than to provide a stock of timber, or by a special class of woodcutters.[57] The ordinary cutting of wood for fire was a part of the farmer's life. Evidently the most important surplus of goods was from agriculture. The same impression is made by an examination of the activity of craftsmen.

Those craftsmen who receive particular notice are the *tekton* and the smith. Although weaving was of great importance, it should not be called a specialized craft, since it was the normal activity of the women in the household. The *tekton*, or master-builder, held a relatively good social position among the people, for he was ranked with seers, bards and doctors as a man who would be welcomed anywhere (*Od.* 17.381–87). We should hardly conclude that he did wander from community to community, but he evidently worked on various commissions and was certainly more peripatetic than a smith who needed a fixed establishment.[58] The *tekton's* craft was skilled and hereditary (*Il.* 5.59-64), devoted, in particular, to shipbuilding (*Il.* 5.59–64; 15.410–12; *Od.* 9.126) and the woodwork on palaces (*Il.* 6.315–16; 23.712–13; *Od.* 17.340–41; 21.43–44). For such building he cut the trees and shaped the lumber himself, as well as doing the actual construction. Presumably he also did cabinet work, since we are told of one *tekton* making a costly chair, and Odysseus' versatility is emphasized by the comment that he has built his own bed (*Od.* 19.56ff.; 23.189).

The smithy, by the nature of its equipment, was a fixed establishment and a place of

[55] *Od.* 4.368–69; we find fishing with a net (*Od.* 22.384ff.), but more frequently by using hooks (*Il.* 24.80-83; *Od.* 4.368–69). Shellfish, too, were obtained (*Il.* 16.746–48). There is no evidence of a specialized group of fishermen.

[56] Gray has pointed out that the poems show familiarity with the working of iron and no other metal; the former is a commonplace (*op. cit.*, pp. 12–13).

[57] *Il.* 5.59–64; 16.482–84. A general word, *drytomoi*, is used of those who fell trees, but it can scarcely be applied to a specialized group of woodcutters (*Il.* 11.86–87; 16.633; 23.112ff.). The large part which wood plays in construction is particularly appropriate to western Asia Minor.

[58] See the remarks of Finley, *op. cit.*, p. 52.

resort as well as a workshop. It offered warmth in the winter and opportunity for appropriate critical comment by the bystanders (*Od.* 18.328; Hesiod *Works and Days* 493). The chief activity of the smith was the manufacture of arms and utensils (*Il.* 12.294–97; 18.410ff.), and some particularly skilled individuals may have turned out articles of precious metals (*Il.* 4.187, a mitra; *Od.* 6.232), but work of this type was usually attributed to the god Hephaestus (*Il.* 18.371ff.) or to a foreign source. It scarcely seems possible to identify the goldsmith as a separate craftsman.[59]

Other crafts receive little notice: the potter is mentioned but once (*Il.* 18.600–01), despite the fact that his products were one of the main articles of use in the community. The only leather-worker noticed is from Hyde (?) in Maeonia (*Il.* 7.220–23). Probably articles of leather were normally made in the household. Ivory is known (*Il.* 4.141–45; *Od.* 18.196; 8.404), but it was of slight economic importance and its working was carried on in a few centers only.[60]

The labor of this community, still largely self-sufficient in its own households, produced a scanty surplus for use in trade, grain, hides, wool and animals in good years on the large estates. Carpenter and smith worked mostly for particular commissions, but the products of a skilled smith might gain repute over a fairly extensive local area. Textiles were produced in excess of need in the larger households, since they were used for a variety of purposes and formed a substantial part of the household wealth.[61] In such a society most of its products were for local consumption, and its few luxuries brought from elsewhere.

Wealth was reckoned by the amount of land and its products, by the quantity and quality of arms, utensils and metal in general, by the possession of a large house and the slaves to staff it. Special notice is given in the poems to any exotic goods from a foreign source, and their rarity is indicated by the detail of the notice. The ordinary agricultural products from the king's land, grain, olive oil and wine were stored in his treasury (*Od.* 2.339–40), and much attention paid to the animals,[62] pigs, sheep, goats and cattle (*Il.* 4.433–34). Their loss particularly distressed Telemachus (*Od.* 1, 2 *passim*; 17.472), and Eumaeus boasted at length about Odysseus' herds. The absence of horses is accounted for by the lack of proper pasture (*Od.* 4.601–08), but horses were a prized possession and probably bred in small numbers only. The produce of the King's own domain was increased by the "gifts" from his subjects,[63] probably a fixed part of their own produce (*Il.* 9.154–56). The King's store then, was the chief concentration point for the agricultural surplus of the community. Yet, in one passage of the *Odyssey* we are told that Odysseus was given barley and wine out of the public store of a Cretan city (*Od.* 19.197–98: δημόθεν). Homer probably refers here to a city-state, properly speaking, where grain, oil and wine were kept as public property, from which gifts to athletes and other heroes were made and food might be

[59] See Gray, *op. cit.*, p. 12.

[60] Barnett, *JHS* 68 (1948) 1–3; below, p. 43.

[61] A dedication (*Il.* 6.90–93); Hektor's ransom (*Il.* 24.229ff.); gifts (*Il.* 16.223–24; *Od.* 8.387ff.; 15.105–08; 24.274ff.); covers for a chariot (*Il.* 5.193ff.).

[62] Finley considers the economy of the poems pastoral rather than agrarian (*op. cit.*, pp. 54ff.). It is perhaps a matter of emphasis in various sections.

[63] See Finley, *op. cit.*, pp. 64ff., for discussion of "gifts" as an institution.

distributed in time of siege. The earliest references to such an institution seem to be Herodotus' account of the siege of Miletus by Alyattes, if not anachronistic (1.22), and a casual reference by Xenophanes (frag. 2.8). This agricultural wealth might be increased as a matter-of-course by raiding. Odysseus announced his intention of restoring his depleted flocks by raids as well as by the gifts of his subjects (*Od.* 23.357–58). Perhaps he felt it entirely justifiable as a matter of recompense. That was the motive of Nestor's famous raid into Elis (*Il.* 11.671 ff.), but Nestor took entirely too much pleasure in the raid for us to consider that recompense was the sole motive. Such raiding was, of course, the peacetime counterpart on land of the piracy by sea.

The King's store of metal, both in bullion and manufactured form, was also a prominent part of his wealth. In the treasuries stocks of metals, bronze, gold and iron, but significantly enough, not silver, were accumulated to be passed down from generation to generation (*Il.* 6.46–50; *Od.* 2.337 ff.; 21.6 ff.; 14.324). Since these are not designated as arms or utensils, the references must be to metals in ingot or some trade form—a modest counterpart of the treasure of iron bars found in such quantity in the palace of Sargon II at Nineveh and mentioned in the Assyrian booty lists.[64] From this stock were made the arms and utensils, and it was used, when necessary, to ransom a captured king. Ransoms were usually paid in metal (*Il.* 2.229–30; 6.46–50; 11.131–34; 10.378–80) with, perhaps, a conventional amount as a start for bargaining (*Il.* 22.340). Aside from arms and armor, the utensils which are particularly mentioned are tripods and cauldrons of bronze and cups of precious metals. The detailed histories of the latter indicate that they were normally of foreign origin and had passed through several hands. They were acquired as gifts or heirlooms, prizes of war and piracy (*Od.* 8.430; *Il.* 24.229 ff.; 7.299, 148–49; 10.267–72; 11.19–20). The standard articles of wealth appear most clearly in such passages as Agamemnon's offer to Achilles, seven tripods, ten talents of gold, twenty cauldrons, seven female slaves and in the lists of prizes at the funeral games of Patroklos.[65]

[64] Below, p. 102. Cf. the mass of iron given as a prize at the games of Patroklos.

[65] Chariot race (*Il.* 23.262 ff.)—prizes: 1st, a woman skilled in weaving and a tripod and cauldron of 22 measures in capacity; 2d, a pregnant mare; 3d, a new cauldron of 4 measures in capacity; 4th, 2 talents of gold; 5th, a new two-handled pot (presumably of bronze). On the result of this race Idomeneus and Ajax laid a side bet of a tripod or cauldron (*Il.* 23.485–88). Boxing (*Il.* 23.657 ff.)—prizes: 1st, a mule; 2d, a two-handled cup. Wrestling (*Il.* 23.701–05)—prizes: a tripod worth 12 oxen and a woman worth 4. Footrace (*Il.* 23.740 ff.)—prizes: 1st, a silver bowl from Sidon of 6 measures in capacity; 2d, 1 ox; 3d, ½ talent of gold. Weight throwing (*Il.* 23.826–35)—prize: the weight itself, a mass of iron. Archery (*Il.* 23.851 ff.)—prizes: 1st, 10 double axeheads of iron; 2d, 10 single axeheads. Javelin throwing (*Il.* 23.885 ff.)—prizes: 1st, a new cauldron worth 1 ox; 2d, a spear.

The standard of value is the conventional one of the ox. To judge from the prizes in the footrace 1 ox probably was equal to 1 talent of gold. This gold talent was probably a pellet of gold like those found at Enkomi in Cyprus or in the Artemision at Ephesus (Enkomi: Evans, *Corolla Numismatica* 365–66; Ephesus: Robinson, *JHS* 71 [1951] 164). If so, a standard of values may be made out with some interesting results: a new cauldron, presumably of bronze, of 4 measures capacity (small) was worth about 4 talents of gold; a female slave, skilled in weaving, was worth 4 oxen (4 talents of gold), much less than the tripod and cauldron worth 12 oxen, given as a first prize in the wrestling. This may well have been a common price for such slaves, for Eurycleia evidently valued herself very highly as a young slave when she says her price was 20 oxen worth (*Od.* 1.429–31). The price paid to Achilles for his captive, 100 oxen worth (*Il.* 21.79–91), was a speculation to get ransom, since the captive was of noble birth; the expectation was realized with a

Trade played a small but definite part in the life of the community, although the professional trader was not regularly recognized. The heroes themselves carried on a form of non-professional trading, which was dignified into various social graces. For example, young Alexander, Priam's son, brought back some *peploi* from Sidon acquired on his Grand Tour (*Il.* 6.289–92); they were probably gifts for which he had given others, thus establishing a guest friendship (*Il.* 6.215ff.; *Od.* 1.311–13; 24.281–86). Another such gift was that made by Polybos of Thebes in Egypt to Menelaos and Helen, metal articles, many of them silver as was fitting in Egypt (*Od.* 4.125–32). Such gifts might pass through many hands, like the silver and gold crater which Phaidimos of Sidon had given to Menelaos and which he gave to Telemachus (*Od.* 4.615ff.; 15.117–19). Another form of gift was that presented by traders to a king for the privilege of trading with his people, a primitive customs toll. The Lemnians made a special present to Agamemnon of choice wine before they traded with the army at Troy (*Il.* 7.467ff.). Phoenicians gave a silver bowl to Thoas; his grandson, Euneos, gave it to Patroklos as ransom for a captive and finally it was offered as a prize in the foot race (*Il.* 23.740ff.) at Patroklos' funeral games. The exchange of these costly articles, however, can scarcely be called trade, for they are pledges of friendship, propitiatory gifts and the like. Although such articles are a large proportion of those of value mentioned in the poems, they were occasionally purchased (*Od.* 15.415ff.). The Homeric king evidently felt free to dispose of his surplus farm products, for Euneos of Lemnos, Jason's son, sold his wine to Agamemnon's army. He might, if opportunity offered, be a slave dealer, disposing of his captives (*Il.* 21.40–41, 102; cf. 21.79–80). Mentes claimed to be a king in his own country, which dignified his transaction in metals. Obviously a king's exchange of products for the services of craftsmen would be a commonplace transaction. Local exchange of surplus agricultural products for metals, slaves and the like was probably equally regular. Agamemnon's army paid for its Lemnian wine by the spoils of war, bronze, iron, hides, oxen and slaves. Wine, too, was exchanged from the regions with a good vintage to those without, as the reputation of the wine from Maroneia in Thrace indicates (*Il.* 9.71–72; *Od.* 9.196–98). This type of local trading approached the professional category, but was still highly respectable, since the kings were merely exchanging the products of their estates for other goods and services. There was, however, no professional middle man. Professional traders were evidently beginning to make their appearance in the *Odyssey*, but were regarded with dislike and suspicion, since they were asked whether they traveled for business or piracy (*Od.* 3.72–74; 8.161–69; 9.253).

This attitude to the trader was based partly on his occasional activity as a pirate or kidnapper but mainly on the fact that he was a foreigner, who came without the credentials of noble birth. After all, piracy and kidnapping were normal activities, but in the tightly

ransom of 300 oxen worth. Evidently 100 oxen worth was very valuable or very costly, for we are told that each gold tassel on Athena's aegis was worth that, and Glaukos' golden armor received a similar evaluation (*Il.*6.236). Presumably 100 oxen worth was the upper limit for transactions, except important ransoms. Exchange was generally on a small scale, and the procurement of a fine set of armor was exceptionally costly.

knit Homeric society the foreigner had no place. Such trading meant roving from place to place by sea and was not essentially different from the life of the clanless man. It might also rouse dislike by a too successful bargain. We hear considerably more of Phoenician (Cypriote?) traders than Greek, because they carried on long distance trade, peddling their goods around the Aegean. The length and route of their voyages is indicated in several passages: Odysseus represents himself on one occasion as having been a passenger on a Phoenician ship from Crete to be dropped at Elis or Pylos on the west coast of the Peloponnesus (*Od.* 13.272ff.); again, he was on a Phoenician ship plying from Phoenicia to Egypt and Libya (*Od.* 14.290ff.). The types of goods carried are interestingly reminiscent of those carried by traders into the Indian country, countless trinkets (*Od.* 15.415ff.) with a few valuable objects for the rulers. In contrast with this, the Greeks probably circulated their agricultural goods locally, exchanging them for what the purchasers had on hand, metals, hides, animals and slaves. The problem of the trade in metal cannot be solved in the light of the Homeric references. It is likely that each surface deposit of iron and copper was quickly worked out as discovered. Perhaps Mentes offers an example of what occasionally happened. Some fortunate landowner, a king, would discover a local supply on his property and go into the business of trading until it was exhausted.[66] At least the metal trade indicates that Homeric exchange cannot be characterized simply as a shifting about of agricultural surpluses and the acquirement of luxuries.

Although the community of the Phaeacians is not very helpful in explaining the character of trade, it does reveal a different way of life than that of the purely agrarian town. The Phaeacians have been identified with various peoples, both Greek and non-Greek, but for our purposes the question is relatively unimportant. They had colonized Scheria, far from men who lived by barley (*Od.* 6.7ff.). The new colony was under the direction of its founder, Nausithous; a wall was built, houses and temples erected and the fields apportioned—some barley was evidently necessary. The siting of the city is reminiscent of many Ionian towns or, rather, of what they wished to be ideally, living in the security guaranteed by the isolation of an island and the defensibility of a peninsula. Around the city were fields and at the base of the peninsula the harbors, between which the narrow entrance led. Each vessel had its own place, and near the harbor the agora was used to prepare gear. The community is called oar-loving, and Nausicaa's friend was the daughter of a famous voyager, Dymas (*Od.* 6.22). They were seafarers who had no care for the bow or quiver (*Od.* 6.270–71). The bow, as Lorimer has pointed out, [67] was an Asiatic weapon. Surely Homer is describing an Ionian city, subject to attack by its Asiatic neighbors, with its defense depending primarily on its position and walls and its livelihood partly on the fields and increasingly on the sea.

[66] Gray (*op. cit.*, pp. 13ff.) accepts an Adriatic locale for this exchange of bronze and iron (iron from the Greek side of the Adriatic for copper on the south Italian coast); it is suggested that the mention of Alybe as a source of silver may be a bit of legendary lore from the Bronze Age, for the Greeks would not know of the silver in Pontus again until the Black Sea was opened in the late seventh century. Probably the gold and silver of Egypt are similar legacies from Mycenean times.

[67] *Homer and the Monuments* 289–300.

The production of the Homeric community was scanty and perishable: some utensils and stocks of metals in the king's treasury, textiles from weaving in the household, some surplus of agriculture. In general, the Homeric household produced by and for itself and its treasure was still for prestige rather than for trade and commerce.[68]

This era was drawing to an end in the latter part of the eighth century when the twin phenomena of specialized agriculture and the pressure of population began to force the Ionians to work out new solutions. In Old Smyrna wider trading contacts are apparent. Early Protocorinthian pottery, some Chiot wine jars and Attic amphoras of the late eighth and early seventh century have been found.[69] Chios, at least, was beginning to produce a surplus of wine for export, so that less land was available for cereals. Evidently Ionian oil production was inadequate, if Smyrna was importing it across the Aegean. The process of urbanization was accelerated. In the seventh century larger and better built houses appeared in Old Smyrna; the city was laid out on a new plan of rectangular blocks with substantial three- and four-roomed stone houses of the megaron-type. During this period Greece was solving the problem of overpopulation by turning to overseas colonization. Ionia, however, had been established on the shores of a continent by conquest. It sought to expand inland before seeking new land across the Aegean. Until the last quarter of the seventh century the main focus of interest in Ionian development is its relations with the new native states of Asia Minor.

[68] Finley, *op. cit.*, pp. 57–58.

[69] I owe this information to J. M. Cook. The same hint of oil scarcity and perhaps of steps being taken to capitalize on it is evident in the well known story of Thales' corner of the market in oil presses (Roebuck, *CP* 45 [1950] 240). Theopompus reports a tradition that Chios was the first to produce wine and cultivate vines (*FGrHist* 2B, No. 276).

CHAPTER III

Ionia and the Interior

Since Ionia occupied the middle ground between the Greek Aegean and Anatolian Lydia and Phrygia, its role as an intermediary between the civilizations of east and west has long been discussed and variously estimated. In the latter part of the eighth and seventh centuries the orientalizing influences apparent in the art products of the period began to affect Greek craftmanship strongly. Their inspiration was obviously the articles of trade, metal goods, textiles, ivories and luxuries of various kinds which moved along the trade routes. At the present time the origin of these orientalizing influences is found in North Syria and, to a less degree, in Phoenicia and Cyprus. Egypt is hardly a factor, except through the medium of Phoenicia, until after 600. Origin is perhaps not the term to use of North Syria and Phoenicia, since they lay between the old centers of Mesopotamia, eventually absorbed into the Assyrian Empire, and the Mediterranean. This area was also heir in some degree to the Hittite Empire and to the Mycenean *koine*. It was the focal point from which contacts might be made by sea with the Aegean to the west and by land with Anatolia to the north. If Ionia was an important intermediary between the orient and the Aegean, it must have been in close contact with North Syria by the long sea route or through Lydia and Phrygia by the more difficult land route. In the early twentieth century this latter was considered to be the case, and Ionia was regarded as the central link between east and west.[1] At present, however, emphasis is placed on the sea route from North Syria to the Aegean, and Ionia has been relegated to a backwater,[2] the last link of a chain which led from North Syria and Cyprus across the Aegean to Athens and Corinth, then to Ionia. Phrygia and Lydia also seem to be on the fringe, for the Hittite Empire was completely broken by the invasions of the Early Iron Age. New political and cultural forms had to be created,

[1] D. G. Hogarth, *Ionia and the East* (1909).

[2] Below, p. 61, n. 2.

and, as yet, we know practically nothing of Lydia before the time of Gyges and are just learning of early Phrygia through current excavations.[3]

Evidently, a fresh evaluation of the role of Ionia will have to be made. On the one hand it received the influences of an individual native Anatolian culture which strongly affected the work of East Greek potters and weavers of textiles.[4] The possibility of influence by land contacts with the older centers of the east is not entirely excluded. Barnett has argued that Ionia was the link for a school of ivory-carving, the center of which is localized in Phrygia and Lydia, where it had survived from the Hittite Empire, the other end in Corinth, of which we see the products in the ivory seals of Perachora and the Argive Heraion. Perhaps Ionia was the center rather than the link, but some Anatolian inspiration is apparent. He has also suggested, more plausibly, that Phrygia transmitted to the west some techniques of metal work, originating in Urartu.[5] On the other hand Ionia and Aeolis were the main agents of Hellenization in Lydia and Phrygia. Their own crafts perhaps developed as much under the stimulus from these markets as from their contacts with the Aegean. The first interest of the Greeks, however, in the interior seems to have been to find new homes and land for their excess population.

PHRYGIA

About 700, to judge from the archaeological evidence, the Aeolian Greeks made a successful assault on Larisa (Map II), which controlled the entrance to the Hermus valley.[6] At about the same time Greek influence became apparent on the native pottery at Sardis.[7] Access to the Maeander valley was a matter of concern to the Ionians, for Ephesus made a series of unsuccessful attacks on Magnesia before its destruction by the Treres *ca.* 650.[8] While it is probable that land was the aim of these assaults, since their time coincided with the start of overseas colonization, it is possible that closer ties with Phrygia seemed desirable. Its king, the legendary Midas, is reported to have married the daughter of King Agamemnon of Kyme[9] and to have dedicated a royal throne at Delphi.[10] Midas is usually

[3] C. H. Émilie Haspels, *La Cité de Midas, Céramique et Trouvailles Diverses, Phrygie* III. Unfortunately very little is preserved at the Midas City that is earlier than the fifth century B.C. The excavation at Gordion, however, is more informative: R. Young, *AJA* 59 (1955) 1–18; 60 (1956) 249–66; see also the reports in *UPMB* from 1951. Excavation has been resumed (1958) at Sardis under the direction of G.M.A. Hanfmann. For a review of Anatolian cultural influence see R.D. Barnett, *The Aegean and the Near East* (ed. S. Weinberg) 214–26.

[4] Hanfmann, *HSCP* 61 (1953) 13–14; Schefold, *JDAI* 57 (1942) 124–42; *Larisa* III *passim*; E. Akurgal, *Ztsch. d. phil. Fak. Univ. Ankara* 8 (1950) 85 ff.; *idem, Phrygische Kunst,* 33 ff.; A. Åkerström, *Sk. ut. av Svenska Inst. i Athen* 1951, 1–105.

[5] Barnett, *JHS* 68 (1948) 1–25; *idem, Iraq* 12 (1950) 39 (a publication of the bronzes from Toprak Kale in the British Museum); the recently discovered architectural sculpture from Gordion, two fragmentary poros lions, seems to reflect Assyrian models of the *ninth* and *eighth* centuries (Young, *AJA* 60 [1956] 262).

[6] *Larisa* I 17 ff.

[7] Below, p. 53, n. 58.

[8] Roebuck, *CP* 50 (1955), p. 38, n. 41; above, p. 9, n. 13.

[9] Pollux 9.83 (Demodike); Aristotle frag. 611.37, Rose (Hermodike).

[10] Her. 1.14.2–3. The name of Midas was synonymous with wealth in Greece as early as Tyrtaeus (9.6). Possibly this reflects Greek knowledge of Phrygia before 700, but, more likely, the association was made

identified with Mita of Muski known from the records of Sargon II of Assyria in the late eighth century, with whom he was in conflict in Cilicia (Que) in 716. He was defeated by the governor of Cilicia to the extent of formally recognizing Sargon's sovreignty in 709/08.[11] Mita was apparently in alliance with the rulers of Tabal (Lycaonia) and the Late Hittite cities of North Syria and with Urartu to the east around Lake Van. He evidently wished to gain access to the sea coast in Cilicia, as his thrust in that region indicates. Whether Mita is correctly identified as the King of Phrygia or not, there seems to be some evidence of trade between Phrygia and these regions. Phrygian pottery has been identified at Carchemish; the influence of Cypriote pottery is noticed in Phrygia, and Cypriote fibulae have been found at Alişar.[12] Urartian metal work of the late eighth and early seventh century has been discovered in east Phrygia. [13] Phrygia loomed in Ionian eyes as the great native power of the interior of which the Ionians had apparently been aware for a long time, as the references to Phrygians in the *Iliad* indicate.

Although the Phrygians were included among the allies of Priam, Phrygia itself was spoken of as a far distant land, which a Greek might pride himself on having visited, as Priam did in his conversation with Helen. It was located on the banks of the Sangarius in the uplands (καθύπερθε; *Il.* 24.545); probably northwestern Phrygia is meant, certainly only its western part. The land is described as vine-covered and containing well-peopled cities whose inhabitants bought the goods of Troy. Horses played a large part in the warfare and movement of the people, for they are described as *hippomachoi* or *hippodamoi* and possessors of swift steeds (*Il.* 2.862–63; 3.184–90, 400–01; 10.431; 16.719; 24.545). Phrygia was evidently agricultural and, along the Sangarius near Gordion, heavily wooded.[14] The cities were the fortified towns of local dynasts, probably in process of consolidation into the kingdom which reached its apogee under Midas. Since there is no mention in the *Iliad* of the disaster which fell upon the Phrygians at the time of the Cimmerian invasion shortly after 700, the references of Homer probably depict the Phrygia which was coming into being in the ninth and eighth centuries. It is unwise to draw any conclusions about trade from the references in the *Iliad*, but perhaps some Phrygian horses were driven down to the coast to be exchanged for easily portable objects of daily use from the coastal cities.

Development of connections with Phrygia, however, was cut short by the Cimmerian invasion.[15] The Cimmerians destroyed Phrygia as an organized state, which event left its

after Lydia had taken over Phrygia as a province in the reign of Alyattes. It is difficult to accept Herodotus' notice of Midas' dedication as literally referring to Midas = Mita. Perhaps he refers to a vassal king of Phrygia when it was under Lydian control. We know, for example, that the young Adrastus came to Croesus' court *ca.* 560 to be trained as a local vassal (Her. 1.35; Koerte, *Gordion* 25).

[11] P. Naster, *L'Asie Mineure et l'Assyrie* 34–38, 53–58; see also K. Bittel, *Grundzüge der vor- und frühgeschichte Kleinasiens* 87 ff.; Bittel and Güterboch, *Abh.*: *Berlin*, 1935, 16–17 (a sketch of early Phrygia); for the condition of Anatolia in the preceding period, Hanfmann, *AJA* 52 (1948) 147–50.

[12] Przeworski, *Die Metallindustrie Anatoliens* 68; Hanfmann, *op. cit.*, p. 150, notes 70,72.

[13] *Anatolian Studies* 3 (1953) 121–24; Hanfmann *op. cit.*, p. 150, n. 70.

[14] At present the terrain is treeless so far as usable timber is concerned, but heavy beams and planks were used in the tumuli at Gordion and with stone in its great gateway (Young, *UPMB* 17 [1953], 4, pp. 19–22).

[15] Below, p. 53, n. 59.

mark on Greek tradition in the story of Midas' suicide by drinking bull's blood.[16] The new Lydian kingdom of Gyges, which had probably coalesced under Greek and Phrygian pressure, was threatened by destruction in 668/67 and in 652, as the king's appeals to Assurbanipal of Assyria for aid indicate. Although the main group of Cimmerians withdrew beyond the Halys after the middle of the century, probably from *ca.* 675 until 625 communication with the interior was hazardous. It could not have been secure and regular again until the reign of Alyattes, when he enlarged his kingdom to include the land up to the Halys. The literary tradition shows that from the eighth century at least Phrygia was known to the Greeks but that from shortly after 700 it no longer had the attractive power of a strong kingdom. Into its place Lydia moved. After *ca.* 600, however, Phrygia was again accessible as a province of Lydia.

So far as the early Greek and Phrygian trading contacts are concerned, it is at present necessary to discuss "influences" and to assume relations rather than to point to specific imports and exports. The scantiness of exchange is well revealed by the early tumuli excavated at Gordion. In those of late eighth century date dug by Young (S1, S2 & G1) and in Tumuli III and IV (Koerte), dated *ca.* 700 and early in the seventh century respectively, there are no imported Greek objects.[17] The earliest are two East Greek bird bowls of *ca.* 650 found in burials at Gordion and Ankara.[18] In the tumuli of the early period were many vessels and utensils of bronze and iron. A large number of fibulae were also found, particularly in Tumuli III and IV. Presumably they were of local manufacture, although some were of types common to the East Greek sites, and one of Phrygian type has been found at Old Smyrna.[19] Since these tombs were burials of the wealthy, which is indicated by their contents and the labor involved in their construction, the absence of precious metals and imported luxury objects, such as are found in the tumuli of the sixth century, is striking.

Yet, the "influences" seem to indicate a certain amount of trade with the East Greek area. A good case can be made out for the export of Phrygian metal ware to the west coast of Asia Minor. The wealth of the tumuli in bronze vessels and tools and some evidence of bronze-smelting from the excavation of Gordion show that it was an important bronze-working center in this early period.[20] Hanfmann has suggested that Samian geometric craters imitated the form of Phrygian bronze vessels, presumably the crater-like cauldrons from Tumulus III. Schefold has commented on the resemblance of basins at Larisa in

[16] Koerte *Gordion* 20, 23. Akurgal prefers to follow the tradition dating the death of Midas in 676/5 as better fitting his classification of Phrygian pottery (*Phrygische Kunst* 124); Young, however, points out difficulties in accomodating the material from Gordion into the scheme and prefers the Eusebian tradition with its date of 696/5 (*AJA* 60 [1956], p. 263, n. 24).

[17] *Anatolian Studies* 2 (1951) 20–21; Koerte, *Gordion* 36–104; no Greek imports were found in the large deposit of Phrygian pottery from a building apparently destroyed at the time of the Cimmerian raid (*AJA* 60 [1956] 263), nor in the royal burial excavated in 1957.

[18] Akurgal, *Ztsch. d. phil. Fak. Univ. Ankara* 8 (1950), p. 60, n. 14; pl. A1; Young, *UPMB* 17 (1953), 4, pp. 32–36, fig. 26.

[19] Akurgal, *op. cit.*, p. 89; Young, *op. cit.*, p. 36.

[20] See, for example, the bronze vessels from Tumulus III at Gordion dug by Koerte. Evidence of bronze-smelting has recently been found at Gordion (*AJA* 60 [1956] 265–66).

Aeolis to bronze examples found at Gordion, and Akurgal has made out a convincing case of influence for plates with spool handles. They are found in bronze at Ankara and Manisa, in clay in the Samian cemetery and in ivory replica in the hand of a figure from the Ephesian Artemision. The handle is the type ultimately used on Corinthian cothons.[21] Perhaps the model of Phrygian bronze dinoi with ring handles traveled even farther, for Hawkes has pointed to clay replicas in Arkades in Crete and in Ithaka.[22] In this case, however, the Ionian link is missing, although the pot from Ithaka may be Rhodian. It has also been suggested by Barnett that Phrygia, rather than North Syria, may have been the medium for transmission of the cauldrons with griffin protomoi and winged human figures as handle brackets. This type of griffin head is found in stone sculpture in Phrygia, and the winged figures seem to have originated in Urartu.[23] Such cauldrons were a very popular form of dedication in the Greek sanctuaries of the late eighth and seventh centuries, and many were found in the Heraion at Samos.[24] If metal vessels were carried from Phrygia to the coast, it is probable that bronze and iron in bar form were brought also until the Ionians were able to solve their metal scarcity by overseas trade. Textiles, too, may have been sent from Phrygia, since Akurgal and Barnett have pointed to textile designs on Phrygian pottery and tomb facades which are reproduced on seventh century pottery in Samos, Ephesus and Rhodes and on the costumes of ivory figurines from Ephesus.[25] The difficult question of the relationship and mutual borrowings between East Greek and Phrygian pottery is best left to experts, but perhaps a few of the better pieces passed in each direction. Hanfmann notes the use of concentric circles to frame the design on late geometric vases found in both Samos and Bogazköy. Bittel has pointed to the use of luxurious plant ornament for each in seventh-century examples. It is striking, too, that the fine sherd from Old Smyrna, representing a lyre with a little bird on top, has a parallel from Gordion.[26] These connections point to the west coast, but the ornament on late Phrygian Geometric vases has affinities with material of the same date from Rhodes and the Cyclades.[27] This might have come through Ionia, but use of a land route through Cilicia or North Syria should not be discounted.

[21] Akurgal, *op. cit.*, pp. 87–88; p. 80, pls. B1 and B2; *Belleten* 10 (1946) pl. 80; fig. 33; most recently, *Phrygische Kunst* 81–86, pls. 57–59. Hanfmann, *HSCP* 61 (1953), p. 14; p. 32, n. 74; comparison is difficult, for the profiles of the Phrygian bronze vessels are not published; Schefold, *Larisa* III, 193.

[22] C. Hawkes, Lecture, Archaeological Institute of America, 1953.

[23] Barnett, *Iraq* 12 (1950) 39; as Barnett observes, the provenance of a large group of the handle-brackets formed of winged figures should place the origin of the type in Urartu rather than in North Syria. He has suggested recently that transmission may have been made through Greek colonies on the Black Sea, such as Trapezos (S. Weinberg, *The Aegean and the Near East* 226–34), but see below, pp. 118ff.

[24] Kunze (*Kret. Bronz.* 267–70) publishes a list; the Samian bronzes have been recently studied by U. Jantzen, *Griech. Greifen-Kessel.* See also P. Amandry, *Études d'Archéologie classique* 1 (1955–56) 1–20 and in S. Weinberg, *The Aegean and the Near East* 239–61.

[25] Akurgal, *Ztsch. d. phil. Fak. Univ. Ankara* 8 (1950) 86; Barnett, *JHS* 68 (1948), p. 9, n. 50.

[26] Hanfmann, *op. cit.*, p. 14 and p. 32, n. 75; I am unable to see the resemblance in type between the Greek and Phrygian horses noticed by Hanfmann. Bittel and Güterboch (*Abh.: Berlin*, 1935, 60) mark the resemblance between Samian fragments (*AM* 54 [1929], fig. 18 and Beil. XIII) and pieces from Bogazköy. Smyrna fragment: Hanfmann, *op. cit.*, fig. 5; the Phrygian sherd: *UPMB* 17 (1953), 4, pp. 34–35, fig. 28.

[27] E. Akurgal (*Phrygische Kunst* 31–32) admits the possibility of influence from Cyprus by land, but

Barnett has also suggested that a school of ivory-carvers, with an offshoot in Lydia and Ionia and a tradition going back to imperial Hittite times, was flourishing in early Phrygia. Little supporting evidence has turned up in the excavation of the tumuli at Gordion, but a seal from Ephesus is of identical type to a Phrygian example from Bogazköy, and the designs on seals from Perachora and the Argive Heraion are akin to Barnett's Phrygian pieces.[28] Perhaps the center of such work was Ephesus rather than Phrygia.

In the trade from Phrygia bronze vessels, fibulae, textiles, bronze and iron may well have been sent to the Ionian cities. By way of return, we can point only to a few unimportant vases and suggest that fibulae and other ornaments of precious metals may have come. Certainly the usual products of Aegean trade, oil and wine, would not have been wanted in early Phrygia. The Phrygians had a reputation as beer-drinkers in the time of Archilochus, and Koerte has suggested that they used butter rather than oil.[29]

In the sixth century, during the period of Lydian control, the connection was evidently much closer. The traffic came up the Hermus river valley through Lydia rather than through the Black Sea colonies of Sinope and Amisos (Map IV). Sinope was probably founded in the late seventh century when the Black Sea was being colonized, and it is likely that its initial purpose was to secure fish rather than to open up trade with the interior. When trade began, its aim was the iron of Pontus and the miltos of Cappadocia rather than the products of Phrygia.[30] Further, the best route to the interior was from Amisos, and there is some indication that the colony, if in existence at all, was weak until *ca.* 560. Perhaps, too, it is significant that the architectural terracottas from Ak Alan, close to Amisos, are much nearer to their Aeolian prototypes at Larisa, if not actually Greek work, than are those of the sixth century found at Gordion and Pazarly.[31]

In the tumuli of the sixth century at Gordion and on the Phrygian sites the variety of Greek pottery is much greater than in the seventh century. Some Corinthian aryballoi and

prefers to regard the regular channel as through the Greeks on the west coast of Asia Minor; Young comments on the parallels between Rhodian and Cycladic Geometric pottery and Phrygian material of approximately the same date (*AJA* 60 [1956] 263).

[28] Barnett, *JHS* 68 (1948) 10–11.

[29] Archilochus frag. 28; Koerte, *Gordion* 85 ff. By the third century B.C., however, Thasian and Rhodian wines were being imported (Young, *UPMB* 17 [1953], 4, p. 6).

[30] For Sinope and Amisos see below, p. 120 n. 27.

[31] The decoration of the architectural terracottas from Sardis, Gordion, Pazarly and Ak Alan shows strong Greek influence, apparently from Aeolis, where the material at Larisa allows comparison. The earliest piece from Gordion is a tile with a representation of Theseus killing the Minotaur, probably to be dated in the first quarter of the sixth century (Young, *UPMB* 16 [1951], 1, p. 8). The Greek influence on the Pazarly tiles has caused some difficulty by their provincial character, and they are now placed in the second half of the sixth century by Akurgal (*Belleten*, 7 [1943] 1 ff.; *Phrygische Kunst*, 69–80, pls. 45–56; see also, Schefold, *Istanbuler Forschungen* 17 [1950] 137–48). The Ak Alan tiles, however, may have been painted by Greeks, although Ak Alan was obviously a native town (Macridy Bey, *Mitt. der vorderasiatische Gesellschaft* 12 [1907] 165–75, pl. X). They are dated to the mid-sixth century by H. Koch (*RM* 30 [1915] 16–23) and are apparently closely related to the Larisa material (Schefold, *JDAI* 57 [1942] 141 ff.). The pottery from Ak Alan, however, is earlier than the mid-sixth century (Bittel, *AA* 48 [1933] 174 and *Kleinasiatischen Studien* 101 ff., "Rhodian" of the seventh century; Schefold, *op. cit.*, p. 141, a Rhodian sherd of the Kamiros group; R. M. Cook, *JHS* 66 [1946], p. 82, n. 138, Rhodian of the last quarter of the seventh century). Probably both sherds and tiles are the products of trade through Amisos.

alabastra of the first half of the century have been found.[32] The number is small, and they were evidently a part of the considerable quantity of Corinthian ware imported into Old Smyrna and to the Aeolian sites. The Corinthians, however, may have been aware of the destination of their pottery, since there is a tradition that the father of the last tyrant of Corinth, Psammetichos, was called Gordios.[33] In any case, they provided an exotic foreign perfume. Attic vases made their appearance with the two little master cups of Ergotimos from Tumulus V at Gordion. The Athenians, too, became aware of Midas at this time, for the first known appearance of the legend on Attic pottery is on a vase by Ergotimos from Aegina. It is apparent that the Persian conquest did not interrupt trade, since there are several fragments of the third quarter of the sixth century.[34] These small cups are the chief type of Athenian pottery found and are evidently a part of the mass of Athenian cups which began to appear in East Greece after 560. Their transport far inland required considerable care in packing, perhaps in wooden boxes, since the stems and handles are very fragile. The amount of East Greek pottery, "Rhodian" and Aeolian, is larger, as might be expected, than the Corinthian and Attic,[35] but on the whole Greek pottery was a very minor article of trade. The Lydians supplied rather more, both their fine marbled ware and the unguent jars known as lydions,[36] but Phrygian native pottery was of good quality and little need was felt to import foreign wares.

With the pottery, however, came luxury items from Lydia and from the Ionian trade into the southeastern Mediterranean. One tumulus excavated by Young, dated *ca.* 550, was particularly rich.[37] It was the burial of a young girl, containing her articles of toilet

[32] Gordion: an alabastron, an aryballos and some fragments were found in Tumulus I by the Koertes (*Gordion* 133–34, fig. 117). This tumulus is grouped with those of *ca.* 550 excavated by Young (*UPMB* 17 [1953], 4, p. 32) in which another Corinthian alabastron was found. Other fragments were discovered in the excavation of the city mound both by the Koertes (*Gordion* 186, No. 48) and in the recent excavations. The fragmentary cup published by the Koertes as Protocorinthian is rather Corinthian of the first quarter of the sixth century. Midas City: a few fragments of Corinthian vases dating 600–550 were found (Haspels, *Phrygie* III, 38, pl. 9, d, 6–10). Bogazköy: neck of a Middle Corinthian aryballos (*Abh.*: *Berlin*, 1935, pl. 16.8; Otto, *MDOrG* 78 [1940], p. 50, fig. 10,6); the pieces from Gordion and Bogazköy are not Protocorinthian as stated by Akurgal (*Ztsch. d. phil. Fak. Univ. Ankara* 8 [1950] 68).

[33] Aristotle *Pol.* v, 1315b, 22; Gorgos or Gorgias is better attested (Nik. Dam. *FGrHist* 2A, No. 60; Plut. *Sept. Sap. Conv.* 17; Strabo 7.7.6; Pseudo-Skymnos 453).

[34] Koerte, *Gordion* 140–43; the burial is dated *ca.* 550; some cup fragments of the same period were also found in the city mound (*ibid.*, p. 187, Nos. 50–52, figs. 177, 178; a fragment of a black-figured lekythos, No. 53). For the Midas legend on Attic vases see Brommer, *AA* 56 (1941) 36 ff. Midas City: Haspels, *op. cit.*, p. 38, pl. 9, d, 1–5.

[35] "Rhodian": amphora and lekythos, *Gordion* 117–18, Nos. 26, 27, fig. 97 (from Tumulus II, *ca.* 600); p. 185, No. 43 (from the city mound, sixth century); Aeolic (Schefold, *JDAI* 57 [1942] 132 and 135): *Gordion* 186, No. 45, fig. 172; 182–83, Nos. 29, 33–36, pl. 9; 185, Nos. 41–42. A piece of a Laconian cup was also found (*Gordion* 186, No. 49, fig. 176). Since the chief influence on Phrygian painting of the sixth century seems to have been from Aeolian Greece, the import was probably larger in quantity than Koerte's publication suggests. Imitations of Ionian pottery have been found also at Kerkenes Dag (Bittel, *Kl. Stud.* 55; *AJSemL* 45 [1929] 264, fig. 60).

[36] Lydian marbled ware: *Gordion* 188–89, Nos. 61–64 (from lydions of the sixth century); striped ware: *Gordion* 189–90, Nos. 65–66; for lydions, below p. 56, n. 70.

[37] Tumulus H: Young, *UPMB* 16 (1951), 1, pp. 17–18; Tumulus I of the same period also contained gold jewelry.

and adornment: gold jewelry, a silver mirror, the ivory inlay from wooden caskets, an alabaster alabastron, a plastic vase and many lydions. The range of the luxury trade is well exemplified by these objects, for the jewelry is probably Lydian, the plastic vase Ionian, the ivory ultimately from Egypt or Arabia, the alabastron of original Cypriote or Phoenician inspiration, if not manufacture. These were a product of the trade carried on by Rhodes, Phocaea, Samos, Miletus and Chios with the southeastern Mediterranean. Similar objects were found in other tumuli of the same date and in Koerte's Tumulus II of the early part of the century.[38] One interesting item is the amber found in Tumulus II, which perhaps came from the northern Ionian region where a considerable amount was found in the sanctuary at Kato Phana in Chios.[39] Evidently the Phrygian upper class prospered under Lydian control, and Ionian merchants were able to provide them with some luxuries. This period of Phrygian history seems to have ended in violent destruction with the invasion of Cyrus. At least the new Persian town was bedded on a layer of clay spread over the ruins of the former Phrygian city.

In the sixth century the character of Phrygian exchange with Lydia and the coast was obviously different than in the previous period. The need of the Ionian cities for bronze and iron seems to have been taken care of with imports by sea, and Phrygian bronze vessels could scarcely compete with the products of local crafts as in Samos.[40] It is possible that textiles were no longer exported, although Miletus perhaps obtained wool for its own textile industry. Greek legend knew of Phrygia as the home of "embroidery," but Herodotus as a country important for agriculture and sheep raising.[41] Another Phrygian export attested for the sixth century, although it may well have been earlier, was slaves. In the poems of Alcman there are said to have been several names of Phrygian flute girls, and Phrygian music is noticed by other lyric poets.[42] Since the music was associated with symposia, it probably came to the Greeks through this medium. Other slaves had a harder life, as Hipponax' notice of Phrygian slaves grinding barley in Miletus indicates.[43]

Generally speaking, the actual trade between Ionia and Phrygia was slight, because of the long distance overland involved. The only effect on Ionian economy was probably in the provision of metals in the early period and of some profit to Ionian merchants in the sixth century. The cultural effects were larger, although this is hardly the place to discuss them. The Phrygians adopted Greek letter forms at an early date, and their sculpture and

[38] For the ivory from the site see Barnett, *JHS* 68 (1948) 18; above, p. 47. Alabaster alabastrons were also very popular in Sardis where many were found in the tumulus of Alyattes.

[39] *Gordion* 128; for the pieces found on Chios see *BSA* 35 (1934–35) 154; most of the Chiot amber was from a geometric deposit, but some from archaic levels. Amber was also found in the Artemision at Ephesus.

[40] Perhaps a sign of the change in direction of the trade is indicated by the lotus bowls found in tumuli of the mid-seventh century (Young, *UPMB* 17 [1953] 34). They are very common on Greek sites of the seventh century.

[41] Her. 5.49.5; the statement is in the speech of Aristagoras to Cleomenes of Sparta.

[42] Alcman frag. 97 (music); Stesichorus frag. 14.

[43] Hipponax frag. 43.2. Phrygia was known as a source of slaves for Athens in the fifth century and later (Koerte, *Gordion* 27).

painting were strongly influenced in the sixth century.[44] The Greeks in their turn took over mythological and religious ideas of some potency, such as the cult of Cybele, but the forms of economic, social and political life were not affected, for the history of the Ionian states was bound up with that of the Aegean and with Lydia. By the time of Herodotus the Ionians knew little of the Anatolian plateau.[45]

LYDIA

The intimate connection which existed between Lydia and the Ionians in the archaic period has often been discussed. Most of the cities on the coast eventually became the subject allies of Croesus, paying tribute and liable to military levies.[46] The cultural relationship between Lydia and Ionia has been described recently as a *koine*.[47] Seemingly the conditions were present for an intimate economic connection, in which the Greeks could use the products of a hinterland to supplement their own slender resources and bring to it the trade-goods of the Mediterranean and of their own industry. This is largely correct, but, as a corollary to the picture, Lydia has been represented as the terminus of long caravan routes across Anatolia which brought the products of the east to Sardis to be distributed in part by the Ionian cities.[48] To judge from Greek-Phrygian relations, that is very doubtful.

Lydia is usually considered to have been a subordinate part of the Phrygian kingdom in the eighth century[49] and to have replaced it as the main power in western Anatolia under Gyges and his successors, reaching its greatest extent in the time of Croesus, when it stretched from the Aegean to the Halys and from the Propontis to Caria. Whatever may have been the political condition of Lydia before the seventh century, it only emerged into history as a strong kingdom under King Gyges, *ca.* 687–652. The chronology of his reign, or at least those parts of it and of that of his successor, Ardys, when they were in contact with Assurbanipal of Assyria, furnish one of the few firm chronological points of the

[44] Ionian influence is apparent on sixth century sculpture: Haspels, *Mnemosyne* 4 (1951) 230–34 (Cybele and the lion on a tomb facade); Bittel, *Grundzüge* 108 (relief from Hamadiye); Bittel, *Kl. Stud.* 103 ff.; *MAMA* VI, p. 138, No. 401, pl. 71; Haspels, *Phrygie* III, pl. 47a; this figure from the Midas City, dated 570–550, is related to the Branchidae figures and to Samian standing *korai*, but is a provincial imitation; pl. 47b is of the same period, but is imported. Recently, fragments of frescoes from a building of Persian Gordion have been found. They show strong East Greek influence of *ca.* 500, like the Etruscan tomb paintings, and possibly were painted by Greek workmen (Young, *AJA* 60 [1956] 255–56).

[45] Jacoby, "Herodotus," *RE Supp.* 2 (1913) 267–68. Herodotus' knowledge of Asia Minor was confined largely to the coast, Caria, Lycia and Lydia. He knew of Phrygia up to Celaenae, but there is no hint of the importance of Achaemenid Gordion (Young, *UPMB* 17 [1953] 9–29).

[46] For studies of the political relationship see D.G. Hogarth, *CAH* III 501–26; Santo Mazzarino, *Fra Oriente e Occidente* 191–252; Roebuck, *CP* 50 (1955) 30.

[47] Santo Mazzarino, *op. cit.*, pp. 168, 180–81, 236, 245, 376.

[48] That is the fundamental thesis of Radet's book, *La Lydie et la monde grecque* (Paris, 1893), which still remains the most comprehensive study of Lydia; Hogarth (*op. cit.*, p. 520) has also interpreted Lydian trade in this manner. Unfortunately, Naster's dissertation, *Histoire de Lydie*, is published only in summary in *Rev. Belge*, 1936, 769.

[49] Hogarth, *op. cit.*, pp. 504–06; Santo Mazzarino, *op. cit.*, p. 369, n. 500. The literary evidence scarcely allows definite conclusions, but there is a tradition of a Phrygian (Hittite?) state around Magnesia under Sipylus (Strabo 12.8.2). O. Seel argues for the existence of a native Lydian tradition about its early kingship (*Wiener Studien* 69 [1956] 212–36).

seventh century, and any discussion of Lydia in historical terms must start with them.[50] In 668 or 667 Gyges made an appeal to Assurbanipal for aid against the Cimmerians; Assurbanipal asserted that none of his predecessors had ever heard of Lydia, and no interpreter could be found at first who understood Gyges' message. Lydia is described as a country "on the other side of the sea." Whether Assurbanipal had ever heard of Lydia and Gyges, Gyges had evidently heard of Assurbanipal and considered his military aid desirable. Although the Assyrian texts do not indicate whether aid was given, it is probable that some help was assigned, for Gyges sent Cimmerian captives and gifts to the Assyrian King as an acknowledgment. Gyges apparently regarded himself as an equal ally of Assyria, rather than a subject, and chose in the latter part of his career to embarass his ally by aiding Psammetichos in Egypt and, perhaps, by intriguing with Samas-sum-ubin of Babylonia in a revolt planned by the latter. This conduct had its proper reward in Assyrian eyes when Gyges was once more attacked by the Cimmerians and killed in battle. His son Ardys again appealed for alliance, but we have no knowledge of further relations. Gyges also attacked several Ionian cities and perhaps controlled part of the Troad.[51] He was plainly in contact with Egypt by sea and presumably with Assyria by land, if he expected Assyrian aid to be of any use against the Cimmerians. Thus, by the first part of the seventh century, Lydia was an organized state, which might act as an intermediary in relations between the Assyrian Empire and the Aegean shore of western Anatolia.

Gyges' accession to the throne is represented in tradition as a revolutionary process directed against an organized government. Hogarth has suggested that his ability to mount raids to the west and north presupposes some organization which Gyges took over and consolidated.[52] Be that as it may, the Greek attempt to expand inland from the west and Phrygian pressure from the east probably spurred the process of consolidation. Gyges was successful in pinning the Greeks to the coast, and Greek influence had to make its way into Lydia by economic and cultural media. Lydia, despite its continual raids on the Ionian cities, showed no desire to annex any one of them as a seaport. Alyattes did not rebuild Old Smyrna, and even Croesus did not construct a fleet or use Ionian ships against their kindred on the islands when he might have done so.[53] Herodotus tells of the situation in a

[50] I have followed the treatment of Gyges by Naster, *L'Asie Mineure et l'Assyrie* 91–98.

[51] Gyges attacked the cities of Miletus and Smyrna and took the *asty* of Colophon (above, p. 11, n. 19). He also made numerous attacks on and eventually captured Magnesia on the Maeander (Nik. Dam. *FGrHist* 2A, No. 62; above, p. 9, n. 13). Strabo has several notices of Lydian activity in the Troad, the most specific of which is that Gyges permitted the Milesians to occupy Abydos (13.1.22); control of the Troad is referred to in 12.4.6 and perhaps implied in the reference to a royal hunting lodge, established by Lydians and used also by the Persians (13.1.17). The plain of Thebe (13.1.8; 13.1.61) and the area of Sidene (13.1.42) were also under Lydian control. Probably, however, much of this refers to the period of Croesus rather than of Gyges.

[52] Hogarth, *op. cit.*, p. 509.

[53] For Smyrna see above, p. 27. It has been suggested that the capture of Colophon was prompted by commercial reasons and that it was politically subordinate to Lydia (Buckler, *JHS* 46 [1926] 36ff.). This view rested partly on the interpretation of the legend on several coins as referring to the River Ales which flowed through Colophonian territory to enter the sea near the harbor. The legend seems better read as the name of Alyattes (*i.e.*, the coins are Lydian; Robinson, *JHS* 71 [1951] 163). For Croesus and the islanders, Her .1.27.

picturesque story, but obviously Lydia had no aspiration to become a sea power. It was an agricultural state controlled by its great landowners who were kept in hand, at times with difficulty, by the king, probably the greatest landowner.

The Maeonians of the *Iliad* were probably identified in the seventh century as Lydians,[54] since they were located under Mt. Tmolus and by the Gygean Lake (*Il.* 2.864–66). These Maeonians are coupled with the Phrygians (*Il.* 3.401; 18.291) and described in similar terms as possessing well-peopled towns whose inhabitants were renowned as chariot-fighters and horse-breeders (*ibid.*; *Il.* 10.431). There is a revealing hint of their lack of luxury in the well known passage in which reference is made to the staining of an ivory cheek-piece for horses by Maeonian or Carian women. This was a very rare object, since the "king" planned to keep it in his treasure house to be envied by other horsemen (*Il.* 4. 141 ff.). Similarly, the archaeological material from Sardis which is dated before the end of the eighth century reveals a rather backward native Anatolian culture with few indications of wealth or foreign contacts.[55] Nevertheless, the people might have been numerous and warlike, organized under their chieftains and concentrated in agrarian villages. Lydia, except for Sardis, seems to have retained this predominantly agricultural character until the Persian period. Herodotus and the early Greek sources do not mention any cities other than Sardis, presumably because there were none to mention.[56] There was also little to see in Lydia, except the gold-bearing Pactolus and the tomb of Alyattes on the shore of the Gygean lake (Her. 1.93). It is rather interesting that Herodotus does not recommend Sardis itself. Perhaps it was like a Greek city in physical form and so of no great interest to a travelled Greek but probably it was mainly drab mud brick and timber. Lydia should be envisaged as a land of peasant and herder villages with one great center, Sardis, which grew as the seat of the king's residence to become the center of the land's industry and trade. Probably this developed largely under Greek influences and was closely associated with the patronage of the king and his feudal nobility, the famed horsemen of Lydia.[57] The trade was based primarily on the mineral and agricultural resources of Lydia itself rather than on any long distance land traffic conducted by the Lydians.

The first evidence of noteworthy foreign contacts appears in the pottery of *ca.* 700, in the generation before Gyges. At that time the Lydian pottery is said to show Greek,

[54] For discussion of the problem of identification see Santo Mazzarino, *op. cit.*, p. 49; Hanfmann, *AJA* 52 (1948) 151 ff.

[55] Hanfmann, *Robinson Studies* I 160 ff.; *AJA* 52 (1948) 151 ff.

[56] Bürchner, "Lydia," *RE* 13 (1927) 2124.

[57] There is an interesting gloss in Tzetzes (*Chil.* V. 456) on the Lydian word πάλμυς which occurs frequently in Hipponax (3,4,34,35); it defines πάλμυς as βασιλεύς ὁ σύμπας. Such a qualification of βασιλεύς implies the existence of other "kings," great landowners who formed the Lydian nobility and provided its famous cavalry. The organization of Lydia is usually described as feudal in character (Santo Mazzarino, *op. cit.*, pp. 182–83; p. 370, n. 514), and we get occasional glimpses of an almost separate "princedom," like that of Adramyttion, and of conflicts for the throne of the sort that brought Croesus to it. The subject is obscure and deserving of special study, for there is a certain amount of scattered evidence. For the Lydian cavalry see Mimnermus frag. 13; Her. 1.27,78,79. A typical landowner of the early Persian period was Pythios of Celaenae who entertained Xerxes' army so lavishly (Her. 7.27–28; below, p. 54).

Phrygian and Cypriote influence.[58] The Greek and Phrygian contacts are easy to understand, but what is the explanation of the Cypriote influence? Possibly it came through the intermediary of the Greek cities, which occasional Cypriote traders visited on a run along the coast, but little Cypriote influence is noticed on the late geometric and early orientalizing wares of Ionia and Aeolis. Perhaps it came by land through Phrygia and was a part of the results of Mita's interest in Cilicia. Either contact accords with Gyges' realization a generation later that he might receive material aid from Assurbanipal. Yet, if a few troops were sent from Cilicia to aid against the Cimmerians, a contact by land is probable. The Assyrian location of Lydia "on the other side of the sea" may be only proper Assyrian disdain. In any case, the difficulties in communications imposed by the Cimmerian raids in the second and third quarters of the seventh century prevented any effective development of the land connection, so that Lydia's growth was associated closely with that of the Greeks. Sardis and several Ionian cities suffered from the raiders, but the damage was apparently mainly of the hit and run variety. Antandrus in the Troad, however, is said to have been occupied by the Trerians, and Lygdamis remained in the Mykale area for several years. It is unlikely that the economic growth of Lydia and Ionia was seriously checked, but the communications with the interior must have been impaired.[59]

[58] Hanfmann, *AJA* 52 (1948) 151–53. The pottery from the excavation of Sardis is only partially published, and any statements about its affiliations and development may need considerable qualification. The most useful accounts are those of Hanfmann, *loc. cit.*; *idem*, *Robinson Studies* I 160 ff. (on the prehistoric pottery of Sardis); *AJA* 49 (1945) 570 ff. (on an orientalizing vase of the third quarter of the seventh century); Schefold, *JDAI* 57 (1942) 134–35 (the orientalizing pottery of the seventh century); Rumpf *AM* 45 (1930) 163–70 (on the lydions; below, p. 56, n. 70); Butler, *AJA* 18 (1914) 432–37 (summary of the pottery found in the excavations of Sardis before the war of 1914–18).

[59] It is probable that the Cimmerian invasions had a paralyzing effect on any potential development of trade by land routes from the Assyrian Empire and Urartu to the western coast of Asia Minor. By *ca.* 700 Cimmerian bands were roving over the whole of Anatolia north of the Assyrian Empire and had destroyed the kingdom of Phrygia as an organized state. They apparently looted and destroyed rather than settled, so that conditions in an area in which they were operating were obviously anything but favorable to the movement of luxury goods over long land routes. In the course of the seventh century two main descents were made to the west. The first, *ca.* 668/7, was turned back by Gyges, who sent some captives as visible evidence of his victory to Assurbanipal. Defeat, however, probably meant only a scattering, so that marauding groups may well have wandered about Lydia and the coast for some years. The Cimmerians returned again in sufficient force to defeat and kill Gyges in 652. At this time, or perhaps slightly later (Naster, *op. cit.*, p. 97, n. 51), the lower town of Sardis may have been destroyed by them. Ardys and later Alyattes were faced with the task of defeating and ultimately driving them out of the area of western Anatolia, which was hardly completed until *ca.* 600.

Attacks against and damage to Greek cities are reported in several sources, which also indicate that further destruction was wrought by a Thracian group, the Treres, who raided into western Asia Minor from the north. To notice the various instances (Lehmann-Haupt, "Kimmerier," *RE* 11 [1921] 419–20): Antandrus, at the foot of Mt. Ida, was apparently taken over by a group of Trerians; Ephesus was raided and the Artemis temple perhaps destroyed. Callimachus (*Hymn to Artemis*, 251 ff.) asserts that Artemis protected her temple, but Hesychius (*s.v.* Lygdamis) states that it was burned. The situation of this temple is an interesting problem, for the Basis of the Artemision, its earliest structure, is now dated *ca.* 600 and the articles in its foundation deposit mostly from 650 to 600. Evidently the Cimmerians destroyed an old shrine, the vestiges of which remain unlocated. Magnesia on the Maeander was also destroyed (Strabo 14.1.40), and its land later occupied by Ephesus. The lines of Callinus should also be cited in this connection, by which he roused his countrymen of Ephesus to war against the Cimmerians

From the time of Gyges an increase of trade and growth of wealth brought both Lydia and Ionia into the mesh of Mediterranean commerce. Above all, Lydia could supply electrum, which was available close to Sardis. In Gyges' own lifetime[60] his name became a byword for wealth, and in the next generation an electrum coinage was invented to serve the needs of the Ionian-Lydian trading area. We might first examine the results of the development of the electrum mining, which seems to have been Greece's chief source of gold well into the fifth century. It also supplied the coinage for western Asia Minor under the Persian regime.

It has been suggested by Radet[61] that the mining industry was a state monopoly in the control of the king. Certainly that is the impression which is given by the literary evidence. The Lydian kings from Gyges to Croesus used the metal to make lavish gifts to the Greeks and, although it receives little notice, to their own sanctuaries; they also subsidized Greek exiles, like Alcaeus, plotting revolution in their homeland.[62] The story of Alcmaeon's visit to Croesus' treasury in Sardis points to the same concentration of gold in the hands of the king (Her. 6.125). Aside from these notices, it is apparent that the king needed money to pay mercenary troops, of which a considerable number was used both on foreign service and probably as a bodyguard for his person.[63] The gold was also disbursed for administrative services and in payment for goods and artistic commissions. The only specific evidence which we have for mineral exploitation, however, is a notice in Plutarch, which refers to the period of Persian control under Xerxes. Plutarch ascribes a large part of the fortune of the rich Lydian, Pythios, to the discovery of a mine which he worked by using the labor of his own peasants and craftsmen. Herodotus, while emphasizing the great wealth of Pythios, gives the impression that he was a very wealthy landowner with many slaves (Plut. *Mul. Virt.* 262d–e; Her. 7.28). While this might be accepted as evidence of the private exploitation of resources, it refers to the period after the fall of the Lydian monarchy. It is likely that the Lydian royal family controlled the mines and probably owed its position in large part to that control. Their first exploitation seems to coincide with Gyges' usurpation. The circumstances were thus favorable to the issuance of the first coinage by the Lydian kings. They had a supply of electrum in their own possession and a strong position in their state. The type which they put on the coins was probably a family seal.

(frags. 1,3,4), and the poetry of Magnes of Smyrna who wrote of Lydian valor against the Amazons, with whom the Cimmerians are identified (Nik. Dam. *FGrHist* 2A, No. 62). Apparently Lygdamis remained for some years after 650 in the Mykale area (Welles, *Royal Correspondence*, No. 7, 16–17). Conditions were thus disturbed in Lydia *ca.* 668 and again from 652–626 (death of Lygdamis). With marauding bands in the countryside at best and great numbers of them in more or less organized attack on occasion it is unlikely that trade into the interior could develop much.

60 Archilochus frag. 22; a dedication of the type described by Herodotus (1.14) would bring Gyges to general Greek attention.

61 Radet, *La Lydie* 225.

62 Alcaeus frag. 42; Alcaeus' faction was given 2000 staters by Lydia.

63 Mercenaries are first heard of in the time of Gyges, when Ionian and Carian soldiers aided Psammetichos I in Egypt; that Gyges sent them is conjectural but by no means improbable in view of Assurbanipal's complaints about the alliance with Psammetichos. For Croesus' use of mercenaries see Roebuck, *CP* 50 (1955), p. 38, n. 29. Probably Greek hoplites were used as a matter of course by the Lydian kings to provide heavy armed infantry to support their cavalry. For the appearance of hoplites in Ionia, above, p. 34.

The invention of coinage has been convincingly ascribed to the generation after Gyges and to the Lydian-Ionian area, if not to Lydia itself. In a study of the coins from the Basis of the Ephesian Artemision and from the related deposits[64] Robinson traces the development step by step from dumps (pellets) of electrum (and some silver), through unpunched dumps, through punched and striated dumps, dumps with a type to coins proper. The whole series is convincingly attributed to a rapid development which starts in the third quarter of the seventh century and reaches its climax *ca.* 600, when the Basis deposit was made.[65] These coins form the earliest hoard of which we know, and, as Robinson observes, the circumstances of their presence in a foundation deposit and as dedications indicate that they are a fair sample of the coins in circulation in the area. Aside from seven silver dumps all (93) are of electrum, which points very obviously to Lydia as the source of the metal. Attribution of the types to particular places is difficult, but those with lion's head and paw are considered Lydian. This series is the commonest of the early electrum issues and is later found not only on the coastal sites of Ionia, but throughout Lydia. It was struck in large numbers to be the ordinary coinage of commerce in the area. Evidently the coins were used in exchange, since money-changers' stamps are impressed on them. The earliest name found is apparently that of Alyattes. Other plausibly identified coins are one of Phocaea and several from Ephesus, while two other Greek states are represented by the types of opposed fighting cocks and a goat's protome. This latter may be the earliest coin proper. Robinson suggests: "Was it...that Lydians were the first to punch the back of currency ingots of their native electron and to give them a striated surface; and Greeks the first to seal them with a device?"[66] The standard on which these coins were struck is that of the stater known as "Milesian" or "Lydian"(formerly "Phoenician"). There are only two certain deviations from it: a Phocaean coin (No. 28) and a "Babylonian" stater (No. 63); No. 65, an unusual 1/10, also may be on a different standard. Almost all are from the same trading area with little indication of alien weights, *i.e.*, of foreign trading. The pieces are mostly fractions with 1/3's, 1/12's, 1/48's commonest; 1/96's are also found.[67] Apparently the money was used in ordinary small-scale transactions and not confined to large purchases. The group shows that coinage in the proper sense of the term originated to serve the needs of the Lydian-Ionian trading area and that the source of the metal was Lydian electrum. It is interesting to speculate on the origins of the idea. The lion's head on the Lydian coins is the Assyrianized Hittite type which appears in Greek art *ca.* 650, and there seems to have been a development almost approximating to coinage in the Assyrian Empire in the reign of Sargon II.[68] It is obscure whether there is a relationship or not, but Lydia was apparently in contact with the Assyrian Empire by land during Gyges' reign.

[64] Robinson, *JHS* 71 (1951) 156–67.
[65] Jacobsthal, *JHS* 71 (1951) 85–95.
[66] Robinson, *op. cit.*, p. 165.
[67] The coins are catalogued by Robinson, *op. cit.*, pp. 166–67.
[68] *NumChron* 2 (1922) 176–85. Dumps of metal without punches or striations were found at Enkomi in Cyprus in Mycenean contexts (Evans, *Corolla Numismatica* 365); apparently the practice could develop in various places at different times, and there need be no connection between them.

Some hint of the character of the exchange of goods is given by the literary and archaeological evidence, scanty as it is. Most useful in this connection is the Ephesian poet Hipponax, although he lived a century later than the period with which we are concerned, at the climax of the interconnection rather than its inital stages. His use of many Lydian words for products, which later commentators had to explain by glosses,[69] shows how intimately they were known to the Ephesians. There is a Lydian word, ἄβδης, which Hesychius explains as μάστιξ, a whip. Probably this was made of leather, since other Lydian leather products are known: sandal thongs (Sappho 17.1–3); perhaps the leather belt referred to by Aeschrio (frag. 3); a shoe, the κυπασσίσκος (Hipponax frag. 24.2,3; Harpokration 117.8). Shoes of some soft material were associated with Lydians, to judge from the epithet of soft-footed given them by the Delphic oracle (Her. 1.55). Wine, too, was apparently traded, since Hipponax knows of a sour Lydian variety, ἀλίβας (frag. 102, Bergk). The most frequently mentioned Lydian product was the βάκκαρις (Hipponax frag. 19; Semonides 14.2) or βρένθιον explained by Hesychius and Pollux (6. 104) as Lydian myrrh. It was apparently the product of a plant found in Lydia and was distributed in the vases known as lydions. They are found in quantity in Sardis, at Gordion, on Ionian sites, where they were imitated, and in Greece and Italy. The distribution seems to have begun in the second quarter of the sixth century and to have continued well into the fifth.[70]

[69] The glosses are listed in Deeters, "Lydia," *RE* 13 (1927) 2155–56; see also *Sardis* VI,2, pp. 85–88. Sayce, *AJP* 46 (1925) 29 ff. I have noted only the words which appear in Greek authors of the archaic period;

[70] Rumpf (*AM* 45 [1920] 163–70) discusses the vases, their use and distribution. The shape indicates that a salve-like substance was packed in them, since they are small, wide-mouthed pots on which the decoration is secondary; the earliest type was found in considerable numbers in the tumulus of Alyattes (Perrot-Chipiez, V, p. 293, fig. 194; A. von Ölfers, *Abh.: Berlin*, 1858, pl. V, 7,8,9). The shape was imitated in Ionian cities and in Italy with some modifications in form and difference in decoration; probably the salve was imitated also. The distribution of the genuine Lydian article in the Aegean was in the hands of the Ionian Greeks, probably of the Phocaeans and of the Samians, while that into the interior of Anatolia and in Lydia was likely carried on by the Lydians themselves. In addition to the lydions found in the tumulus of Alyattes a considerable number were found in the excavation of Sardis (*Sardis* I, p. 150, fig. 168; *AJA* 18 [1914] 433, 434, fig. 6; 26 [1922], p. 389, pl. 6). Lists are given by Dragendorff, *Thera* II, p. 218, n. 180; by Rumpf, *op. cit.*, pp. 164, 167, 168, n. 2 and by Kunze, *AM* 59 (1934), p. 100, n. 1. To these should be added: Athens, Kerameikos graves—Karo, *An Attic Cemetery* 21 (Karo apparently regards them as genuinely Lydian); Agora graves—Young, *Hesperia* 20 (1951) 88–89, No. 5,1, pl. 39a (possibly Lydian); p. 92,10,5–7, pl. 41a (probably Greek); p. 92, 10,4, pl. 41a (a lekythos, perhaps Lydian; a similar one in Samos, Boehlau, pl. VII, 5); Italy—E. von Mercklin, *RM* 38 (1923), p. 75, 6 (Greek imitation); A. Blakeway, *JRS* 25 (1935), p. 132, pl. XXI, D1 (a lydion [?] from Vulci of Etruscan manufacture with Greek geometric decoration, early seventh century in date); *AA* 51 (1936) 382, No. 33 (an Ionic imitation from Praeneste); Corinth—*AJA* 34 (1930) 422, fig. 15 (from a grave and identified as a Lydian import); Rhodes—*Clara Rhodos* III, p. 31, fig. 15; IV, p. 266; Aegina—Welter, *AA* 53 (1938) 496, 508, fig. 24 (Samian imitation). The whole area of Aegean trade, as well as Italy and the Black Sea, was covered by the distribution of genuine lydions or their Ionic imitations. Perhaps merely by accident of excavation Samos is the provenance of most examples in Ionia. One is reported from Emporion in Spain, which points to Phocaea as a distributor. This Lydian-Ionian product of the sixth century was evidently a serious competitor of Corinthian, Rhodian and, later, Attic unguents. The Lydians did not compete in decoration of the package but only in the content. It is probably correct to say that most of those found on Aegean and Italian sites are Ionian imitations, while those from Lydia and Phrygia (there are many from Gordion) are genuine Lydian articles. It is possible that the unguent which filled the Ionian pots was exported in bulk from Lydia to be packaged in the Ionian vases, the shape of which branded their contents as Lydian.

Most revealing, however, is a Lydian word for a little coin (*maulisterion*), which was used metaphorically of a trifle (Hesychius *s.v.*). A type of headdress, the mitra, was also probably of Lydian origin (Alcman 1.67–68). These products mentioned by the Ionian writers of the archaic period were mainly products of Lydian agriculture. The character of the land in Ionian eyes is well summed up by Aristagoras of Miletus for Cleomenes of Sparta (Her. 5.49.5): Lydia is a fertile country, rich in gold.

Other products, not so specifically attested, may be added to these: horses (Her. 1.78.1), metalwork (Daimachos, *FGrHist* IIA, p. 16, No. 4) and, above all, textiles. Archilochus commented on the sheep of Lydia (frag. 23), and a Greek tradition ascribed the invention of dying cloth to the Lydians (Pliny *NH* 7.56[196]; Hyginus *Fables* 274). The textile industry centered at Sardis is known only from the fifth century (Scholia to Aristophanes *Archarnians* 112; *Peace* 1174) but was probably much older and developed from small beginnings as a household craft under the patronage of the Lydian and Ionian nobility. A remarkable confirmation of the industry has been supplied recently by the discovery of tapestries of the mid-fifth century in southern Siberia at Pazyryk near the border of Outer Mongolia.[71] They were apparently imported from the Near East as trade articles or gifts for Scythian chieftains with whom they were buried. Those decorated with animal friezes of stags and lions are the first tangible evidence of the tapestry work which Greek legend ascribed to western Anatolia and which, it is suggested, inspired the animal-style decoration of East Greek orientalizing vases. To this list we should also add ivory-working.[72] Whether Lydian work of the archaic period was an offshoot of imperial Hittite traditions or developed under Greek influence is not clear, but Barnett seems correct in recognizing some Lydian pieces among the ivories of the Artemision. It is likely that only the textiles and the unguents went very far beyond the boundaries of Lydia and the Ionian states. What did the Greeks offer in exchange for these products?

Pottery, although rather more important than in the case of Phrygia, was still a very minor article of trade. Greek imports appear in the seventh century and their influence on the local style is remarked. Hanfmann specifically notes a Samian connection.[73] In the case of the orientalizing pottery Schefold stresses the strong Aeolian influence and identifies some pieces from Sardis as Aeolian imports.[74] In his publication of the Horseman vase from Sardis, dated 650–625, Hanfmann finds the major influence East Greek and Island, although the vase shows some interesting parallels in technique to the Pazarly (Phrygia) tiles.[75] In the sixth century the range of imports is greater, and the effect of

[71] *ILN*, July 11, 1953, pp. 69–71; S. I. Rudenko, *Finds in the Gorny-Altai and the Scyths.* Leningrad, 1952 (in Russian).

[72] Barnett (*JHS* 68 [1948] 18 ff.) identifies as probably Lydian the crouching goat (pl. XI a,b) and perhaps the walking lion from the Artemision. An ivory female head from Sardis (*Sardis* XIII, pl. VIII, 87) is very similar to a terracotta head found at Praisos in Crete (*BSA* 8 [1901–02] 279), and we should perhaps identify the latter as a Lydian export.

[73] Hanfmann, *Robinson Studies* I 175; *AJA* 52 (1948), p. 153, n. 87. Hanfmann compares Sardian craters to the Samian *AM* 58 (1933) Beil. XXI,11.

[74] Schefold, *JDAI* 57 (1942) 134–35.

[75] *AJA* 49 (1945) 570–81; Hanfmann regards the vase as a product of an unknown Ionian workshop or made by a Greek potter working in Sardis.

Greek shapes on the local pottery very marked.[76] Yet the quantity is still very small, and there is none of high quality. Evidently the Lydian nobility, unlike the Etruscans, were not interested in fine Greek pottery, which could have been easily obtained. Corinthian appeared in the early sixth century, but only three aryballoi, an olpe and a few scraps of other vases are reported.[77] Interestingly enough, two Laconian cups of the mid-sixth century were found in a grave.[78] They are probably a trickle from the large amount of Laconian found in Samos, but perhaps we should recognize in them some of the gifts brought by the Spartan envoys who came to Croesus to procure gold for a statue of Apollo. Towards the end of the century a few unimportant Attic black-figured vases appear, and a little red figure was imported in the fifth century.[79]

Probably the Ionians paid for their Lydian goods by imports brought by sea and by services. Among the former we may list ivory, the metals which Lydia did not have, iron(?), tin and copper, and the miscellaneous faience and bric à brac of the southeastern trade. Probably, too, the products of Ionian industry should be added, not only those made to order for Lydian kings,[80] but the lesser products of craftsmanship which have left little trace in the plundered Sardian graves. It is noticeable that in Croesus' reign there was a generally widening net of relationships with the Aegean Greeks. Among the services performed by Greeks that of mercenaries was probably most important in draining off Lydian electrum, but orders were placed with Ionian master craftsmen as early as the time of Gyges.[81] Out of all this interconnection developed the need for a medium of exchange, which was satisfied by the invention of coinage in the latter part of the seventh century. This trade was quite unlike the limited land traffic over the frontiers of two small Greek states or from island to island in the Aegean. In the Lydian area goods and animals and people could move relatively easily by the land routes.

In his brief description of the Lydians Herodotus has an interesting section on coinage and commerce: "(The Lydians) were the first of mankind in our purview to strike and use a coinage of gold and silver, and they were the first also to become *kapeloi*" (1.94.1). Although the first part of this statement has been referred to the innovation of a bimetallic coinage by Croesus to facilitate the exchange of gold and silver on a fixed ratio (between Lydia and the Aegean), it is better interpreted as attributing the actual invention of coinage to the Lydians.[82] Herodotus considered that the Lydians became *kapeloi* about the

[76] *Ibid.*, p. 579; for some imitations (?) of Ionian cups of the second quarter of the sixth century see *Abh.*: *Berlin*, 1858, pl. V, from the tomb of Alyattes. It is striking that in this royal burial the pottery, so far as we can tell from the excavation account, is mostly native Lydian. It contained many alabaster alabastrons.

[77] *Sardis* I, 154; p. 119, fig. 125 (grave); *AJA* 18 (1914) 432.

[78] *AJA* 25 (1921) 111–14, pl. IV; Lane, *BSA* 34 (1933–34) 151.

[79] *AJA* 18 (1914) 432—some 20 Attic b.-f. and r.-f. vases, "for the most part small and carelessly painted." A late black-figured Attic oinochoe is illustrated, *Sardis* I, 118, fig. 124.

[80] For example, the work done by Glaukos of Chios for Alyattes (Her. 1.25.2).

[81] Nik. Dam. *FGrHist* 2A, No. 62 (Magnes of Smyrna).

[82] J. G. Milne (*CR* 63 [1949] 85–87) has interpreted the passage as referring to the innovation of a bimetallic coinage by Croesus. Brown (*NumChron* 10 [1950] 179), however, considers the passage refers to the invention of coinage (cf. Xenophanes, quoted in Pollux 9.83). In this latter article the Aeginetan

same time, although the two parts of the statement are coupled rather loosely. That is, with the innovation of a monetary exchange there began the development of a merchant and trading group in Lydian society.[83] It might be objected that elsewhere (Her. 1.155.4) this is associated with the Persian conquest: Cyrus advised Croesus "that he should order the Lydians to train their sons to play the kithara, enjoy games and to become merchants." While the loss of independence may have turned the Lydians perforce to peaceful activities, that would hardly have started such a process. In fact, a trading class seems to have been clearly defined in Lydia before the time of the construction of Alyattes' tomb.[84] Herodotus refers to the three groups among the people who built it: οἱ ἀγοραῖοι ἄνθρωποι in whom we may recognize the *kapeloi*, οἱ χειρώνακτες, the craftsmen, and αἱ ἐνεργαζόμεναι παιδίσκαι, the temple prostitutes. Evidently a corvée was decreed and each group made liable for a specific part of the work, which was recorded for Herodotus to see. The *kapeloi* began to emerge in society as a definable group when the use of money increased between 650 and 600. How they were organized we do not know. Possibly the unit was a guild of workers in various crafts and of traders in particular goods, for guilds seem thoroughly entrenched in the social and economic organization of Asia Minor at a later date. It is likely that the new group appeared in the Ionian cities at the same time as in Lydia, for they were a part of the same economic area. This was only a part of the transformation in Ionia during the last part of the seventh century, for it was accompanied by the great

coinage is studied, and its earliest issuance placed in the last quarter of the seventh century. The study of the Aeginetan coinage *per se* thus supports the implications of Robinson's study of the Artemision coins. Brown's conclusion, however, about the date of the beginning of Corinthian coinage, *ca.* 575, needs further examination in the light of Corinthian trade; E. Will prefers a date of *ca.* 620–600, which seems very reasonable (*Korinthiaka* 488–91).

83 There is some dispute over the meaning of *kapelos* in Herodotus, which affects the characterization of Lydian trade. Radet and Hogarth considered the *kapelos* a tavern (=caravanserai) keeper in accordance with their view of Lydian trade as servicing long caravan routes to eastern Anatolia and North Syria. Radet's picture of the trade was formed by a seeming analogy with conditions in the seventeenth century after Christ when Tavernier went overland to the east (Radet, *op. cit.*, pp. 91–98, 108 and *passim*). Hogarth admits, however, that this specialized meaning of *kapelos* is later than Herodotus; it is not met with before the late fifth century (Liddell and Scott, *s.v.*). Accordingly, Radet's picture of the Lydians practicing it in the eighth century has no validity. Nikolaos of Damascus (*FGrHist* 2A, No. 44) tells of a Lydian king of the Heraclid dynasty in exile acting as a lowly laborer and tavern keeper. The story has a familiar oriental ring and the language cannot be taken at its face value, for it is of the author's own period. Herodotus obviously uses *kapeloi* to mean traders and merchants. In the passage, 2.35.2, it is said that women in Egypt ἀγοράζουσι καὶ καπηλεύουσι instead of men: they engage in trade and commerce in the internal life of the country; in 3.89.3 Darius is compared to a *kapelos*. For the system of tribute established by him, in which payment was made in kind and in metals, coined and by weight, elaborate weighing of the metals and account keeping were necessary. Darius looked after this like a merchant (*kapelos*), checking his exchanges carefully. In discussing Egyptian society Herodotus associated the *kapeloi* (not women this time) with the χειρώνακτες καὶ ἀγοραῖοι and contrasted them to warriors (2.141; 164.1). Finally he tells of a group of *kapeloi* who lived above Massalia (5.9.3), evidently trading with the Celts of the region. The only pre-Herodotean usage is in Hipponax (frag. 47.2), where a changer of coins is meant.

84 Her. 1.93. It is evident that these great royal tumuli in both Phrygia and Lydia must have been built by large numbers of laborers whose service was made available by a highly centralized political organization. The tomb of Alyattes was *ca.* 61m. in height and *ca.* 355m. in diameter on its stone socle (von Ölfers, *Abh.*: *Berlin*, 1858, 545).

expansion overseas and a change in the character of trade. In the sixth century the results of this change in the structure of society began to appear with the "tyrants," stasis and new political institutions.

While the economic relationship with Lydia was very important and profitable to the Ionians, it did not solve their two main problems, scarcity of food and of the various metals which were needed. There is no hint in the sources that grain was imported from Lydia. In fact, it was a part of Lydian policy to deny the Ionians the use of their own production by frequent razzias. Lydian electrum partly paid for Ionian goods and services, but the cities also needed silver, tin, copper and iron. To satisfy these needs they had to orient their trade to the Aegean and the Mediterranean.

CHAPTER IV

Ionia, Syria and Cyprus

In the obscure period which preceded the revival of regular Greek trade with the south-eastern Mediterranean in the late eighth century, connections with the Aegean were by no means entirely broken. For example, Cypriote influence has been noticed on Greek Protogeometric pottery, and sailors from the northern Cyclades probably began to make occasional voyages to Syria before 850. By the first half of the eighth century their typical small cups were widely distributed along the Syrian coast and inland.[1] This era of sporadic visiting culminated *ca.* 750 in the establishment of a small trading factory at Al Mina on the mouth of the Orontes River. The Ionians of Asia Minor, who met their Cycladic kindred at the Delian panegyris, could scarcely have been ignorant of this new trade, but Ionia's place in it remained slight until well after its regular establishment.[2] From *ca.* 700, Samos, in particular, seems to have taken some part, perhaps at first through the medium

[1] Cypriote influence on Protogeometric pottery: E. Gjerstad, *Swedish Cyprus Expedition* IV, 2, 315; Cycladic in the Near East: Desborough, *Protogeometric Pottery* 180–85, 303–04; *idem*, *JHS* 77 (1957) 212–19; Ch. Clairmont, *Berytus* 11 (1955) 98–100; G.M.A. Hanfmann, "Eastern Greek Wares at Tarsus," *The Aegean and the Near East* (ed. S. Weinberg) 167, 173–75.

[2] Poulsen regarded the Phoenicians as the agents and largely the source of the oriental influences (*Der Orient und die frühgriechische Kunst*, 1913). Karo enlarged on this by pointing to Urartu as the source of certain techniques of metal work carried to North Syria and thence to Italy and Greece (*AM* 45 [1920] 106–56). The links in the westward chain were traced by Kunze and Payne: Cyprus, Rhodes, Crete and the Cyclades to Corinth and Athens (H. Payne, *Necrocorinthia* 5–7, 67–69, 170–73; E. Kunze, *AM* 55 [1930] 141–62; *Kretische Bronzereliefs* 248–64; *AM* 60–61 [1935–36] 218–33). P. Démargne has stressed the role of Crete and the legacy from the Mycenean period (*La Crète dédalique*), while E. Gjerstad has emphasized the importance of Cyprus as a link between the Mycenean and orientalizing periods and between east and west (*op. cit., passim*). On the Late Hittite art of North Syria in this connection see, in particular, E. Akurgal, *Späthetitische Bildkunst* (1949). With the discovery of Al Mina at the mouth of the Orontes River it seemed that the first Greek link in the chain had been found, but Gjerstad stresses its Cypriote, rather than Greek character. As a result of this expanding knowledge of the process of orientalization Ionia's role, of course, diminished: R.M. Cook, *JHS* 66 (1946) 67–98; G.M.A. Hanfmann, *HSCP* 61 (1953) 1–37.

of Rhodes and Cyprus, and after the middle of the seventh century direct Ionian commerce to the southeast began to grow rapidly. Its main goal was Egypt where the emporion of Naukratis was established in the last quarter of the century. Perhaps the fact that Rhodes and Cyprus were already very active in the Syrian trade deterred the Ionians, but it is likely that Egyptian wheat bulked larger in their eyes than Syrian luxuries. Egypt could provide the latter and, in addition, linen and papyrus.[3] Thus, the focus of interest in the Syrian area is rather the role of the islanders, Rhodians and Cypriotes, than that of the Ionians of Asia Minor.

Nevertheless, the name given to all Greeks by the Assyrians was Iamani, Ionians.[4] Presumably it was used of themselves by the Cycladic Greeks, the first with whom the easterners came into contact aside from those of the Mycenean period and their descendants in Cyprus and Cilicia. The earliest evidence of its use is in an inscription, dated in 711, of Sargon II. It is possible that the name became familiar in Syria in Mycenean times, when it was borne by the Achaeans, but the epigraphical evidence for that is slight. From these early contacts in the ninth and eighth centuries "Ionian" was evidently applied to all of Greek speech, just as Egyptians used it of any Greek, even after they had learned that there were differences of origin among them.

AL MINA AND CILICIA

While the Cycladic Greeks were probably the first to settle at Al Mina, their factory was soon reinforced by Rhodians and Cypriotes.[5] The site, possibly to be identified as Posideion, is considered to have been the main port of departure to the Aegean for the oriental products of North Syria and the regions farther east. It is situated on the delta of the Orontes (Map I), where Mt. Kasios in the background provides a convenient landfall and the Orontes valley a means of access to the Fertile Crescent by way of Aleppo and Apamea. The Greek pottery found there presumably identifies the site as a Greek trading factory, where traders obtained eastern goods directly rather than through the medium of Phoenicians or Cypriotes, yet its architecture is entirely eastern in type. The excavator has suggested that, in a sense, Al Mina never ceased to be Greek—it was an Achaean foun-

[3] For the Ionian trade with Egypt see Roebuck *CP* 45 (1950) 236–47; 46 (1951) 212–20.

[4] On the problem of the oriental references to Ionians see H. Bengtson, *Philologus* 92 (1937) 148–55 and C. F. Lehmann-Haupt, *Klio* 27 (1934) 74–83. The first certain references to Ionians (Iamani) belong to the period of Sargon II in the late eighth century (711), by which time the term was evidently well established, but its precise reference is not clear. Bengtson concludes that Iamani was a very old designation for the Greeks, which was learned from the Ionians proper after the conclusion of the great Aegean migrations. If so, the archaeological evidence points to the Ionians of the Cyclades rather than to those of Asia Minor and to direct contacts by sea rather than by land (despite Santo Mazzarino, *Fra Oriente e Occidente* 112–16). Hrozny, however, interprets a reference in a document from Ras Shamra of the thirteenth century as to Ionians, *i.e.*, raiders from Cilicia or Cyprus (*Archiv Orientální* 4 [1932] 169 ff.). If correct, the name may have been established in the Near East by Mycenean colonists and continued in use to be applied to Greek-speaking islanders when they appeared in the ninth century.

[5] C. L. Woolley, *JHS* 58 (1938) 1–30; 133–70; S. Smith, *Antiquaries Journal* 22 (1942) 87–112; M. Robertson, *JHS* 60 (1940) 2–21 (early Greek pottery); *idem, JHS* 66 (1946) 125; R. M. Cook, *JHS* 66 (1946) 78–79, 82–83, 86.

dation of the late Mycenean period.[6] If it is correctly identified as Posideion, it does have the tradition of being founded before the Trojan War. The possibility of such a survival is strengthened by the revelations of the Karatepe inscriptions and given some material support by the discovery of Mycenean sherds at Sabouni, an "acropolis" three miles upstream from Al Mina. At Al Mina itself, however, the earliest pottery belongs to the eighth century.

There is some question whether the foundation should be dated in the first or second half of the eighth century, but, on the whole, historical circumstances in the Near East seem to favor the earlier dating.[7] At that time the dominant power in North Syria was Urartu, itself non-Semitic and favoring the non-Semitic elements of North Syria. This might have had an effect in directing trade from Aleppo to Al Mina rather than south to Byblus and the Phoenician coast. The opportunity for settlement was present soon after 800, and Cycladic Greeks with some prior knowledge of local conditions then established the trading post. If we may identify the traders by their pottery, from the foundation until *ca.* 700 the trade was in the hands of the islanders. There is some East Greek material in the early levels (10 ?, 9, 8), but it is very small in quantity; the only other sherd which belongs to this early period is a stray piece of Protocorinthian, which dates from the last half of the eighth century, possibly near its middle.[8] Probably these traders of the eighth century were mainly Cycladic Greeks with a few Rhodians.

The character of the factory changed *ca.* 700. A considerable amount of Cypriote pottery, imported or made locally, appeared, and at the same time the settlement was enlarged. Gjerstad has suggested that Cypriotes virtually took it over as the result of the Assyrian conquest of Cyprus and the Mediterranean coast.[9] Along with the Cypriote, however, East Greek pottery (mainly bird bowls) was found in increasing volume until, in the second half of the century, it definitely predominated. Evidently Assyrian domination was not incompatible with Greek use of the port in increasing momentum. This East Greek pottery was accompanied by a steady but not large importation of Protocorinthian and Corinthian until *ca.* 600.[10] The latest Corinthian, however, was outlasted by the East Greek, which extended to *ca.* 580. Throughout most of the seventh century Al Mina was a Rhodian center but used also by Corinthian and perhaps Aeginetan traders. Other pottery fabrics are negligible:[11] 1 piece of Chiot, 1 piece of Attic (?) and a few fragments

[6] C. L. Woolley, *JHS* 58 (1938) 1–9, 28–30; Smith, *op. cit.*, pp. 90, 96–98.

[7] Smith, *op. cit.*, pp. 91–95, 99; Robertson (*op. cit.*, p. 21) and R. M. Cook (*op. cit.*, pp. 78–79) consider that the pottery need hardly extend far back into the first half of the eighth century; so, too, Desborough, *Protogeometric Pottery* 183, 194; Hanfmann suggests an earlier date, *ca.* 800 (*The Aegean and the Near East* 175).

[8] On the identification of the pottery see Robertson, *op. cit.*, pp. 2–21.

[9] Gjerstad, *Swedish Cyprus Expedition* IV, 2, 462–63.

[10] There is a fair quantity of Corinthian of the seventh century, but Rhodian, with some Cycladic, is predominant among the Greek wares (Robertson, *op. cit.*, pp. 16–18).

[11] Chiot: Robertson, *op. cit.*, fig. 4, k; Attic (?): *ibid.*, fig. 8, e; Laconian (?): *ibid.*, fig. 8, l–n. On the break in the ceramic evidence see Smith, *op. cit.*, pp. 105–10 (result of Nebuchadrezzar's foreign policy) and Robertson, *JHS* 66 (1946) 125. The gap is difficult to account for, since the pottery from Tell Sukas only a short distance down the coast belongs to the period 605–540 (below, n. 37).

of Laconian (?). The evidence further indicates that the post was not used throughout most of the sixth century, for there is a gap in the ceramic sequence from *ca.* 580 to 520. It is filled only by a sherd of Fikellura (Samian ?) pottery which is hardly enough to serve as a point of departure for speculation. Nothing at Al Mina indicates that Ionia was in early and direct contact with North Syria by the sea route.

The apparent tardiness of Rhodes in using Al Mina is somewhat puzzling. The position of the island off the southwest tip of Asia Minor (Map I) made it a focal point in communication between the Aegean and the southeastern Mediterranean, and Cycladic and Cypriote traders must have stopped in the course of their journeys. The island was large and fertile; it could both offer hospitality and collect the tolls on ships using its harbors. Yet the orientalizing influences which were a product of this new trade appeared in Rhodian craft products rather later than in Crete, Corinth, Athens and the Cyclades. Probably at first the Rhodians were content to profit from tolls on shipping and felt little compulsion to take to the sea, since their island offered them a good living from its own soil. Shortly after 700, however, the Rhodians began to play an active part in the trade.

The foundation of Phaselis and Soloi along the south coast of Asia Minor is probably one mark of that activity. The Eusebian chronology sets the foundation of Phaselis in 691, and that of Soloi is considered contemporary. These could serve as way stations for ships, but Phaselis grew into a thriving town in its own right, for it had a place in the organization of Naukratis.[12] Other evidence of Rhodian trading is to be seen in the imported pottery of Tarsus and Mersin, which indicates that a coasting trade along the south shore was in operation.

At Mersin only a limited area of the Early Iron Age town was dug, and few architectural remains discovered. The pottery of the seventh and sixth centuries, however, was plentiful, with more imported than local fabrics, so that the town probably had a group of Greek residents. The excavator suggests that it had become a small trading station in the Rhodian orbit and comments on the resemblance of the pottery to that from Vroulia on Rhodes. Most of the material was East Greek marked by the characteristic bird and rosette bowls of the seventh century and a large amount of the so-called Ionian ordinary ware. There was relatively little Cypriote and Corinthian and no Attic of the seventh and sixth centuries. A few pieces of Fikellura and grey bucchero are reported, but the pottery gives the impression that it was imported for use, mainly from one center, which we may conclude from the resemblance to the Vroulia pottery, was Rhodes.[13]

The imported pottery from Tarsus gives the same impression of Rhodian activity beginning *ca.* 800(?) and continuing throughout the century. A few bird bowls and a bird jug are said to occur in levels earlier than the Assyrian destruction of 696, but the bulk of such pottery was found in the Assyrian levels themselves. Late examples of this subgeometric ware occur in a floor level dated by an Assyrian tablet of 636. This is presumably a part of the house complex referred to in the preliminary report, in which Rhodian Orientalizing

[12] Phaselis: W. Ruge, "Phaselis," *RE* 19 (1938) 1874–83; Soloi: W. Ruge, "Soloi," *RE* 3A (1927) 935–38.

[13] J. Garstang, *Prehistoric Mersin* 253–59; R. D. Barnett, *LAAA* 26 (1939) 98–130.

pottery was found and many iron tools came to light. Other identified Greek imports mentioned in the preliminary reports include "Ionian" cups among which Hanfmann singles out the largest number as Rhodian, but suggests that some are of Samian and local origin.[14] Most of the pottery from these levels was a local imitation of Cypriote types, but the imported material seems to point definitely to Rhodes as the carrier, as might be expected from the finds at Mersin. Apparently these imports found little reception inland in Cilicia. Not only is the Tarsus material scanty, but there seem to be no Greek imports among the pottery found at Karatepe. To the descendants of the Achaeans in this area Greece was something alien. They looked mainly to Cyprus[15] and retained only a legendary tradition of their origin.

CYPRUS

In the Early Iron Age Cyprus (Map I) was a wealthy and flourishing island which carried on an extensive trade with the adjacent coasts of Palestine, Syria and Cilicia.[16] It was dominated by Phoenicians in the eighth century, absorbed into the Assyrian Empire in 719, but regained its independence once more in 664 to retain it until the Persian conquest of *ca.* 540. Its "great" period as established by the archaeological evidence was in the seventh and early sixth century. The basis of the economy was agriculture, the chief products of which were grain, olives, wine and cattle, but, in addition, metal production was developed, mainly of copper and iron. A partial index of the production for export may be seen in the tribute lists of Sargon II which record payment in gold, silver, utensils and furniture. These products, however, were also typical of the booty lists of Syria,[17] so that probably Cyprus' trade to the coast was mainly in copper, iron and agricultural products with some pottery for its own trading stations there. Through these factories the Cypriotes were able to obtain eastern goods, both Syrian and Phoenician, for sale to the Greeks. In Greek tradition, however, Cyprus was known as the great producer of copper. Throughout the eighth century Cypriote trade was partly in Phoenician hands, both of those settled in Cyprus and of those from Phoenicia itself, but probably after the Assyrian conquest Cypriote traders and Greeks carried the exports to the west.

Gjerstad has plausibly suggested that Rhodes was the distributing point of Cypriote goods to Greece, for about ninety per cent of the Cypriote pottery which has been reported from the Aegean was found on that island. Only sporadic finds have been made along the coast of Asia Minor, but probably Cyprus traded directly with Samos, to judge from the quantity of terracottas of Cypriote origin found in the Heraion.[18] On Rhodes itself the distribution of Cypriote material is not uniform. Most of the pottery was discovered at

[14] Assyrian tablet: Hanfmann, *HSCP* 61 (1953), p. 33, n. 85; preliminary reports: *AJA* 41 (1937) 276–77; 42 (1938), p. 44, fig. 33; Hanfmann, *The Aegean and the Near East* 167–75.

[15] Karatepe: Mellink, *Bib. Or.* 7 (1950) 141–50; R. D. Barnett, *JHS* 73 (1953) 140–43; Cypriote influence: Hanfmann *AJA* 52 (1948) 138–43.

[16] This account of Cypriote trade is based, with some reservations, on Gjerstad, *Swedish Cyprus Expedition* IV, 2, *passim*; for iron and copper, below, pp. 102–04.

[17] D. D. Luckenbill, *Ancient Records* II, Nos. 70, 186.

[18] Rhodes: Gjerstad, *op. cit.*, p. 316; Samos: below p. 68.

Ialysos on the northwest corner of the island, farthest from Cyprus; at Kamiros farther down the west coast there is virtually none, but at both Lindos and Vroulia on the southeast, nearest to Cyprus, a moderate amount. Probably Cypriote ships put in at Lindos, then sailed up the east coast, rounding the tip of the island to discharge most of their cargo at Ialysos. The large amount of pottery there should indicate the presence of Cypriote metics engaged in the business of forwarding Cypriote goods to the north and west. A little Cypriote trade along the west coast of Asia Minor and into the Propontis is perhaps indicated by the scattered finds of pottery at Cnidus, where a group of Cypriote figurines also came to light, on Chios and in Aeolis.[19] Probably some pieces were carried north in the eighth and early seventh century by Cycladic and Cypriote traders, and the later pieces brought by Ionians from Samos or Cyprus itself. The pottery, however, was not an important article of trade. In general, the distribution of the Cypriote figurines is similar to that of the pottery. Many were found in the Athena sanctuary in Lindos where there may have been a resident group of Cypriote metics. Some are reported from Ialysos, and there is a group at Kamiros, the origin of which is disputed; they were perhaps made in Rhodes rather than in Cyprus. A few figurines have also been found along the Ionian coast.[20] To judge from the distribution of this material, Cypriote trade with Rhodes was early and continuous, starting in volume from *ca.* 700; with Samos it probably began *ca.* 650, but with the rest of Ionia it was never intense. There was also a strong Cypriote influence on Samian sculpture which Gjerstad considers set in *ca.* 550 when Cypriote sculpture was also imported into Rhodes and Naukratis.[21]

The importation of Greek pottery to Cyprus began in the eighth and early seventh centuries with a few pieces of Cycladic, Rhodian and Attic origin. The general course of the traders in this and the succeeding period was along the west and south coasts, where the important harbor towns with easy access to the interior were situated. Most of the pottery, however, remained in the coastal towns. The Greek traders of this early period were the Cycladic and Rhodian Greeks with the former probably carrying the Attic material. After the middle of the seventh century, as the volume of shipping increased, Rhodians and Ionians seem to have taken over most of the trade. The imported pottery is almost all East Greek, mainly Rhodian, but with some Ionian. It is obviously an article of trade, since it is found in fair quantity and consists mostly of simple bowls and cups. Two Chiot pieces are reported from Marion, which should probably be associated with the East Greek amphoras found in tombs there, indicating import of wine. The greatest volume of this trade was reached toward the middle of the sixth century, when it was probably incidental to East Greek commerce with Naukratis in Egypt. The trade was almost wholly in East Greek and Cypriote hands, for very little Protocorinthian and

[19] Rhodes: Gjerstad, *op. cit.*, pp. 262–66; Cnidus (Dadia): *ibid.*, p. 268; *JHS* 2 (1882) 305. I have noticed Cypriote pots in the museum in Chios. Miss Mellink informs me that some Cypriote sherds were found in the excavations under Hagia Sophia in Istanbul.

[20] Rhodes: Gjerstad, *op. cit.*, pp. 327–31; Cnidus (Dadia): *ibid.*, p. 332; Halicarnassus: Higgins, *BMC Terr.* 301; Lycia: Gjerstad, *op. cit.*, p. 332; Ephesus: Pryce, *BMC Sculpture* I, 1. B2; Smyrna: Walters, *BMC Terr.* C413.

[21] Gjerstad, *op. cit.*, pp. 369 ff.; Naukratis: *ibid.*, pp. 318–22.

Corinthian has been found; there are only four pieces of Protocorinthian reported (one is an imitation), and a few sherds of Corinthian aryballoi. There does appear, however, to be a direct connection between Cyprus and Aegina, for some Cypriote figurines have been found in temples on the latter island.[22]

In general, to judge by the pottery distribution on Cyprus, the pattern of Greek trade was similar to that in Cilicia and Syria. There is sporadic material left by Cycladic traders of the eighth and early seventh centuries, and then a steadily increasing amount of East Greek material, most of which is Rhodian. Unlike Al Mina, however, the amount of Corinthian is negligible. The pottery is primarily for ordinary use rather than of high quality. Evidently Cyprus was included in the orbit of Greek trade with the adjacent coast and played its part in the transmission of eastern goods and metals as well as its own products. It remains to discuss the place of Ionia in this area dominated by Rhodes and Cyprus.

IONIAN TRADE

Samos, as might be expected from its location (Map I), was the first of the Ionian states to become interested. There is some literary evidence to indicate that Samos colonized Amorgos in the first half of the seventh century.[23] This island was a useful port of call on the regular lane of traffic from southwestern Asia Minor into the Cyclades and across the Aegean. Yet, Samian interest in it seems to have been shown after the line of trade had been long in operation, for the Samians were forestalled by a Naxian colony. Perhaps the foundation of two Samian colonies on the southwest coast of Asia Minor, Nagidus and Celenderis, should be placed in this connection also. There is no evidence for their date of foundation, but it seems clear that both were Greek and in existence in the archaic period. Celenderis issued a coinage which is attributed to the fifth century, and Nagidus is mentioned by Hecataeus (*FGrHist* I, No. 266).[24] They would provide stopping points en route to Syria or to Cyprus and lairs for the favorite Samian occupation of piracy. It seems extremely doubtful that Samians had a share in Al Mina at this time. One subgeometric pottery fragment found at Al Mina is perhaps Samian,[25] but we can hardly postulate the presence of Samian traders on that evidence.

Samos, however, did share, even if indirectly, in the growing commerce. In the excavation of the Heraion several objects were found which are either oriental imports or

[22] Geometric: Gjerstad, *op. cit.*, pp. 274–75; East Greek: *ibid.*, p. 270, n. 6, pp. 276–78; Chiot: *JHS* 66 (1946) 5–7, pl. 1; Corinthian: Gjerstad, *op. cit.*, p. 270, notes 4, 5, p. 275; Aegina: Gjerstad, *op. cit.*, p. 336.

[23] Amorgos is one of the few Samian colonies. Although the Samians were anticipated on the island by Naxians, there is no evidence of discord between the two. The chronological evidence is slight: Suidas (*s.v.* Simonides) states that the Samian poet Simonides took part in the colonization as *hegemon* and that he lived 490 years after the Trojan War (in the early seventh century). According to Stephanus, Naxians had colonized the island before Samos (*s.v.* Amorgos). The testimonia are collected in *IG* XII, 7, pp. vii–viii.

[24] Celenderis: W .Ruge, "Kelenderis, 2," *RE* 11 (1922) 138; *ATL* I, 500. Nagidus: *idem*, "Nagidos," *RE* 16 (1935) 1582–83. Side in Pisidia claimed to be a foundation of Aeolian Kyme (Arrian *Anab. Alex.* 1.26; Strabo 14.4.2). This tradition may indicate a Mycenean colonization (Magie, *Roman Asia Minor* II, p. 1132, n. 3), one of the archaic period or merely the aspirations of a Hellenized barbarian town seeking to claim a Greek origin.

[25] Robertson, *JHS* 60 (1940), p. 14, fig. 7, h, j.

close imitations: a bronze statuette of a bearded man identified by Kunze as "a Greek work of Assyrianizing style" and dated to the beginning of the seventh century; an ivory lion's head recognized as mainly Late Hittite in inspiration but showing some Assyrian influence. Barnett has discussed the ivories from the Heraion which show a strong Phoenician influence and has suggested that they are the product of a school of Phoenician ivory-carvers established in Samos, where the Heraion offered a favorable market.[26] By 650 the first of the series of Cypriote stone and terracotta figurines appeared in the Heraion. Their number was so great by *ca.* 600 that local and other Greek figurines were apparently excluded from the market for a time. Whether their presence indicates a group of Cypriote metics or not,[27] there was obviously from 650 a direct trading connection with Cyprus. Another import of this period from the Syrian area is a metal cheek-piece for a horse, which is paralleled by one in Lindos.[28] On the whole, the evidence seems to indicate that Samos' early contacts with this Syrian trade were indirect, for we do not know the foundation dates for Nagidus and Celenderis, and there is no quantity of identifiable Samian pottery in Al Mina. Phoenician workmen may have established themselves in Samos, where the Heraion offered a market. Probably the more valuable objects, if trade articles and not loot taken by Samian pirates, were brought by Cycladic, Rhodian and Cypriote traders. This implies, of course, that Samos was not a distributor of such goods on any scale to the rest of Ionia. It was on the fringe of the main current of trade to the west, either from Rhodes to Crete or into the Cyclades and to the mainland. After 650, however, the discovery of the Cypriote figurines hints at a substantial trade in Cypriote goods, probably copper and iron, for which Samos could serve as the distributor to Ionia. They would replace the tenuous supply from Anatolia, where communications had been disrupted by the Cimmerian attacks.

Probably the Milesians took over their adjacent islands (Map I) in the first half of the seventh century as the importance of the new trade routes became apparent. Ikaros, west of Samos, was convenient for access to the Cyclades, while Leros, Lepsia and Patmos could serve as ports of call on the route south to Rhodes.[29] We do not have any evidence about Milesian motives, but the situation of the islands suggests a consideration for trading interests rather than a spilling-over of Milesian population. The islands are very small and rocky, and Milesian colonization of the Propontis had already begun *ca.* 700.

Few oriental imports which can be dated before 650 have been found on the other Ionian sites, but evidently some were brought. No Late Hittite nor Assyrian objects are reported from the excavation of Old Smyrna. There is a faience figurine, paralleled by one on Rhodes, and a few other small objects of Phoenician origin, statuettes, amulets, seals, scarabs and bone figures, but their date is difficult to fix and may well fall for the most part after 650. They are small luxury objects of the type that characterizes the current of southeastern

[26] Kunze, *Kret. Bronz.* 238–39, Beil. 5a+5b; Akurgal, *op. cit.*, I, 75, 133–34, pl. XXXVII; Barnett, *JHS* 68 (1948) 3–4, 6.

[27] Gjerstad, *op. cit.*, pp. 332–35; Ohly, *AM* 65 (1940) 57 ff.

[28] *JHS* 50 (1930) 249, fig. 7; *Lindos* I, No. 621; II, pl. 25.

[29] Above, p. 13.

trade and need not indicate any early or direct trading connection.[30] Similar material has been found in the sanctuary of Kato Phana in Chios: a Cypriote figurine, a bone or ivory seal of the late geometric period, faience scarabs and figurines of Naukratite and Phoenician origin, which belong to the latter half of the seventh and sixth centuries.[31] The material from the Artemision at Ephesus is now considered to date mainly from 650 to 600. It is of a very specialized nature appropriate to the goddess Artemis and is mainly of local manufacture and tradition. Akurgal notes a Late Hittite lion type among the ivories, but most are considered to be Anatolian. The type of lion head, however, used on the Lydian coins is Assyrian in origin and perhaps came by direct land contact in the first part of the seventh century.[32]

About the middle of the seventh century the Ionians became aware of Egypt. Probably this was the result of mercenary service there under Psammetichos I, to whom Gyges had sent some troops. Gradually a regular line of traffic, in which the Ionians called at Rhodes and Cyprus, was established, and shortly before 600 the new emporion at Naukratis was founded. It is likely that the Ionians obtained most of their Syrian goods from this traffic rather than going directly to the Syrian ports. There were certain exotic products beyond the range of Greek traders which could only have come through Phoenicia. Ivory probably did so from the first, for the North Syrian elephant herds seem to have been killed off by the eighth century.[33] Herodotus lists exotic spices, perfumes and unguents which came from Arabia through the Phoenicians in the fifth century (3.107,111). While a Spartan bronze of *ca.* 550 is reported to have been found in South Arabia, it is hardly possible to assume that Greeks were in direct contact with that area.[34]

It remains to notice what the Greeks offered in exchange for Syrian goods. At first they can have had little but their agricultural surpluses, hides, wine and olive oil. Their pottery was mainly a useful article of exchange in their own factories. By the end of the sixth century, however, when its origin is recognizable in coinage, a flow of Greek silver was entering Syria and the Persian Empire. The coins are mainly Thraco-Macedonian, Aeginetan and Athenian.[35] Probably at an earlier date the silver was carried in ingot form. Since the

[30] Akurgal, *Ztsch. d. phil. Fak. Univ. Ankara* 8 (1950) 82 ff., pl. 13a; *ILN*, Feb. 28, 1953, 328–29, figs. 1, 2, 7 (the very fine ivory lion is apparently Greek work).

[31] *BSA* 35 (1934–35) 153–54, pl. 33, 1–4; pp. 155–56, 163–64; 156, pl. 33,15.

[32] *The Archaic Artemisia* pl. 21,3; pl. 25; fig. 12 a–c; pl. 3; fig. 7; Akurgal, *Späthet. Bild.*, p. 78, n. 231; Barnett, *JHS* 68 (1948) 8 ff. For the lion head on Lydian coins see Robinson, *JHS* 71 (1951) 159–61.

[33] Barnett, *JHS* 68 (1948), p. 1, n. 4.

[34] Beazley, *BSA* 40 (1939–40) 83–84; B. Segall (*AJA* 59 [1955] 315–18) comparing a similar statuette found in the Heraion at Samos, suggests that these were tokens of Spartan military strength circulated in connection with an anti-Persian coalition at the time of the Persian conquest of western Asia. This particular piece may have come to South Arabia through Tema siezed by Nabonidus of Babylonia in 550. Nabonidus was anti-Persian in 539, but the Spartan position is difficult to make out. The latter objected to the Persian conquest of Asia Minor, but were hostile to the Samian tyranny and friendly to the Samian oligarchs. The problem is chronologically involved with the date of the Samian tyranny and thus very complicated.

[35] C. F. A. Schaeffer, *Mélanges Dussaud* 30 (1939) I, 461–87; Willy Schwabacher, *Skr. ut. av. Svenska Inst. i Rom* 15 (1950) 139–49; E. S. G. Robinson, *Iraq* 12 (1950) 44–51. A few Greek fibulae were imported to Sendschirli (*Sendschirli* V, pls. 22, 43), to Nineveh (G. Loud, *Palace of Sargon* II, pl. 59; before 705) and to Carchemish (*LAAA* 26 [1939], pls. 19, 21; late eighth and early seventh century). For the Greek pottery

Ionians used silver to finance their purchases of wheat in Egypt,[36] it was probably used also for this Syrian trade. They could have bought for Lydia, too, carrying electrum for purchases.

Toward the end of the sixth century there began a changeover in the Syrian area from an East Greek to an Attic trading connection. At Al Mina the pottery sequence failed from *ca.* 580 to 520. When it resumed, Attic red-figure had taken the place of the East Greek wares, although there was no large quantity until after 475. At Sabouni Woolley reported some good, early Attic black-figured pottery, but it is not published and, to judge from the finds at other sites, would not be earlier than the mid-sixth century. At Tell Sukas an Attic "Tyrrhenian" amphora of *ca.* 550–540 has been found, but that site seems to have come to a temporary end at that time.[37] Interestingly enough, the Greek material from the mounds in the Amk plain, excavated by the Oriental Institute, follows the pattern of the pottery at Al Mina, although its scantiness indicates that Greek pottery was imported into the interior in very small quantity. The earliest Attic is black-figure of the late sixth century. At that time, too, Attic pottery began to predominate among the imported material on Cyprus. The scattered material from Palestine also falls into the same pattern. A few East Greek pieces belong to the late seventh and early sixth century. There is a little sixth century Corinthian, while the Attic begins only at the end of the century.[38]

This pattern of distribution probably indicates that East Greek trade with the coast became indirect or tapered off after 580, although it remained strong with Cyprus. By the end of the century it evidently lapsed for a time at least. The explanation is probably to be found in historical circumstances—the trade received a blow from the aggressive policy of Nebuchadrezzar in Syria and Palestine. When a more lenient Persian occupation favored trading conditions in the area, the East Greeks were faced with a fight against Persia from 546–40, then found it more profitable to trade in Thrace, the Black Sea and Italy. At the time of the Ionian Revolt, in which Cyprus joined, trading probably lapsed almost entirely. Into this vacuum, which history provided, the Athenians stepped. Their earliest pottery in the region may have been carried by Rhodians or Cypriotes, but after the Persian Wars they probably traded directly in their own ships. In general, the appearance of Attic pottery along the Syrian coast lags about two generations behind its appearance in Samos, Rhodes and Naukratis.

found at sites in the interior see Ch. Clairmont, *Berytus* 11 (1955) 98 ff. It is very scanty in quantity and was probably imported as a novelty by some traders from the coast.

[36] Roebuck, *CP* 45 (1950) 236–47.

[37] E. Forrer, *Bericht über den VI Internationalen Kongress für Archäologie, Berlin, 1939*, pp. 360–65, pls. 32–33. The Greek pottery begins *ca.* 605 with some Rhodian. The site is only partially excavated.

[38] Al Mina: Robertson, *JHS* 66 (1946) 125; Beazley, *JHS* 59 (1939) 1–44; Sabouni: Woolley, *JHS* 58 (1938) 21; Tell Sukas: Forrer, *op. cit.*, p. 64; Cyprus: Gjerstad, *op. cit.*, p. 270, n. 7, 278–79. The stray finds of Greek pottery in the Near East, with the exception of Anatolia, have been collected by Ch. Clairmont, *Berytus* 11 (1955) 85–141. Clairmont notes that the quantity of Greek pottery in southern Syria and Palestine is very small and that the Attic black-figure is late, all after 500. The Corinthian in Palestine is mostly Late Corinthian II.

CHAPTER V

Ionia and the Aegean

Ionian trade of the late eighth and seventh centuries has usually been represented as closely knit with that of the Aegean and the cities of mainland Greece. This historical reconstruction was formed under the influence of the view that Ionia was the chief agent for the distribution of oriental goods into the Aegean and a leader in the process of trade and colonization, which characterized Greek history in this early period. A further assumption was that out of this trading and colonial activity grew inter-state combinations and rivalries, forming a political framework in which our very fragmentary knowledge of events could be included. Yet it seems no longer possible to consider Ionia as the terminus for routes by which trade goods moved from eastern Anatolia, Mesopotamia and North Syria to the Aegean. Ionia and Lydia, however, did form a closely linked economic area in the seventh and sixth centuries, which gave the Ionian cities some share in a large and fertile hinterland organized under a vigorous, centralized authority. Their position in this respect was quite unlike that of any other Greek state. Since Ionia's relation to the east has been reinterpreted, perhaps some modification of its position in the Aegean is necessary to set Ionian relations with Greece in proper perspective.

The scanty information from the historical traditions of the seventh century links Samos and Miletus to certain Greek states in the Aegean and on the mainland. From this evidence has been developed a picture of Greek trade proceeding along certain lines of travel between friendly states knit into loose groups, the trade leagues, whose conflicts are traced more or less directly to trade and colonial rivalries. For example, A. R. Burn has constructed three major "leagues" for seventh-century Greece, a Samian, a Milesian and a south Dorian (Rhodian). Recently this view has been given fresh currency by an examination of the connection of Pheidon of Argos with the groups. The starting point for such a reconstruction is the war between Chalcis and Eretria over the Lelantine plain in

Euboea.[1] It was probably a local and long-protracted struggle between two neighboring states for the possession of land, similar to that between Samos and Priene over land around the Panionion. Yet Thucydides (1.15) singles it out of the obscurity of early Greek wars as being the first occasion on which the rest of Greece took sides, and Herodotus tells us, in an incidental reference (5.99), that Samos was allied to Chalcis and Miletus to Eretria. Perhaps Thucydides referred only to a decisive phase of the war, and the extent of Milesian aid to Eretria is indicated by Eretria's repayment of its debt with five ships in the Ionian Revolt. Even so, the sources seem to attest a system of alliances extending across the Aegean in the early seventh century, if that date may be accepted for the war.

Herodotus' evidence links Samos with Chalcis and Sparta, Thucydides' with Corinth. The link to Corinth is given by the notice (1.13) that a Corinthian, Ameinokles, built four ships for Samos about three hundred years before the end of "this (Peloponnesian) war." It is unlikely that these ships were triremes, but apparently a Corinthian builder did introduce some new technique of ship construction, perhaps the penteconter, to Samos in the late eighth century (721 or 704, depending on the interpretation of "this war").[2] For Sparta, Herodotus tells us (3.47) that Samos aided that state against Messenia. Possibly the reference is to a war against Messenia in the late eighth century, although there is some difficulty here, too, in accepting the war as more than local.[3] Yet the Messenian hero, Aristomenes, showing an unusual knowledge of the east, is said to have fled for refuge to Rhodes and to have contemplated going on to Sardis and ultimately inland to Ecbatana (Paus. 4.24.2). Samian hostility to Aegina is mentioned by Herodotus (3.59.4), who refers to a raid on Aegina in the time of the Samian King Amphikrates. In the Cyclades Samos was on good terms with Paros and Andros, since it participated in an arbitration along with Paros and Erythrae at the invitation of Andros and Chalcis over the ownership of the colony Akanthos (Plut. *Quaest. Gr.* 30). Samos, too, colonized Amorgos, apparently without antagonizing its previous Naxian settlers.[4] Probably Samos and Thera were on good terms from *ca.* 638, when Colaeus, in his famous voyage west, aided the new Theran colony near Cyrene (Her. 4.152). Of the Greek states in the Aegean, Samos seems to have been friendly with Erythrae in Ionia, with Paros, Andros and probably Naxos in the Cyclades, and with Corinth, Sparta and Chalcis in Greece.[5]

Miletus' association with Eretria is affirmed by Herodotus (5.99). In addition, it may have been friendly with Argos,[6] with Aegina, since Samos was hostile to it, and with Megara (Plut. *Quaest. Gr.* 57); at least there is no record of friction in the colonization of

[1] A. R. Burn, *JHS* 49 (1929) 14–37; D. W. Bradeen, *TAPA* 78 (1947) 223–41. The problem has been discussed recently from the point of view of Corinthian participation by E. Will, *Korinthiaka* 391–404. Will is severely critical of Bradeen's treatment and suggests that the war, or rather its final phase, took place in the early sixth century. This seems most unlikely, but the present context is hardly the place for the lengthy discussion which the question requires.

[2] R. Carpenter, *AJA* 52 (1948) 7–8.

[3] Bradeen (*op.* cit., p. 231, n. 41) argues for the validity of the lists of allies on each side.

[4] Above, p. 67.

[5] Bradeen, *op. cit.*, pp. 231 ff.

[6] *Ibid.*, pp. 229–30.

the Propontis between Megara and Miletus, although Megara and Samos fought. In Ionia Chios and Miletus were military allies in the seventh century, since Miletus helped Chios in a war against Erythrae and Chios returned aid against Alyattes (Her. 1.18). The Milesian group consisted of Chios, Eretria, Megara, Argos and Aegina. Miletus' relations with the Cyclades are difficult to make out. It raided Melos and Karystos, perhaps in the Lelantine War, but was probably on good terms with Paros.[7] The Archilochus monument mentions an embassy from Miletus to Paros, but gives no hint of its business. Parian arbitrators, however, were called in to settle Milesian internal difficulties in the early sixth century. All the Ionians met, of course, at Delos for the panegyris.

These scraps of information are disjointed and difficult to interpret or date precisely and they may indicate only a very temporary condition of friendship or hostility, but we know how prominent a place traditional enmities and friendships had throughout Greek diplomatic history. Since these connections could be recorded in writing in the seventh century, it is probable that they had sufficient longevity to make that seem proper. They do not fully accord with later relationships, particularly those between Corinth and Miletus, whose tyrants, Periander and Thrasyboulos, were on good personal terms. That, in itself, is probably a confirmation of their validity. They are scraps of information from an earlier period which were not incorporated and reconciled into later tradition.

The connections seem to have been political and military for the most part, but perhaps two reveal a trading interest, Ameinokles' ship-building for Samos and the Samian visit to the island of Plataea off Cyrene. It is possible to work joint colonial projects into the groups, but, since that presupposes an intimate trading relation with the colonial areas, it is best left aside until such a relationship can be established on other grounds. Bradeen felt the need of supplying an economic cause to explain the hostility between them and suggested that it is to be sought in Samian-Milesian-Aeginetan rivalry in the trade with Egypt.[8] This is plausible, but unfortunately breaks down on chronology. Our earliest literary reference to Greek commercial relations with Egypt places their inception in the reign of Psammetichos I, but the emporion of Naukratis was not founded until the last quarter of the century, well after the date (704–670) suggested by Bradeen for the Lelantine War. If trade relationships are to be connected with the groups, it is necessary to point to specific archaeological material which falls into their pattern, the distribution of pottery

[7] Melos and Karystos: Roebuck, *CP* 50 (1955), p. 39, n. 57; Paros: *IG* XII, 5, No. 445, lines 10 ff.; Her. 5.28–29.

[8] Bradeen, *op. cit.*, p. 236. On Greek relations with Egypt see Roebuck, *CP* 45 (1950) 236–47; 46 (1951) 212–20. There is considerable controversy about the date of the Lelantine War, for our chief sources give no chronological indication beyond Thucydides' "long ago" (1.15) and the inference from Aristotle's information (Plut. *Moralia* 761a) that it is to be placed after the colonization of the Chalcidice (itself uncertain in date). The problem is well discussed by Bradeen (*op. cit.*, pp. 223 ff.), who concludes that the war should be placed between 720 and 660 as outside dates, and more specifically, between 704 and 670. This conclusion accords well with certain considerations about conditions in Ionia. Between *ca.* 670 and 625 the Ionian states and Lydia were faced with the problems of the Cimmerian and Trerian invasions (above, p. 53, n. 59). Towards the end of the seventh century Miletus and Corinth were on good terms, which does not seem to have been the case earlier. Thus, general considerations favor a date before 670, if Samos and Miletus were really concerned in the war.

and the like. Unsatisfactory as pottery distribution may be as an index for trade, it is our only archaeological evidence in this period.

It is necessary to distinguish between fine pottery of various degrees of quality and coarse pottery for trade and household use. The former might be used for dedication in a shrine or distributed by sale in a community. If a dedication, it could be made by a passing visitor[9] or bought for the purpose by a citizen. While the fine pottery has received considerable attention from archaeologists, its use as economic evidence is very complex. The coarse wine and oil jars are unmistakeable evidence of trade in those commodities, but unfortunately have only recently received much care in excavations. The ordinary pottery for household use is usually locally made, but, if it can be established as imported, there is evidence of a volume trade in pottery. With these distinctions in mind let us see whether the picture of Ionian trade in the Aegean accords with that of the literary sources.

THE CYCLADES

Ionian trade with the Cyclades (Map I) should have been earlier than with any other part of Greece, since the islanders seem to have taken to the sea in the tenth century to trade and were making lengthy voyages in the ninth. Also, the Ionians of Asia Minor met with them in the Delian panegyris. The hymn to Apollo, apparently the oldest of the Homeric hymns, was traditionally composed by a Chiot, Cynaethus. Its date cannot be established, but the evidence indicates that the festival was being celebrated before the mid-eighth century.[10] This festival, which brought Ionians and islanders to Delos at least once a year, included a fair as well as the usual games, dances and musical contests, thus providing an occasion for an exchange of goods. Some of the trinkets and the pottery which were found on Delos should be an archaeological testimony of this exchange. Islanders, for their part, probably attended and brought dedications to the local festivals held in Ionia, to the Heraion at Samos and the panegyris at Ephesus. Such trading was largely an exchange of small luxury items, like fibulae and other jewelry. In addition to this, however, there does seem to be definite evidence from the mid-eighth century onward of a more regular trade which was probably initiated by the islanders. We might first notice the indications of definite contact between the islands and the Ionian cities and then the converse of the process in the islands.

In northwestern Asia Minor (Map III) fibulae of island type have been found in the Troad and in the sanctuary of Apollo at Kato Phana in Chios. They are geometric in style but date from both the eighth and seventh centuries.[11] In the Chiot sanctuary the pottery found with the fibulae was of local manufacture only, which indicates that the latter may be articles from the Delian festival brought back by the Chiot visitors rather than articles of trade. The latter, of course, is by no means excluded (nor the fact that they may be local

[9] The East Greek pottery found in the little shrine at Aetos in Ithaka was probably left by passing sailors (S. Benton, *BSA* 39 [1938–39] 27).

[10] T. W. Allen, W. R. Halliday, E. E. Sikes, *The Homeric Hymns* (2d ed., 1936) 183–86.

[11] Troy: Blinkenberg, *Fibules grecques*, p. 89, IV, 1b; 98, IV, 10b; IV, 10d; Chios: *BSA* 35 (1934–35) 152; *Deltion* 1(1915), p. 79, fig. 16; 2 (1916), p. 209, fig. 32.

imitations), since Cycladic pottery was imported into the Troad and Aeolis. From Antissa in Lesbos a small amount of ninth and eighth century date is reported, and some later material has been found in Samothrace, Troy and perhaps in Larisa in Aeolis.[12] To judge from the amount of Protocorinthian and Aeolian pottery found at Troy, the city still had some importance as a trading center in the late eighth and seventh centuries.[13] It was a natural port of call for a trading tour starting perhaps from Paros, which had colonies in Thasos and Thrace, proceeding eastwards to the Hellespont and then south along the coast of Asia Minor to run back to the Cyclades from Samos. In Samos itself very little imported pottery was found earlier than seventh-century pieces from Corinth, but several geometric vases have been identified as Cycladic, and Cycladic, as well as Rhodian, influence is noted on the local pottery.[14] In this region fibulae of island type have been found both in Samos and in the Ephesian Artemision, but most are reported from the sanctuary at Lindos on Rhodes, carried along the trade route which led from the Cyclades to North Syria.[15] Very little from the southern islands of the Aegean has been found on the Ionian sites, only some Cretan (?) pottery at the Samian Heraion and a Cretan shield in Miletus.[16] These are probably products of the Rhodian-Cretan trading connection rather than of any direct trade between Crete and Ionia. All these objects reflect the contacts of the eighth and early seventh century. Cycladic Orientalizing wares have not been found on the Ionian sites as yet, and it is probable that from the early seventh century onwards the balance of trade was in favor of Ionia. The Cyclades were soon outdistanced by the larger Greek states after their initial period of activity.

Aside from the considerable amount of East Greek pottery found in Delos and Rheneia and in Thera and Crete, there is only a scattering to report from the other islands:[17] Melos—some stray fragments have been picked up at Prophetes Elias; Ikaros—some sherds of Chiot; Paros—one sherd of Chiot; Naxos—a little "Rhodian" geometric. From Siphnos, on which the Acropolis and several small sites have been excavated, there is rather more, but no great quantity: perhaps four late geometric skyphoi are East Greek; only a small quantity of seventh-century pottery was found, but in it were a few bird bowls and sherds of Chiot; there were also some fibulae of Asia Minor type. Siphnos is probably an example for the other small islands, on which there has been less excavation. The bulk of the pottery was local and the greatest part of the imported material, Naxian and Parian, while the main influence was Cycladic, from these centers and Melos. Protocorinthian and Corinthian were considerably more important than East Greek. A similar impression is made by the

[12] Antissa: *BSA* 32 (1931–32) 44–45, 57; Samothrace: *Hesperia* 21 (1952) 35–37; Larisa: *Larisa* III, p. 170, pl. 57.3 (from Kyme); Hanfmann (*AJA* 53 [1949] 222) suggests that it is Cycladic.

[13] Schefold, *JDAI* 57 (1942) 138.

[14] Technau, *AM* 54 (1929) 17, Beil. VIII, 4 and 5; Eilmann, *AM* 58 (1933) Beil. XVIII, 6 and 10 (perhaps also XVIII, 9); cf. Hanfmann, *HSCP* 61 (1953), p. 31, n. 64.

[15] Artemision: Blinkenberg, *op. cit.*, p. 98, 10e; Jacobsthal, *JHS* 71 (1951), p. 85, n. 2; Samos: Blinkenberg, *op. cit.*, p. 103, IV, 14b; Rhodes: *ibid.*, pp. 87–106, *passim.*

[16] Technau, *op. cit.*, Beil. II, 3; Eilmann, *op. cit.*, p. 53; Miletus: Kunze, *Kret. Bronz.* 281; 243, Group C.

[17] Melos: *FastiA* 1 (1946), p. 105, No. 828; Ikaros: *JHS* 64 (1944) 89; Paros: H. Prinze, *Naukratis* 88; Naxos: *AM* 54 (1929), p. 155, fig. 8, 6 (?); Siphnos: *BSA* 44 (1949), p. 44, Nos. 35–38 (?); pl. 15:27, 31, 33, 34 (geometric); p. 50, pl. 15:19, 22, 21, 26 (bird bowls); pp. 26–27, Nos. 3, 4, 5 (fibulae).

pottery found in the Heraion at Delos and that published from the purification trench at Rheneia.

The vases from the Heraion[18] were dedicated to the goddess Hera and are particularly appropriate to her. Their date ranges from *ca.* 650 to 520 with the greater part *ca.* 600. About 60% of the vases are perfume and unguent containers of various types, appropriate for a goddess and perhaps easy to sell at a festival fair, where visitors like to buy small souvenirs. The relative proportions of the fabrics represented are instructive: 56 vases are Cycladic, 376 Corinthian, 120 Attic and 51 "Rhodian" (East Greek). Of the 51 East Greek pieces, 34 are perfume vases and the others various small types. Evidently East Greek unguents competed with difficulty against Corinthian. Probably most of the East Greek vases are Ionic rather than Rhodian, since Delos was a peculiarly Ionic sanctuary. There are also 7 Chiot pieces, one of which is a chalice of exceptional quality (No. 121). In addition there are 10 pieces of polychrome bucchero, perhaps originating from Samos. Most of the other East Greek material from the area was found on Rheneia,[19] where the greater number of vases was Cycladic and large shapes predominated. The East Greek material extends from the late eighth century throughout the seventh, with skyphoi being the favorite shape among the late geometric vases and bird bowls among those of the seventh century. From the purification trench came a varied group: 15 amphoras, 1 oinochoe, 2 hydriae, 8 plates, 8 cups, 5 pinakes, 1 skyphos, 1 phiale, 18 ring vases, 4 aryballoi, 4 plastic and 1 plaque. These belong to the latter part of the seventh century and form a poor contrast to the Cycladic Orientalizing vases found in the trench.

While the number of East Greek pieces of the late eighth and seventh centuries is far smaller than of those from Corinth and the Cyclades, it is large enough to indicate that pottery was one of the articles of trade. Presumably some costlier articles of Ionian manufacture, like textiles and metal work, were brought for dedication and sale.

A large amount of East Greek pottery of the eighth and seventh centuries has been found in Thera and Crete.[20] It is mainly Rhodian rather than Ionian. Since there is very little from Crete on the Ionian sites, it is probable that Ionian contacts with the southwestern Aegean were slight until the long voyages to Spain and Italy began in the latter part of the seventh century.

This pottery distribution shows that Ionian trade with the Cyclades was on a rather small scale. The islanders themselves probably initiated it, and Ionia's main part was to bring dedications and some small objects for sale to Delos. The Cyclades were, of course, a very unimportant market. The islands were poor, and their sailors engaged actively in a carrying trade of their own. The importance of the contact was to keep the Ionians in touch with their kindred on the islands through the Delian festival. Also, it led to the adoption of some Cycladic motifs in their art products, a forerunner of the influence which was to come later from Corinth and Athens and blend with those from Anatolia. Pre-

[18] *Delos* X, *passim*.

[19] *Delos* XV, XVII, *passim*; chronology, *Delos* XV, 95 ff.; purification trench, *Delos* XVII, 53 ff.

[20] E. Will (*Korinthiaka* 62–64) notes Thera's function as a meeting place for the exchange of oriental goods, although Thera's own part in the exchange must have been slight.

sumably, too, the Ionians would hear stories of the coasts visited by Cycladic traders, which they could put to use in due time.

THE DISTRIBUTION OF CORINTHIAN POTTERY IN IONIA

The best general guide to trade across the Aegean in the early archaic period is furnished by the distribution of Corinthian pottery. It was widely scattered with the greatest amount and the finest vases found in the cemeteries of Rhodes. Its import there is well known, the earliest pieces appeared shortly after the middle of the eighth century, and the volume continued strong until *ca.* 575 or possibly as late as 550.[21] As well as the ubiquitous perfume and unguent containers, aryballoi, alabastra and pyxides, other shapes are found, which indicates that the pottery was welcomed for its own sake as well as for its contents. The Rhodians began to imitate its shapes and design motifs, and by 600 the Corinthian had virtually ousted the local wild-goat style of decoration. That picture is familiar, but it changes as we move northwards into the Ionian area. The contrast in quantity and quality is considerable enough to have some significance, at least in the case of the more fully excavated sites. Caution should be exercised in drawing conclusions, as a consideration of the case of Old Smyrna indicates. Practically no Corinthian was found in Miltner's investigation, while the more recent excavation has produced a considerable amount. Nevertheless, there seems to be some significance in the pattern of distribution.

The earliest pieces from the Samian Heraion,[22] some fragments of large vases, an oinochoe and a lid, are in the Middle Protocorinthian style (700–675). Throughout the seventh century a small but steady amount was imported and dedicated in the sanctuary, with aryballoi prominent among the shapes. This small quantity of Corinthian, mostly unpublished, is the only import from across the Aegean, until it is replaced by Laconian and Attic in the early sixth century. Boehlau also found a few aryballoi and some later pieces[23] of the Middle Corinthian style (600–575) in the cemetery. Samos seems to have imported Corinthian pottery from *ca.* 700 to 575. On the other hand, there is no Protocorinthian and very little Corinthian reported from Miletus.[24] In the excavations of 1938 only one Corinthian sherd was found in what seems to have been a largely sixth-century filling. Although the archaic pottery from the early excavations has not been published in detail, Wiegand commented on the scarcity of Corinthian. It is not surprising to find little from sixth-century contexts, when it is infrequent in the whole of Ionia, but its absence in the

[21] The tables in J. Benson, *Die Geschichte der korinthischen Vasen* (Basel, 1953) 110–40 are most useful, although not complete for the material found in East Greece and the Black Sea. See also F. Johansen, *Les vases Sicyoniennes* 18 and *passim*; H. Payne, *Necrocorinthia* 186; R. J. Hopper, *BSA* 44 (1949) 171–76, 194 ff.; R. M. Cook, *JHS* 66 (1946) 95; E. Will, *op. cit.*, pp. 51–54.

[22] Eilmann, *AM* 58 (1933) 53–54, Beil. XIX, 4, 5; Technau, *AM* 54 (1929) 26, Beil. XVI, 5–10; fig. 20, 1. Technau considered the pieces Beil. XVI, 5–10, East Greek imitations, but Payne (*op. cit.*, p. 342, X) and Kunze (*AM* 59 [1934], p. 80, n. 3) have identified them as genuinely Corinthian.

[23] Payne, *op. cit.*, p. 62; Boehlau, *Aus ionischen Nekropolen* 39–40, grave 21; 136 ff., pl. 4, 1–3, pl. 5, 1 and 3.

[24] Johansen, *op. cit.*, p. 88; Payne, *op. cit.*, p. 186; Wiegand, *Abh.*: *Berlin*, 1908, Anhang 8; Weickert, *VI Int. Kon. Berlin, 1939*, 332.

seventh century seems significant. The literary evidence indicated that Samos was on friendly terms with Corinth at that time, but Miletus was not.

In Ephesus,[25] probably on friendly terms with Samos, a little Protocorinthian and Corinthian pottery has been found. The import was very scanty, but it coincides in time with that to Samos. In both cases we are dealing with sanctuaries of a peculiarly local character, those of the patron goddess of the cities, to whom trifling dedications of foreign origin might not have seemed appropriate.

The import into Old Smyrna[26] started in the latter part of the eighth century and continued steadily throughout the seventh. The excavators report Early Protocorinthian kotylai, Late and Transitional pieces in some quantity and Early Corinthian to the time of the city's destruction by Alyattes (*ca.* 610). The earlier pieces, of the late eighth and early seventh century, are mainly cups, the later, the usual aryballoi and alabastra. The pottery was imported for ordinary use as well as for dedication. The Corinthian pottery found in the interior probably was distributed from Smyrna, Phocaea or Aeolian Kyme. It has been found widely scattered in Aeolis, at Sardis and in Phrygia.[27] Corinthian traders also sold their pottery at Troy in the Hellespont and on the island of Lesbos from the late eighth to the end of the seventh century.[28] At Antissa in Lesbos there was a considerable quantity of Protocorinthian and a smaller quantity of Corinthian, dating from the late eighth to the early sixth century. Cups and aryballoi were predominant among the Protocorinthian, but there were some fragments of large craters among the Corinthian.

In contrast to this wide distribution in the northeastern Aegean, the excavations on Chios have yielded practically no Corinthian.[29] From Kato Phana Kourouniotes has published a Middle Corinthian aryballos, but Lamb reported that Protocorinthian was very scarce and Corinthian scarce in her excavation of the sanctuary. Very little has been found in the recent excavation at Emporion and on Kofina Ridge in the town of Chios. This exception in a Corinthian area of trade may again have some significance. Chios was traditionally an ally of Miletus and in the anti-Corinthian group of states in the seventh century.

From this brief review of Corinthian pottery distribution several important conclusions emerge. In the first place, there seems to be some support for assigning an economic

[25] Hogarth, *The Archaic Artemisia* 229, Nos. 29–30; p. 230, fig. 257; p. 231, fig. 60; Johansen, *op. cit.*, pp. 88, 94, No. 23; p. 102, No. 80; Payne, *op. cit.*, pp. 186, 271, No. 26; p. 276, No. 114A.

[26] Åkerström, *Sk. ut. av Svenska Inst. i Athen*, 1951, p. 80, n. 75; *JHS* 67 (1947) 43; 70 (1950) 10; 71 (1951) 249; Hopper, *BSA* 44 (1949) 176; Akurgal, *Ztsch. d. phil. Fak. Univ. Ankara* 8 (1950), pp. 66–69.

[27] Larisa: *Larisa* III, 171; Kebrene: a Protocorinthian skyphos with subgeometric decoration (Johansen, *op. cit.*, p. 88); Myrina: Pottier-Reinach, *Myrina* I, 505; Pergamon: Conze, *Kleinfunde* 15; Neandria: Koldeway, *Neandria* 16; Aegae: *BCH* 15 (1891) 231, No. 3; Samothrace: Payne, *op. cit.*, p. 283, No. 366 (an Early Corinthian alabastron); Sardis: *AJA* 25 (1921) 114; Phrygia: above, p. 48, n. 32.

[28] Troy: H. Schmidt, *Schliemann's Sammlung*, Nos. 3772–74, 3815–17; *AJA* 41 (1937) 44, 47; 43 (1939) 223; Koile: Payne, *op. cit.*, p. 274, No. 67A (a Transitional alabastron of *ca.* 640; Cook, *JHS* 66 [1946] 82); Elaious: Payne, *op. cit.*, p. 187; Antissa: Lamb, *BSA* 32 (1931–32) 58–59. Many vases are recorded by Payne as Smyrna purchases, which probably indicates that they were found in Ionia and Aeolis.

[29] *Deltion* 2 (1916), p. 206, fig. 26; *BSA* 35 (1934–35) 162–63; Hopper, *BSA* 44 (1949) 252 (21); *BSA* 49 (1954) 135, No. 4; 140, No. 67.

as well as a political character to the groupings of states indicated by the historical tradition. There is sufficient Corinthian pottery along the west coast of Asia Minor from Rhodes to the Hellespont to show that Corinthian traders were active throughout the whole of the seventh century. The inception of the trade was as early as in Al Mina, if not in Rhodes, but, to judge from the superior quality of the vases found in Rhodes to those farther north, the latter area was secondary. Corinth was evidently aware of the orient which lay behind Ionia as well as that beyond Rhodes. Perhaps this explains the presence of the Lydian dedications in the Corinthian treasury at Delphi.[30] It is apparent that the Corinthians found a market for their pottery as such, since the cups are fairly frequent, as well as for the usual perfumes and unguents.

THE DISTRIBUTION OF ATTIC POTTERY IN IONIA[31]

In the seventh century the chief pottery fabric imported into the East Greek region had been Protocorinthian and Corinthian. In the sixth century its place was taken gradually by Attic, which, in its turn, influenced the local wares strongly in the latter part of the century.

While stylistic connections have been pointed out between Attic and East Greek pottery in the late eighth and seventh centuries, there does not seem to be any imported Attic pottery found on an Ionian site until the end of the seventh century, except for a few geometric sherds and oil amphoras in Old Smyrna. There may be Athenian influence in the prothesis scene on a late geometric Samian vase, and Kübler has noted some East Greek influence in Attic pottery of *ca.* 630,[32] but it seems probable that mutual borrowings were made through the Cyclades, where both Athenians and Ionian Greeks attended the Delian panegyris. The possibility of direct trade seems to be ruled out by the fact that, when imports of fine Attic pottery begin *ca.* 600–575, they are in small quantity and a variety of shapes for a generation. This may indicate that other traders, Corinthians or Aeginetan, brought them. There is also hardly enough East Greek pottery found in Athens to indicate direct trade in the seventh and very early sixth century. It has been suggested on the evidence of the pottery found in Cyprus and the popularity of ship scenes on late geometric Attic pottery,[33] that Attica was trading actively into the southeastern Aegean in the late eighth century. The pieces in Cyprus, however, may well have been brought by

[30] Below, pp. 88, 92. Possibly no political or commercial significance should be ascribed to this storage of Asiatic dedications in the Corinthian treasury—it was merely a matter of convenience after the fire in 548 which destroyed the temple (E. Will, *op. cit.*, pp. 550–53); yet there is more archaeological evidence of connection between Corinth and western Asia Minor than Will has noticed.

[31] For studies of the distribution of Attic pottery see B. L. Bailey, *JHS* 60 (1940) 60–70; Åkerström, *Sk. ut. av. Svenska Inst. i Athen*, 1951, *pp.* 79–80; Kübler, *Altattische Malerei* 20.

[32] J. M. Cook has informed me of the Attic pottery found in Old Smyrna; the amphoras are of the type discussed by D. B. Thompson, *Hesperia* 2 (1933) 570–71. Influence on Samos: *AM* 54 (1929), pl. II; Åkerström, *op. cit.*, pp. 79–80; East Greek in Athens: *Kerameikos*, Inv. 56, fig. 13; Kübler, *op. cit.*, pp. 20–21.

[33] The ship scenes on geometric vases are discussed by G. S. Kirk, *BSA* 44 (1949) 144–53; Kirk argues that their popularity with Athenian artists is the result of the scenes' suitability for geometric artistic treatment.

Cycladic Greeks, and it is difficult to understand why, if Athens was a maritime power in the eighth century, it did not continue along such a line in the seventh, when trade was developing and new areas opening up. In East Greece as elsewhere the evidence shows that Athens began to engage seriously in trade only in the Peisistratid period.

The earliest fragment of Attic black-figured ware reported from East Greece is a piece from the rim of a large pot found at Troy, decorated in the Vourva style.[34] Bailey has suggested that there may be some connection between the appearance of this vase in the Troad and the expedition of Solon against Sigeion, which is usually dated *ca.* 607. The vase is, however, an isolated example, and no trade followed on it immediately. Other Attic pottery in this region dates from near the middle of the sixth century, and the earliest Attic ware in the Black Sea (from Istria) is placed *ca.* 570. Thus the piece was probably brought to Troy by Corinthian traders, whose activity we have noted there in the seventh century.

In Aeolis and northern Ionia the earliest Attic imports appear before the middle of the sixth century, but there is no great amount until its latter part. From Antissa in Lesbos come fragments of a crater and of another large vase dating about 550. These were votive offerings, but five lekythoi dating from *ca.* 500 were found in the cemetery and four fragments of large vases of the same period came from the town.[35] The lekythoi, of course, imply the import of high-grade olive oil. From Larisa the earliest piece of Attic is to be dated 550–40, and it ushers in a small number of imports to the end of the century.[36] Large vases are very sparingly represented, as are lekythoi, but the cup fragments are relatively numerous. From this contact came the influence noted on the architectural terracottas, which replaced the earlier Corinthian influence.[37] In the sanctuary at Kato Phana in Chios[38] a very small quantity of Attic black-figure of the last half of the sixth century was found; from the almost completely plundered cemetery at Latomi, Kourouniotes has published two small lekythoi, an amphora and an amphoriskos of the same period. This evidence from Chios is probably of little value, for the sanctuary at Kato Phana was of local importance only, and the cemetery at Latomi had been virtually stripped of its contents. Although the city of Old Smyrna was destroyed by Alyattes *ca.* 610, a small town grew up about a generation later, some houses of which were excavated. From its sixth-century levels has come a fairly large amount of Attic pottery, which indicates that it was being imported into the area in some quantity.[39] The earliest pieces are contemporary with those found on Samos; they are attributed to the manner of the Gorgon Painter and to other groups of that period, and there is a crater by Sophilos. From the deposits of the

[34] *Schliemann's Sammlung* 3828; Bailey, *op. cit.*, pp. 62, 64; below, pp. 110–12.

[35] *BSA* 32 (1931–32), p. 59, pl. 24: 9, 15. Bailey (*op. cit.*, p. 66) incorrectly dates the red-figured bell crater and fragment (pl. 24: 12, 13) to 530 and 530–20 quoting Lamb's text (pp. 59–60), which is obviously in error for 430 and 430–420. Lekythoi: *BSA* 31 (1930–31) 176; town: *BSA* 32 (1931–32), pl. 24: 5, 6, 10, 14.

[36] Larisa III, 174 ff.; pl. 59, 4; pl. 58: 21, 23, 18, 20, 24, 22, 19.

[37] Åkerström, *op. cit.*, pp. 81–83; Åkerström comments also on the Attic influence apparent in Klazomenian sarcophagi (p. 83) and on the Northampton amphoras (p. 79, n. 67; p. 82).

[38] *BSA* 35 (1934–35), p. 163, pl. 37, 32–33; *Deltion* 1 (1915), pp. 68–69, 71, fig. 6.

[39] *JHS* 70 (1950) 10; Akurgal, *op. cit.*, pp. 69–70; *JHS* 67 (1947) 43.

mid-sixth century came a considerable number of cup fragments, and the import continued into the fifth century. Some of the Attic pottery, like the Corinthian, was distributed from the coastal sites far into the interior, to Sardis and to Phrygia.[40]

In southern Ionia and Rhodes the Attic imports perhaps began a little earlier and came in greater volume. A large amount has been found in the Heraion on Samos.[41] Its import began early in the sixth century, and it soon predominated over other imported wares. The earliest pieces, a crater and a lid, are in the Vourva style, and in the first two generations of import there is much of good quality, vases by Sophilos, the Amasis painter and many fine cups. Little master cups were very popular and were imitated by various Ionian workshops, one of which is localized on Samos by Kunze.[42] To judge from the volume indicated by the published pottery, direct Attic trade with Samos started *ca.* 575, when it began on some scale to the Cyclades, and reached considerable quantity by the middle of the century. The Athenian traders did not bring back much Samian pottery to Athens, but probably procured eastern goods from Naukratis, Cyprus and Rhodes as well as the textiles and metal products of the southern Ionian region. There is little to report from Miletus,[43] for the Attic pottery has not been published. On Kalabaktepe, where there was an archaic settlement, numerous black-figure sherds were found, and from near the Athena temple in the harbor region came some little master cups. Although the Artemision in Ephesus produced no Attic pottery, some fragments of little master cups were found near the stadium, where Keil suggests the archaic city may have been located.[44] In the Rhodian graves of the sixth century a very large amount of Attic ware has been found—sufficient to justify a study in itself. For our purposes, however, it is sufficient to note that the imports began at about the same time as on Samos and continued in volume throughout the sixth century. Among the early pieces are some of Sophilos' products.[45]

Attic pottery began to enter the southern East Greek area soon after 600, about a generation earlier than to the north. Before direct trade set in *ca.* 575, the pottery probably came through the Cyclades, where it was acquired by East Greek traders, or was carried by Corinthians and Aeginetans from Athens itself. Before 550 the Athenian vases show considerable variety in shape and are mostly large and fine pieces. From 550, however, by the time Athenian trade had set in fully with Rhodes and Naukratis, Athens seems to have flooded the East Greek area with a specialized product, the fine little master cups which were carried far inland to Sardis, Gordion and the Carian towns. Apparently the Athenians could not compete with the Ionian cups before that time nor with the perfume and unguent trade developed in the early sixth century by Lydians and their Ionian agents. They met it in Delos on equal grounds but not in East Greece itself. The

[40] Sardis: *AJA* 25 (1921) 114; 18 (1914) 432; Gordion: above, p. 48, n. 34.

[41] It is partially published by Technau, *AM* 54 (1929) 38 ff., Beil. XXI–XXV; see also *AM* 56 (1931), p. 109, No. 23, pl. III (amphora fragments by the Amasis Painter); *AM* 62 (1937), p. 133, No. 20, pl. 57, 1 = *AM* 54 (1929), pl. 4 (Sophilos' cup); *AM* 62 (1937) 135 (Sophilos); *AM* 58 (1933) 54.

[42] *AM* 59 (1934) 81 ff.; Vourva style: *AM* 54 (1929), p. 38, Nos. 1 and 2, Beil. XXI.1 and XXI.2.

[43] *Abh.*: *Berlin*, 1911, Anhang 6; *VI Int. Kon. Berlin, 1939*, 330–31.

[44] *JOAI* 23 (1926), *Beibl.*, pp. 255–56, fig. 47; above, pp. 8–9.

[45] *Lindos* I, p. 635, No. 2629; II, pls. 126–27.

fragility of the little master cups indicates that they were a luxury article of some value, for their boxing and transport over long distances were costly. The bulk of pottery for ordinary and fine use was still furnished by local East Greek workshops, but after 550 strong Attic influence asserted itself in the East Greek black-figure fabrics, in Fikellura, Klazomenian and less important local classes like the Northampton amphoras. Only at the end of the century did the Athenian lekythoi with their high-grade oil appear to challenge the Ionian production.

THE DISTRIBUTION OF LACONIAN POTTERY IN IONIA

Although it is by no means so important a fabric as either Corinthian or Attic in quantity, a considerable amount of Laconian ware has been found in the East Greek area. Most of it is reported from Samos, both the Heraion and the cemetery, so that probably the Laconian found on other sites was distributed from there. This export to Samos is usually and reasonably accounted for by the political connections between the two states, which are attested from the eighth(?) century, when Samos is said to have aided Sparta against Messenia. In addition to the pottery there are Spartan dedications in the Heraion.[46] Since there is considerably more Laconian ware in Samos than Corinthian, it is probable that Sparta traded directly with Samos rather than through the medium of Corinth. If so, the eastern material and influences in the votives from the sanctuary of Artemis Orthia at Sparta are accounted for by this Samian connection. It may also help to explain the Samian contacts with Thera and Cyrene.

The earliest Laconian on Samos is dated *ca.* 640, and the import lasted for about a century with the greater part of the material coming after 600, when it and the Attic imports replaced Corinthian.[47] Evidently the tyranny of Polycrates, *ca.* 540, marked a break in relations with Sparta and an intensification of relations with Athens. The disappearance of Corinthian on Samos in the period *ca.* 575–50 and its falling off on Rhodes have been explained by H.R.W. Smith as the result of agressive Samian piracy, but Hopper has pointed out that the decline in Rhodes is more apparent than real. It is probable that this is a part of the same phenomenon as in the western Mediterranean and in the Black Sea, where Corinthian pottery lost ground to the technically better and more attractive Athenian black-figure.[48] Corinthian held the Rhodian market to some degree by its cheap small and miniature vases, but could not compete with Attic and the new black-figure Fikellura of southern Ionia. The Laconian material, too, was not only attractive as pottery, but had the advantage of being marketed by the traders of a powerful state whose political friendship was an asset to Samos. A considerable variety of shapes is represented in the Laconian on Samos: craters, bowls, aryballoi, oinochoai, chalices, but above all, cylixes. As in the case of the Attic, many are of high quality.

[46] Kunze, *AM* 59 (1934), p. 99, n. 2.

[47] *AM* 54 (1929) 38; *BSA* 34 (1933–34) 178 ff.

[48] H.R.W. Smith, *Univ. Cal. Pub. in Cl. Arch.* 1 (1944) 256–58, 263–66; R. J. W. Hopper, *BSA* 44 (1949), n. 43 on p. 173.

The Laconian on Rhodes began shortly after 600, the oldest piece being a Laconian II cylix from a grave at Papatislures.[49] A few other vases, which span the period to 540, have been found. Thus, while import did not begin quite as early as in Samos it ended about the same time. Since the quantity is small, probably these Laconian pieces were traded from Samos to Rhodes. On other East Greek sites there is only a scattering of Laconian, at Ephesus, Sardis, Gordion, Old Smyrna, Antissa on Lesbos and Pergamon.[50] No Laconian has been found on Chios as yet, although Chiot imitates some Laconian motifs of the early sixth century, possibly from contacts in Naukratis.[51] It is hardly surprising to find Sparta engaging in a liaison with Samian aristocrats expelled by Polycrates or to find the Ionians asking Sparta for aid against Persia *ca.* 540. Sparta was well known to the Ionian Greeks, and we may wonder how imperfectly informed Cleomenes really was about Persia at the time of the Ionian Revolt when Aristagoras showed him the famous map.

IONIAN MATERIAL IN GREECE

In attempting to trace the lines of East Greek trade with Greek cities by the distribution of imported objects we are at a considerable disadvantage. Pottery was not an important article of trade, for it could not compete with both local products and Protocorinthian and Corinthian wares, which were the chief export fabrics of late eighth and seventh century Greece. Many of the Ionian imports must have been perishable, textiles and articles of precious metal and bronze of which the fibulae give some hint of early trade. Presumably most of the trade went into the two centers of Corinth and Aegina until the latter part of the sixth century, following the lines indicated by the literary evidence and the distribution of Corinthian pottery on the east side of the Aegean.

The best example is afforded by the Chiot pottery which has received the expert attention of R. M. Cook.[52] Most of that known from the western Aegean has been found in Aegina, where it was dedicated in the Aphaia temple. The earliest piece is dated *ca.* 650, while a considerable amount of the inscribed pottery belongs to the first half of the sixth century. It is likely that this pottery was not for purposes of trade, but made to order for Chiot merchants to be dedicated when their voyage was successfully completed. Their cargoes may have contained a small amount of pottery to be traded as a novelty, but no evidence of large scale importation has come to light from well excavated sites. Yet, if the above interpretation is correct, we do have evidence of a Chiot-Aeginetan trading connection which accords with the other evidence. Very little Chiot has been found

[49] *Clara Rhodos* VI, Papatislures II; it was found with a Middle Corinthian alabastron; Lane, *BSA* 34 (1933–34) 179–80.

[50] Ephesus: Lane, *op. cit.*, p. 180; Sardis: *AJA* 25 (1921) 111 ff. (Lane, *op. cit.*, pp. 151, 180); Gordion: above, p. 48, n. 35 (Lane, *op. cit.*, p. 180); Old Smyrna: *JHS* 70 (1950) 10; Akurgal, *Ztsch. d. phil. Fak. Univ. Ankara* 8 (1950) 70–71; Antissa: *BSA* 32 (1931–32) 59; Pergamon: *BSA* 49 (1954), p. 304, No. 7.

[51] Lane, *op. cit.*, p. 186; various East Greek influences are noticed in Laconian pottery (pp. 122, 131, 170–72).

[52] Cook and Woodhead, *BSA* 47 (1952) 159–70; Cook *BSA* 44 (1949) 154 ff.

elsewhere in mainland Greece.[53] There is one chalice from Rhitsona, but that is all from central Greece. A group of fragments from Athens, from both the Acropolis and Agora, belong mostly to the early sixth century, when Athenian potters seem to have imitated the chalice shape (*ca.* 580) and when Athenian pottery was just beginning to replace Corinthian on the other side of the Aegean. Yet the earliest piece is dated *ca.* 625; perhaps it came by way of Aegina. There are also a few pieces, as yet unpublished, found at Perachora and one piece from Ithaka. Evidently in the seventh and early sixth century Aegina was the main goal of Chiot traders.

The other pottery imports into mainland Greece are very scanty. In Eretria several large skyphoi of the seventh century are probably Samian, and Samian influence has been noticed on Eretrian pottery of that period.[54] Yet these are the only East Greek vases in the material from the temple of Apollo Daphnephoros and from the cemetery excavated by Kourouniotes. From Corinth there is a rosette bowl of the last quarter of the seventh century with a graffito, apparently recording the owner's name, a trader from Rhodes or Miletus.[55] Also, several imitations of East Greek bowls have been found there, dating from the same period. In a well, the contents of which belong mainly to the second quarter of the sixth century, there were some fragmentary Chiot wine amphoras and Ionian cups. In Sparta sherds of about a dozen bowls which imitate East Greek wares have been found. The Argive Heraion has also produced a bird bowl. Aegina has yielded a few bird bowls dating from the beginning to the late seventh century, as well as some "Rhodian" pieces, but certainly not enough to assume that the pottery was a significant article of trade. From Delphi, too, a few pieces of Rhodian are reported. In all, there is only a scattering of East Greek pieces from sanctuaries and from sites like Corinth, Aegina and Sparta,[56] whose eastern connections are attested by other evidence. Possibly they are the dedications of East Greek merchants or occasional purchases brought by Aeginetan and Corinthian traders. The activity of the East Greeks in the far west is confirmed by the pottery of that origin found in the little sanctuary of Aetos in Ithaka on the trade route to Italy,[57] where sailors stopped to make dedications en route. The pottery is undistinguished and may represent that carried for their own use. There are the usual bird and rosette bowls (Nos. 576–81; 583–84), two early oinochoai (Nos. 590–91) and some later ones (Nos. 593–95) dating from near the end of the seventh century. One piece is perhaps Chiot (No. 586). There is much variety in the shapes, but all are small pieces. In addition to the bowls and oinochoai are a pyxis, kyathos, crater, ring-vase and a bottle.

[53] Rhitsona: Cook, *op. cit.*, p. 160; Athenian Agora: *Hesperia* 15 (1946), p. 136, No. 34 (and a few unpublished pieces); Athenian Acropolis: Graef-Langlotz, I, Nos. 450–53; Ithaka: *BSA* 43 (1948) 97, No. 586.

[54] Boardman, *BSA* 47 (1952), p. 12, Nos. 2–7; see also p. 23, n. 124.

[55] Corinth: *Corinth* VII, p. 71, No. 307, pl. 37; No. 308; p. 69, No. 287; *Hesperia* 25 (1956), pp. 352–53, Nos. 95–101; Sparta: Lane, *op. cit.*, p. 115, fig. 9; Heraion: *Heraeum* II, p. 135, fig. 66; Aegina: Kraiker, *Aegina*, p. 33, Nos. 103–04 (Cook, *AJA* 56 [1952] 221); p. 34, No. 105, pl. 7; Delphi: *Delphes* V, p. 145, Nos. 142–43, figs. 602–03; p. 146, No. 144, fig. 604.

[56] The earliest imports seem to have come into Aegina, Corinth and Athens; Aegina: above, n. 55; Corinth (Perachora): Jacobsthal, *JHS* 71 (1951), p. 86, n. 5; Athens: *ibid.*, pp. 86–87; p. 85, n. 2 (Cycladic?).

[57] Robertson, *BSA* 43 (1948) 97 ff.; *BSA* 39 (1938–39) 27.

To judge from this pottery, East Greek interest in the western trade began little before 650. The earlier visitors are from the Cyclades and Crete.

Some information about early connections across the Aegean is given also by the fibulae found on mainland sites. A rather large number of East Greek type (Blinkenberg's XII), dating from the eighth to the sixth century, have come to light at the large Peloponnesian sanctuaries and in Perachora and Aegina.[58] The earliest, from geometric contexts of the first part of the eighth century, presumably indicate some casual contacts before the development of more regular trading connections. It is interesting that practically no mainland types are found on the East Greek sites and that these small imports start so early in the eighth century. They are probably trinkets sold throughout the Peloponnesus from the centers of Corinth and Aegina, typical of the objects acquired by these traders on their eastern run. The oriental objects, faience and the like, which began to appear from *ca.* 725 onwards were presumably brought directly from the eastern centers or through Rhodes rather than by Ionians. Probably, however, the ivory in Sparta is to be accounted for by a Samian medium. It remains to notice one remarkable find mainly of Eastern Greek origin, which is hardly an article of trade, the ivory and gold dedications found under the Sacred Way at Delphi. The only example as yet fully published, the little statuette of the "lion-tamer," is considered by Amandry to be Ionian, but Barnett has suggested that it is rather Rhodian.[59]

The archaeological evidence of cross-Aegean trade, while very meagre, does support the lines of connection made out from the literary evidence. The center of trade for Ionians in the Cyclades was Delos, where a fair was part of the panegyris. The scarcity of Corinthian pottery in Miletus and Chios and the inscribed Chiot sherds on Aegina indicate that one line of trade ran from Miletus and Chios to Aegina; the Corinthian in Samos and Ephesus suggests that the other line connected these states with Corinth. Miletus, however, because of its position in southern Ionia close to Samos, probably traded with that island also, crossing the lines to some degree. We can hardly speak of trade "leagues" organized for commercial purposes in seventh-century Greece, but it is likely that there were ties of friendship of a quasi-political character between individuals in the states mentioned. These may have afforded security for their ships in each other's harbors and immunity from the privateering, which was probably as frequent as trade at this period. These tenuous connections hardly survived into the sixth century, when changes of government from the aristocracies to tyrannies involved the formulation of something like a firm foreign policy by the individual rulers. Thus, Periander and Thrasyboulos drew together, and Sparta became hostile to Samos when Polycrates expelled the Samian aristocrats. The develop-

[58] *Perachora* 33, 171; *Artemis Orthia* 198–99, pls. LXXXIII–LXXXIV; Mycenae: Blinkenberg, *Fibules grecques* 209, XII, 1a; Aegina: A. Furtwängler, *Aegina*, p. 403, Nos. 118–21; Argive Heraion: *Heraeum* II, p. 246, Nos. 895, 896, 897, 899; p. 247, No. 905; p. 244, Nos. 887–89; p. 245, Nos. 890–94; Olympia: *Olympia* IV, p. 56, Nos. 375–76; p. 55, Nos. 370–72, pl. XXII; Delphi: *Delphes* V, p. 114, No. 603, fig. 409; Tegea: *BCH* 45 (1921), p. 385, No. 154; Thebes: Blinkenberg, *op. cit.*, p. 225, XII, 14n.

[59] P. Amandry, *Syria* 24 (1944–45) 163–64; Barnett, *JHS* 68 (1948) 16–17. The objects in the find are not homogeneous; Stillwell has pointed out that some of the heads (*BCH* 63 [1939], pl. XXXV, lower left, 3) show strong Corinthian influence of *ca.* 575 (A. N. Stillwell, *Corinth* XV, 2, p. 81).

ment of Athenian trade under Peisistratus introduced a new factor into the Aegean, and the old alliances of aristocratic Greece dissolved.

In the seventh century the volume of trade was evidently small. From Ionia came small trinkets and probably some electrum, ultimately from Lydia, a very little pottery and some costly luxury goods like textiles, ivories and jewelry. We should probably add wine from Chios. From the mainland some pottery, perfumes and unguents, mainly from Corinth, were sent to Ionia. There was no trade in bulk goods on either side. As in the case of the Cyclades the Ionians were dealing with states which carried on a trade of their own. There was some room for the special products of Ionia, but ships and traders were few, and trade was still largely confined to local areas and to occasional long distance ventures. Ionia had to find solutions to its scarcity of metals and food elsewhere than in the Aegean.

CHAPTER VI

The Search for Metals

PRECIOUS METALS: GOLD, ELECTRUM, SILVER

The growth of archaic Greece was facilitated by a renewed use of the precious metals and the seeking out and development of new sources of supply. To judge from the present archaeological evidence, there had been a great scarcity of gold and silver both in the Aegean area and in Anatolia during the "Dark Ages" which followed upon the collapse of the Mycenean and Hittite Empires.[1] This resulted from the almost complete cessation of the trade and production which brought gold and silver to Mycenean Greeks and Hittites.[2] For this period there are only a few small, plain pieces of jewelry to set beside the treasures of Mycenae and those of the Artemision of Ephesus and of the tombs of Kamiros in Rhodes. A change is apparent in the eighth century, when the quantity of precious metals began to increase and local centers of metal-working came into existence. Evidently this is to be connected with the growth of trade with the Near East and in the

[1] H. L. Lorimer, *Homer and the Monuments* 71–72; there is not a complete lack of gold as Lorimer implies, although the quantity is very small and the objects plain and trifling articles of jewelry. Desborough (*Protogeometric Pottery* 308–12) lists 1 gold ring (p. 310), beads and disks of gold leaf from Skyros (p. 130), 1 gold spiral from Tiryns (pp. 208, 311), 1 gold ring from Vrokastro in Crete (p. 311) and 6 gold rings from Kos (p. 311); they were in Protogeometric and near Protogeometric contexts (*i.e.*, tenth and ninth centuries B.C.). A few similar objects have been found in Sub-Mycenean and Protogeometric tombs in the Kerameikos in Athens (Kübler, *Kerameikos* IV 25), on Salamis and at Marmariane (*BSA* 31 [1930–31], pp. 33–34, fig. 14, 1–5). For Anatolia see S. Przeworski, *Die Metallindustrie Anatoliens* 180: 1 gold ring from Konya, 1 silver ring from Samsun, gold pendants from Gözlü Kule, a few small silver pieces from Alişar Hüyük IV. There appear to be no silver objects from the Aegean area, although a fibula of silvered bronze is reported from Skyros (Desborough, *op. cit.*, p. 311).

[2] Lorimer (*op. cit.*, pp. 56, 59) considers that the ultimate source of most of the Mycenean gold was Nubia, whether directly from Egypt or from a Syrian trading center like Ugarit. The Hittite records reveal the existence of stocks of silver, which may have been of Anatolian origin.

Aegean area, and it is suggested that imports of raw metal were brought to Greece from Phoenicia or Cyprus along with manufactured goods.[3] The present state of the evidence indicates that this renewed use of gold appeared first in Athens; Eretria, Corinth, Crete and the Cyclades were not far behind, but Rhodes and the Ionian area seem to have produced little until after 700.[4] In any case, the use of precious metals on a growing scale was re-established in the Aegean as a whole by the early seventh century, and the supply had to be satisfied by trade and the exploitation of new mining areas.

The Ionian states had to import their supplies of gold, electrum and silver, for apparently there were no substantial deposits in their own territories.[5] Regular processes of trade were established to provide the metals for the various uses to which they were put, the manufacture of jewelry and precious objects for personal use and dedication, the accumulation of wealth and, after its invention, for coinage. The metals were also sought for exchange, and problems of supply and use are complex and interrelated. In the case of gold and electrum the evidence points to Lydia in particular as the source both for Ionia and for Greece as a whole.

In Lydia the native gold contained a varying and sometimes considerable amount of silver;[6] while deposits are referred to in the sources as "gold," the gold had to be refined. Herodotus distinguished between refined and "white" gold (= electrum),[7] and the electrum coinage of the Lydians and Ionians has considerable variation in its gold and silver content.[8] The criteria for distinguishing were apparently color and weight, but, since the general word, gold, was used to describe the Lydian metal, any conjectures about Croesus' wealth should be tempered by the reflection that it was by no means "pure" gold. To judge from the metal used in the Artemision treasure[9] and the fact that the Ionian coinage was predominantly electrum, exports from Lydia were normally in that form. Refined gold was the exception, as Herodotus' description (1.50.2) of Croesus' dedication for Delphi shows. The chief source of supply in Lydia in the archaic period was the Pactolus River which flowed from Mt. Tmolus through the market-place of Sardis to empty in the Hermus. In addition, mines may have been worked on Mt. Sipylos and near Atarneus in the

[3] Lorimer, *op. cit.*, pp. 71 ff.

[4] Walther Reichel, *Griechisches Goldrelief*; see the review by Kunze, *Gnomon* 21 (1949) 1–11 and the remarks of J. M. Cook, *BSA* 46 (1951) 47–49; D. Ohly, *Griechische Goldbleche des 8 Jahrhunderts v. Chr.* (review by J. M. Cook, *Gnomon* 26 [1954] 107–10). Ohly identifies a group of gold bands as Eretrian in manufacture.

[5] Above, pp. 20–21.

[6] J. Forbes (*Metallurgy in Antiquity* 152–53) points out that this is the normal condition of native gold; the amount of gold in the metal from Lydia is stated by Przeworski (*op. cit.*, p. 185, n. 6) to be *ca.* 73%.

[7] Her. 1.50.2; Herodotus describes the making of ingots for Croesus' dedications: "gold" (χρυσός) was melted down and from it 117 ingots made, 4 of which were of refined gold (ἄπεφθος) and weighed 2½ talents each, 113 of white gold (λευκὸς χρυσός) which weighed 2 talents each. Apparently the "gold" was the native metal from which Croesus extracted some refined gold but left the rest in a condition which could be described as pale gold (electrum). Herodotus uses χρυσός of the native metal (1.93; 5.101, in the Pactolus; 6.125, in Croesus' treasury); cf. Strabo 13.1.23, 4.5; 14.5.28.

[8] *BMC*, *Ionia*, xxv–xxxi; Head, HN[2] 643; J. G. Milne, "Phocaean Gold in Egypt," *JEA* 20 (1934) 193–94 (Hellenistic Period).

[9] Hogarth, *The Archaic Artemisia* 94.

neighborhood of Pergamon. Probably, however, the latter only came into production in the reign of Croesus.[10]

Davies has suggested that the Lydian deposits were not exploited before the Iron Age,[11] and several considerations point more precisely to *ca.* 700. No objects of Lydian gold work have been found that can be dated earlier than the seventh century, and most of it is much later.[12] The most recent study of the Basis deposit in the Ephesian Artemision dates it mainly to the latter part of the seventh century, and only one object may be of the late eighth century.[13] Since the metal of which the objects were made came from Lydia, a date after 700 is indicated for the inception of a regular trade in gold, which coincides with the other evidence about Ionian-Lydian trading relations.[14] Lydian gold was first mentioned by Archilochus who describes Gyges as πολύχρυσος (frag. 22). From the early seventh century, then, Lydia was well known to the Greeks as a producer of gold.

Probably analyses of the various gold objects of the archaic period found in Greece would be of little aid in this problem, for all native gold contains some silver, and the composition of the Lydian electrum varied considerably. Close stylistic analyses might identify the various centers of gold work and allow the lines of trade to be traced, but could not determine the source of the raw metal. The complexity of the question is illustrated by the study of the gold jewelry of the seventh century from the tombs in Kamiros. Probably the metal used for them came from Lydia, since its description is very similar to that used for the objects in the Ephesus Basis, and Rhodes was certainly trading with the Ionian states at this time. Marshall found a close stylistic connection between the

[10] Herodotus knows only of the Pactolus, which he lists among the wonders of Lydia (1.93; 5.101; see Strabo 13.4.5), but the mining area of Atarneus is connected with Croesus by the Pseudo-Aristotelian *De Mir. Ausc.* 52 (834 A) and attested as a former producing area by Strabo (14.5.28), although worked out in his own time. Mt. Sipylos is usually mentioned as a source of gold (e.g., Przeworski, *op. cit.*, p. 185, n. 6), but even in antiquity its mines were legendary (Strabo 14.5.28). All these mines were probably exhausted in the Hellenistic Period.

[11] Davies, *Nature* 130 (1932) 985.

[12] The jewelry from the Sardis tombs is published in *Sardis* XIII. Unfortunately, since the context of pottery was lost in the war of 1914–18, the dating depends on stylistic considerations. While many of the tombs were found to have been pillaged, it is likely that their remaining contents give a sample of production; none of the jewelry was earlier than the seventh century and most belongs to the sixth and fifth (Karo, *AM* 45 [1920] 146). The gold objects found near Aidin are considered by Poulsen to be of Greek rather than Lydian workmanship and are related by him to Rhodian gold work (*Der Orient* 146, 159). While electrum was known in the Bronze Age in both Anatolia and Greece (Hissarlik II, Alişar Hüyük III, Mycenae), it was perhaps manufactured by alloying rather than mined. In any case, we cannot trace it to a Lydian source. In Anatolia metal-working revived again in the eighth century with centers of production in Urartu, Tabal and Phrygia; they were crippled by the Assyrian expansion and Cimmerian raids, but opportunity was thus afforded to Lydia and the Ionian states. There seems to be little basis for the view that gold came to the Aegean from Colchis at the eastern end of the Black Sea (below, pp. 117–18). Any regular trade had to await the foundation of the Greek colonies in the late seventh and sixth centuries, by which time both Lydia and Thrace were centers of production. The metal of the Caucasus went southwards to Urartu and Media rather than the length of the Black Sea to compete with Aegean metals.

[13] For the dating see Jacobsthal, *JHS* 71 (1951) 85; there seem to be no earlier pieces among the objects found outside the Basis.

[14] Above, pp. 52–54. Przeworski (*op. cit.*, p. 182) couples the development of Ionian and Lydian metal work and considers that Ionia began to export in the last half of the eighth century.

Kamiran material and that from the Artemision, but Kunze relates it to gold work from the Doric Cyclades.[15] Accordingly, it seems necessary to rely on the literary evidence and general considerations.

It is hardly necessary to examine the evidence for Lydia's reputation for wealth among the Greeks, since the fables and facts connected with the name of Croesus indicate that Lydia was to them the producer of gold *par excellence*.[16] A more specific indication is Herodotus' story of the Spartan attempt to purchase gold from Croesus to make a statue of Apollo.[17] He gave it to them freely, no doubt for its propaganda effect, but the story underlines the fact that Sardis was the market for obtaining any unusual amount of gold. In comparison to it other sources were scanty and probably served only local needs.

The other sources of which we have some knowledge are the North Syrian area, for which the outlet would have been Al Mina or some Phoenician port, the mining region southeast of Abydos in the Troad, Siphnos in the Cyclades, Thasos and Thrace. The annals of the Assyrian kings record the large stores of gold and other metals in the treasuries of the temples and palaces of northern Syria and on the coast.[18] Greeks, however, had to purchase it at the ports or from eastern traders, competing with the local demand. Possibly some was distributed in the Aegean before the Lydian deposits were worked, but evidently on a very small scale and hardly to Ionia, since no Phoenician objects of precious metal have been identified among the votives of the Artemision.[19] After *ca.* 700 it is likely that the need for gold was satisfied from the nearby sources in Lydia and the Aegean rather than by trading for it in Syria.

The mining region in the mountains southeast of Abydos (Map III) was traditionally the source from which Priam obtained his wealth. Since, however, the mines are first mentioned in the fourth century B.C. and Gyges is said to have permitted Greek settlement in Abydos, their exploitation probably started subsequent to its colonization in the early seventh century. Small attention is paid to the mines in the sources, and they were probably of only local importance.[20] The same is true of the Siphnian mines. They are said by Herodotus to have produced both gold and silver, but their richest yield seems to have been in the last half of the sixth century. At that time their exploitation gave the Siphnians considerable, if temporary wealth with which they built an agora of Parian marble and the lavish treasury at Delphi. The mines were evidently exhausted or flooded in the fifth

[15] The jewelry from Kamiros is published by E. H. Marshall, *BMC, Jewelry*, pp. xxii,85 ff., Nos. 1103–1211, pls. XI–XIII; Kunze, *Gnomon* 21 (1949) 11; Jenkins (*Daedalica* 89–92) dates the material *ca.* 650–620, which Kunze considers too rigid (*op. cit.*, pp. 10–11). Presumably the metal of the jewelry from Assarlik and Aidin is also Lydian.

[16] Radet, *La Lydie et le monde grecque* 215, 225.

[17] Her. 1.69.4.

[18] For the ninth century see the record of Assurnasurpal's expedition (Luckenbill, *Ancient Records* I 479).

[19] Note the absence of Phoenician analogies among the objects studied by Jacobsthal, *op. cit.*, pp. 85–95.

[20] Xenophon (*Hell.* 4.8.37) referred casually to the mines at Kremaste as in operation, but Strabo (13.1.23, Astyra) indicates that they had a scanty yield in his own time and shows some scepticism about their use by Priam (14.5.28). It was Troy II of the Early Bronze Age which yielded the large treasure, not Mycenean Troy. For the foundation of Abydos see below, p. 112. The mining area is probably that referred to by Pliny as near Lampsacus (*NH* 37.193).

century and, at their best, probably yielded no more than 100 talents per year.[21] It is likely that these and other small deposits on the Cyclades were the source of the gold for the gold-working crafts, such fine examples of which have been found on Melos and Delos. Possibly, too, we should see in them, rather than Syria, the source of some of the metal for the early work from Crete, Thera, Corinth, Eretria and Athens. There is no reason to suppose, however, that they supplied the Ionians.[22]

The mines of Thrace (Map III) were evidently one of the most plentiful sources of precious metals for the Aegean area, but it is difficult to differentiate their production of gold from that of the silver which they sent so copiously into the trade channels. Leaving aside the difficult question whether Phoenicians obtained gold before the Greek colonization,[23] it seems clear that the mines on Thasos and possibly on the mainland were being worked in the first half of the seventh century. Archilochus referred to quarrels between the Parian colonists and the natives over the exploitation of the mines on Thasos, and possibly the same motive led to warfare when the Greeks settled on the mainland.[24] Export, then, would have started before 650, when the varied pottery found at Kavalla shows that Corinthian and Ionian traders were active, as well as the settlers from the Cyclades.[25] Probably Thasos served as an emporion for the district, and Herodotus'

[21] Her. 3.57–58; Paus. 10.11.2. Herodotus tells us that 1/10 of the revenue paid for the treasury in Delphi. Probably a rich vein was struck, for which the Siphnians exuberantly rendered their thanks to Apollo by a tithe of the immediate yield, as Colaeus did after his successful voyage to Spain. The mines were producing when Polycrates seized the tyranny in Samos, for some of his exiled opponents sailed to Siphnos, tried to borrow 10 talents and, failing that, seized 100, the contents of the city's treasury. The mines have been examined by Bent (*JHS* 6 [1886] 195–98) and Davies (*Nature* 130 [1932] 985) who reports a sherd of the sixth century.

[22] For the Melian jewelry see *BMC, Jewelry*, p. 103, No. 1232, pl. XIV; *AA* 55 (1940) 124–25; *BCH* 63 (1939) 285–86; for Thera, *AM* 28 (1903) 91–93, 225–29; for Delos, *BCH* 71 (1947) 148 ff.; for Perachora, *Perachora* I 73 ff.; for Crete, D. Levi, *AJA* 49 (1945) 313 ff. and Démargne, *La Crète dédalique*, 126–28, 340. This early material is discussed by Reichel and Kunze (above, note 4). The Aegina treasure, dated *ca.* 700, is currently regarded as Phoenician (*BMC, Jewelry*, pp. 51–56, Nos. 683–768; Lorimer, *Homer and the Monuments* 71). There is little evidence for trade with Ionia from the excavation of the Siphnian acropolis (above, p. 75).

[23] Herodotus reports (6.47) very precisely that the Phoenician mines were on Thasos between Ainyra and Koinyra, opposite Samothrace. The site was called Phoenix and a large pile of slag from the workings was visible; Davies' inspection of the area did not bear this out (Lorimer, *op. cit.*, p. 76). Other sources mention Phoenician or legendary exploitation of the mines on the mainland: Pangaeus was said to have been exploited by the Phoenician Kadmos (Pliny *NH* 7.197; Strabo 14.5.28; Strabo rejects the tradition); Mt. Bermion was the legendary source of the Thracian Midas' wealth (Strabo 14.5.28), but Davies (*JRAI* 62 [1932] 147) reported that the mountain is mainly limestone and found no trace of gold or of workings.

[24] The *Monumentum Archilochum* (*IG*, XII, *Supp.* 212 ff.) represents the Thracian natives as mining and transporting gold, for the Parians made an agreement to restore any gold taken from them, but did not keep their promise (lines 40 ff.). This passage evidently refers to Thasos itself, but, if the natives were exploiting mines on the island, they were probably working those on the mainland also. In the light of this evidence of native exploitation of the mines, it seems probable that some gold came out of the region before the colonization of Thasos, either as a result of pre-colonial Greek trade or that of the Cypriotes and Phoenicians (*i.e.*, in the eighth century). The date of the colonization of Thasos and Archilochus' connection with it is controversial, but the evidence favors the second quarter of the seventh century (680–640; Jacoby, *CQ* 35 [1941] 97–109; Cook, *JHS* 66 [1946] 71; A. R. Burn, *JHS* 55 [1935] 132; J. Pouilloux, *Études Thasiennes* III, c. 1).

[25] See below, p. 108.

figures for its revenue from the mines are an index to the production attained by the late sixth and early fifth centuries. He reported the revenue from the mines on the island itself as less then 80 talents per year, but from all the mines, both gold and silver, controlled by Thasos the annual revenue was 200–300 talents.[26] The gold deposits made the greater impression, for Herodotus lists several in the Pangaeus area, Mt. Pangaeus (gold and silver), Skapte Hyle (gold to the value of 80 talents per year) and Daton. Probably the mines at Krenides north of Philippi and those near Akanthos were exploited first by Philip II rather than in the archaic period.[27] The Ionian interest in this region, attested from the eighth century to the Persian conquest, was probably mainly in the silver.[28]

There is unfortunately no definite information about the yield of the Lydian mines, which can be contrasted with Thasian (200–300 talents) and Siphnian (100) figures, but certainly Herodotus' lists of the dedications of the Lydian kings show that it was the paramount source of gold in Greek eyes.[29] These impressive lists merely record calculated generosity to the Greeks, and, in addition, there were dedications in Lydian shrines and furniture in the Lydian palaces.

The Ionian states were in an advantageous position to act as the middlemen between Lydia and the rest of Greece, since all exports had to go from their harbors. They acquired electrum in various ways, in payment for artistic commissions and by service as mercenaries, as well as through the normal course of trade.[30] Probably, too, transit tolls were charged on Lydian goods passing through their ports, for, until Croesus' time at least, the Ionian cities were fully independent. Some Lydian gold work, like the mitra which Sappho wished to buy for her daughter,[31] evidently passed through Phocaea. Other Greeks could probably buy small amounts of electrum in Ionia, and Ionians themselves distributed it in their Aegean trade. It was a desirable commodity for the Rhodian and Corinthian traders who were active along the coast. As mentioned above, the metal in the Kamiran jewelry is probably Lydian, and stylistic affinities have been pointed out between East Greek work and some of the objects found at Perachora.[32] It is rather interesting that

[26] Her. 6.46–47.

[27] The mining areas and the ancient sources referring to them are listed by A. S. Georgiades, *EphArch*, 1915, 88–93; Davies has inspected most of the area and reported on the deposits (*JRAI* 62 [1932] 145–62), correcting Casson's account in *Macedonia, Thrace and Illyria* in numerous respects. Herodotus refers specifically to Mt. Pangaeus (7.112), to Skapte Hyle (6.46), which was the region of Thucydides' mines, to Daton (9.75) and to Dysoron (5.17) for its silver mines.

[28] Roebuck, *CP* 45 (1950), pp. 238–40, 246, n. 47, where it is argued that Chios was the chief carrier of Thraco-Macedonian silver for the trade with Egypt; Pouilloux's view (*loc. cit.*) that there was a direct trading connection between Thasos, Paros and Egypt is rejected by Fraser (*AJA* 61 [1957] 99; review of Pouilloux).

[29] Gyges: Her. 1.14.1–3; Alyattes: 1.25; Croesus: 1.50–52, 54, 92.

[30] See above, p. 58.

[31] See above, p. 3.

[32] *Perachora* I 73–75. This material is from the Geometric temple of Hera Akraia and was apparently dedicated in the period 800–725. J. M. Cook has suggested to me that Lydia may have been the source of the metal from which some of the earliest Attic gold bands were made. They seem to be of pale gold. This would account very well for the few scraps of Dipylon vases and the abundant Early Protocorinthian pottery found in deposits of the second half of the eighth century at Old Smyrna.

Herodotus' story of Megacles, the Alcmaeonid, in Croesus' treasury coincides in time with the appearance of Athenian pottery in some volume on the coast. Yet, on the whole, export must have been small, for Greece was poor in gold throughout the archaic period. A large project, such as Sparta's for the construction of a statue, needed diplomatic negotiation with Croesus, and dedications, such as the latter made at Delphi and Branchidae, were the exception.[33] Probably the Greeks had little to exchange for the gold. In Lydia, as in Syria and Egypt, the ordinary products of Greek craftsmanship did not find a large market. While Ionia was in a position to draw some profit from the nearness of Lydia's gold, it had to procure its silver by developing other trade connections.

If we may judge by the votives in the Basis at the Artemision of Ephesus, silver was by no means in such demand in Ionia in the seventh century as was gold. The proportion of silver to gold objects is striking, about 40 to 600.[34] This seems to be true of the rest of the Aegean area also. The number of gold objects in the small list of precious metals from Perachora far outnumbers those of silver, as in the other treasures of the archaic period.[35] Perhaps the general ratio of the use of various metals in mainland Greece is correctly mirrored in the catalogue of decorated fibulae compiled by Hampe. He lists 156 fibulae of the type with decorations on their large clasp plates. Of these, 147 are bronze, 3 are silver, 2 are gold and 4 are of iron.[36] The need for silver, however, obviously increased to a marked degree from the late seventh century, when the states of mainland Greece and of the Cyclades began to coin.[37] While the Ionians for the most part coined in electrum, they needed silver for the trade with Egypt in which grain was purchased.

There were deposits close at hand both in the Aegean and in Asia Minor. A part of the the production on Siphnos was in silver, but, aside from the Siphnians, only Aeginetans may have used it.[38] Deposits are reported on the other Cyclades, but there is no evidence for their working.[39] A deposit on Lesbos was exploited in the archaic period, which may have taken care of the needs of that island.[40] Workings have also been found near Myndos in Caria, but it is possible that they are medieval rather than ancient.[41] The mines in Laureion in Attica probably came into production *ca.* 600, but until the Persian Wars exploitation was limited and served Attic needs primarily; the yield was probably eked out

[33] The finds made under the Sacred Way at Delphi in 1939 indicate, however, that there must have been many small, costly dedications (above, p. 85).

[34] *The Archaic Artemisia* 232–33. Most of the silver objects were found outside the Basis (p. 116).

[35] *Perachora* I 73–75; 184–86.

[36] R. Hampe, *Frühe griechische Sagenbilder in Böotien* 90–111.

[37] Robinson has pointed out the implications of his study of the coins from the Artemision for the history of Greek coinage: since its development began in Ionia only *ca.* 650 and the Aegean coinages are derivative, the use of silver for the purpose of coinage began only toward the end of the seventh century (*JHS* 71 [1951] 165–66).

[38] Above, pp. 90–91; Cary, *Mélanges Glotz* I 137; Aegina and Siphnos were on friendly terms (Her. 3.59), and Siphnos and the other Cyclades coined on the Aeginetan standard (Head, *HN*² 479 ff.).

[39] Forbes, *Metallurgy in Antiquity* 198.

[40] Davies, *Nature* 130 (1932) 985. Davies reports bucchero pottery of the archaic period.

[41] Paton and Myres, *Geog. Journal* 9 (1899) 46 ff.; Gowland, *Archaeologia* 69 (1918) 156; Davies, *op. cit.*, p. 986, suggests that the workings are medieval.

by Peisistratus from Thrace.[42] Thus, the Ionians had to look elsewhere for their silver. The evidence indicates that they found it in Thrace rather than Asia Minor, despite the traditional wealth of that land in silver.[43]

The existence of Thracian silver was known from the exploitation of the gold mines in the seventh century, but it is probable that production was only developed in the sixth century in response to the new need. Herodotus notices three silver-producing areas in Thrace in his own time, Pangaeus, Dysoron and Lake Presios. Thasos controlled production to some degree, but much of it seems to have been in the hands of the native tribes whose large coins of the late sixth and early fifth century have been found in such quantities in Egypt, south Italy and elsewhere in the Mediterranean.[44] Chios and the northern states of Ionia in particular seem to have traded with them and with Thasos, as the Chiot foundation at Maroneia and the pottery found at Kavalla indicate. This, in itself, raises doubts about the importation of Spanish silver to the Aegean. The trade for metals in Spain was rather for high grade bronze and tin.

TIN AND BRONZE

The regular traffic which was established between Ionia and Spain in the late seventh century is one of the most interesting and important examples of Ionian enterprise. The carriers had to traverse the whole length of the Mediterranean, running not only the risks of storm and remote waters but those of piracy and the rivalry of Etruscans and Carthaginians. Then, too, the trade seems to have been almost exclusively in the hands of the small state of Phocaea. Without such a trade, Phocaea would have been a small and unimportant harbor town sharing the obscurity of Lebedos and Myus. With it, the city found an outlet for its surplus or restless population in the founding of trading posts and colonies in the west, above all, of course, at Massalia. It provided itself with a finely built city wall, which evoked the admiration of Herodotus, and bred a type of citizen whose merits in leadership were recognized by the other Ionian and Aeolian cities. For example, a Phocaean was selected to head the delegation of Ionians and Aeolians to Sparta to ask for aid at the time of the Persian conquest, and another Phocaean, Dionysius, was chosen to lead the fleet of the Ionian rebels at Lade in 494.

Although they were probably not the first Greeks to reach the far western Mediterranean, the Phocaeans moved in to organize its regular trade. The question of Greek primacy in

[42] Cary, *op. cit.*, p. 137.

[43] Probably the silver from the land of the Alybes mentioned in Homer is a reminiscence of the Late Bronze Age (above, p. 40, n. 66). There were deposits in Mysia, but we do not have any evidence of their working until the Roman period (Forbes, *op. cit.*, p. 192, Nos. 18–19; Magie, *Roman Rule* II, pp. 803–04, notes 27 and 28); perhaps the silver in the treasure of Troy II came from this area. There are also silver deposits in Lydia, at Yenekoi near Tralles, but evidently Lydia's efforts were directed mainly to the exploitation of the electrum (Gowland, *op. cit.*, p. 156; Forbes, *op. cit.*, p. 192, No. 22). The main source of supply for Assyria was probably in the Cilician Taurus, referred to as the "silver mountain" (Luckenbill, *Ancient Records* I, No. 579; Forbes, *op. cit.*, pp. 191–92), whence some may have come into the Aegean before the Thracian mines were developed.

[44] Above, pp. 91–92; many were found in the Tarentum hoard, Noe, *Numismatic Notes* 78 (1937), No. 1052.

the far west is obscure, partly because of the difficulty of the evidence and partly because two separate areas and types of trading were involved. There was, first, the region of southern Spain and Tartessus, on the Atlantic side of the straits of Gibraltar, where metals were to be obtained; second, the northeastern part of Spain, where the colony of Emporion was developed, at first probably as a port of call, then as a part of the Massaliote trading area. To south Spain a direct route from Sicily might be followed, across to Sardinia and through the Balearics to make a landfall at Cabo de la Nao in southeast Spain; another, less direct, could be taken up the Italian coast to strike Provence by way of Corsica, then followed up to northeastern Spain and down the length of its east coast.[45] Each of these areas has a certain claim to primacy for the interest of the Greeks, but it is probable that the journey down the coast of Spain was only regularly taken after the ultimate goal became clear, the metals of the southwest.

A passage in Strabo (14.2.10) states that many years before the founding of the Olympic Games (776) the Rhodians had established the colony of Rhode in northeast Spain, and East Greek Subgeometric and Protocorinthian pottery has been found in Provence;[46] the earliest Greek object, however, found in northeastern Spain (in a grave at Emporion) is a Corinthian aryballos of *ca.* 600.[47] While the site of Rhode has not been found and excavated, this presumed Rhodian activity in the ninth and eighth centuries B.C. seems highly improbable in view of the evidence of Rhodian trade in Sicily.[48] There, only a few fragments of Rhodian pottery of the early seventh century have been found, and the bulk of the material falls after 650. If some venturesome captain did push on from Provence in the eighth or early seventh century to northeastern Spain, it was probably only an exploratory venture which led to nothing for the time being. The archaeological record at Emporion gives the impression that it was founded as a port of call and remained a small trading factory throughout the sixth century.[49] It and other similar small stations on the

[45] For a description of the route via Sardinia and the Balearics see Carpenter, *The Greeks in Spain* 12–36; Greek knowledge of the route is recognized by its place names terminating in *-oussa* and by the Ionian awareness of Sardinia which Bias of Priene (*ca.* 540, after the Persian conquest) and later Aristagoras (*ca.* 494) advocated as a suitable place for a new Ionia. Both routes are discussed by A. Garcia y Bellido, *Hispania Graeca* I 66–78, and the Phocaean activity along the Italian coast by L. Pareti, *La Tomba Regolini-Galassi* 28–33, 501–09.

[46] Garcia y Bellido, *op. cit.*, I 64–66; A. Blakeway, *BSA* 33 (1932–33), p. 199, Nos. 85–87, pl. 33.

[47] Garcia y Bellido, *op. cit.*, II, p. 150, No. 6; Smith, *AJA* 57 (1953) 35.

[48] Garcia y Bellido (*op. cit.*, I 57 ff.) argues very strongly for Rhodian and Chalcidian contact with Spain in the ninth and eighth centuries; their archaeological traces in Sicily offer no support for this view (Dunbabin, *The Western Greeks* 228 ff., 340, 472–73). See also Smith, *op. cit.*, p. 32.

[49] The site of the earliest settlement at Emporion has not been found, but is reasonably conjectured to have been on the small promontory of San Martin de Ampurias, formerly an island. Its existence before the middle of the sixth century and its probable foundation *ca.* 600 by the Phocaeans (not by Massalia) have been argued by Garcia y Bellido on the evidence of the pottery from its cemetery on the mainland at Portitcol. He reasonably suggests that the colony was moved from its site on the island to the mainland towards the end of the sixth century. There, pottery, if not buildings, of that period has been found near the city wall (*op. cit.*, I 164–67; II, p. 28, fig. 10). Thus, Emporion seems to have existed as a small port of call for two generations before being converted into a regular colony and growing to some prosperity as a part of the Massaliote trading area after the battle of Alalia. There is no archaeological evidence or definite foundation dates in the literary evidence for the other Greek colonies along the east coast.

east coast owed their existence primarily to the development of the route by Provence as an alternative to the Balearic route rather than to any market facilities in northeastern or eastern Spain. The object of Greek trade with Spain was its metals, possibly brought to the Aegean or to Syria before this by Phoenician traders.

The first Greek voyagers possibly found the Phoenicians established at Gadir;[50] perhaps the welcome given them by the Tartessian ruler was the warmer on that account. Herodotus ascribes the opening of this trade to Colaeus, the Samian, whose voyage to Tartessus we may set *ca.* 638,[51] but the Samians did not follow it up to develop the profits of the new market. Probably their trade with Egypt and in the eastern Mediterranean was sufficient for their needs or, perhaps, they reaped too much profit to come to terms with the Tartessian king. Herodotus emphasizes the personal nature of the relationship of the Phocaean traders with Arganthonios, the King of the Tartessians.[52] The story is similar to others about early trade in a new market, where the personal qualities of the traders are a decisive factor in obtaining the lion's share. Obviously any traders coming from the eastern Mediterranean in small numbers had to establish friendly relations with the native Tartessians rather than to colonize and occupy by force. According to Herodotus, the Phocaeans enjoyed this most favored position from their first contacts after 620, until their trade was broken by Persian conquest in Asia Minor *ca.* 544 and by their expulsion from Corsica after the battle of Alalia *ca.* 535. The Tartessians allowed them to establish a trading factory at Mainake,[53] and the trade, if not Arganthonios himself, paid for a city wall. Probably, as Herodotus observes, it was to the use of the speedy penteconters rather than the slower merchant ships that the Phocaeans owed their ability to carry on this long

[50] The literary evidence supports a Phoenician settlement at Gadir (Cadiz) *ca.* 1100 and at Ibiza in 654. Archaeological evidence from the latter at least indicates the existence of a Punic (Carthaginian) colony in the sixth century, but the question of Gadir is more difficult. Carpenter (*AJA* 52 [1948] 475, 478–80), stressing the negative character of the evidence for Gadir (the earliest graves found are Punic, of the sixth century), argued that the Greeks were first in the market for Spanish metals and did not follow the Phoenician voyaging west. Albright, however, considers the Phoenician inscriptions in Sardinia are to be dated in the ninth century and the ivories from Carmova in the Guadalquivir valley to be not later than the tenth century. Thus, he argues for trading and colonial activity on the part of the Phoenicians in the western Mediterranean in the tenth and ninth centuries (*AJA* 54 [1950] 174–76). Carpenter has amplified his views in a thorough study of Phoenician activity in the western Mediterranean (*AJA* 62 [1958] 35–53), but the Sardinian inscriptions still remain a difficulty to their acceptance.

[51] Her. 4.152. There seems no valid reason to doubt the fact of Colaeus' voyage, of which Herodotus probably saw the record on the crater dedicated in the Heraion at Samos. The miraculous storm which blew Colaeus from Plataea, off the Libyan coast near Cyrene, through the Mediterranean and the Straits of Gibraltar is the proper sort of detail to mark a new discovery, and veil it for a time. The discovery of the Jerez helmet (Greek of the seventh century) gives some color of veracity to early Greek voyaging in the area, but who brought it and who wore it can only be conjectured. The voyage of Colaeus is dated by its connection with the preliminaries of the foundation of Cyrene (Dunbabin, *op. cit.*, p. 339, n. 1).

[52] Her. 1.163–65; the chronology may be worked out from the passage: Arganthonios died shortly before 565 when Alalia was founded (165); he is said to have reigned for 80 years, thus from *ca.* 645, shortly before Colaeus' voyage. The Phocaeans are said to have established their relationship with him personally, probably in the last quarter of the seventh century. Anacreon attests his longevity even more excessively than Herodotus, since Arganthonios is credited with a life-span of 150 years (Strabo 3.2.14).

[53] Strabo 3.4.2; Garcia y Bellido, *op. cit.*, II 3–19; its precise location near Malaga has not been found (see Smith, *AJA* 57 [1953] 33–34). The foundation is dated *ca.* 600 by Garcia y Bellido.

distance trading. While Phoenicians from the eastern Mediterranean may not have offered much danger in the sixth century, Etruscans from Caere and possibly Carthaginians did; it is probable that the Greeks had to run or fight on many occasions.

The aim of the trade is usually regarded as the metals of Spain, but there are many problems about its organization which remain obscure. It is clear on general grounds that metals must have been the object of trade, for only small and extremely valuable cargoes could justify the long voyages of both Phoenicians and Greeks. The mountainous area of southwestern Spain was rich in copper and silver, while its northwestern area produced tin.[54] It would hardly have been worthwhile to transport copper the length of the Mediterranean, since ample supplies and an experienced mining industry existed already on Cyprus, but silver, tin and high-quality bronze, probably made in the region of Tartessus, were a different matter.

Evidently in the Early Iron Age there was a general scarcity of tin in the Mediterranean as a whole. While deposits are known in Etruria, they do not seem to have been worked before the second century B.C.,[55] and tin or high quality bronze could find a market in Italy and Sicily for their developing bronze industry. The need must have existed also in the Aegean area and western Asia Minor, where tin was unknown or existed in very small deposits. For example, only a few veins of tin stone are reported in the Greek coastal area at Darmanlar, southeast of Smyrna, and it is unlikely that they were worked.[56] The variable and scanty tin content in Anatolian bronzes of the Late Bronze and Early Iron Age have led to the conclusion that tin was imported into that region.[57] It is significant also that the Hittites imported bronze from Cyprus.[53]

Perhaps this condition is reflected in the Homeric poems. In the *Iliad* tin is a precious metal used by itself for decoration on metal work, while in the *Odyssey* it is not mentioned at all, but bronze or copper is imported from Cyprus(?).[59] The *Iliad* may reflect the state of supply in the Late Bronze Age, while the *Odyssey* represents a shortage of tin in the Early Iron Age. While tin was available in the Caucasus and in northwestern Iran and, in fact, was obtained from there by the Assyrians before the reign of Assurnasurpal, its transport to the west was a long and costly process, carried out only by Assyrian permission. It seems significant that in Assurnasurpal's reign Assyria procured it from the Phoenicians.

[54] For the sources of Atlantic tin see Cary, *JHS* 44 (1924) 167–68 and Forbes, *op. cit.*, pp. 241–42.

[55] Forbes, *op. cit.*, p. 243. While it is possible that tin was brought from the central European fields to Italy, it is striking that there are no references to Bohemian tin until the twelfth century after Christ; they are regarded as a source of tin, however, for Hissarlik (Hissarlik VII b; Przeworski, *Die Metallindustrie Anatoliens* 102–03).

[56] Other small deposits are known in western Asia Minor, but there does not seem to be any evidence of their working in antiquity (Forbes, *op. cit.*, p. 238; Przeworski, *op. cit.*, pp. 91, 101–02). Quite possibly, of course, small deposits were discovered and quickly exhausted, so that they had little significance for trade; to judge from the decline of Hissarlik in the archaic period, any importance which the supposed central European tin trade may have had dwindled away completely.

[57] Przeworski, *op. cit.*, pp. 100–02.

[58] *Ibid.*, p. 92.

[59] *Iliad* 11.34; 18.474, 574; 23.503, 561. *Chalkos*, which may be bronze or copper, is imported from Temesa (perhaps Tamassa), *Od.* 1.184, but see Gray, *JHS* 74 (1954) 3, 5.

Evidently their trade was supplying tin to the eastern Mediterranean,[60] and the tin fields of the Atlantic region began to take over the function of supplying the Mediterranean area as a whole. It was into this trade that the Phocaeans moved.

It is not surprising, then, that Pliny picked up from some source the statement that Midacritus was the first to bring tin to the Mediterranean from the Cassiterides.[61] The Cassiterides have a distressingly evasive character, but at this time Tartessians were presumably the intermediaries in the trade. They obtained the tin from northwest Spain and brought it to Tartessus. Midacritus' voyage to the ultimate source of supply was hardly duplicated by other Greeks.[62] The role of the Phocaeans was that of distributors rather than users, for Chios and Samos are the traditional centers of Ionian metal work. Part of the cargoes was probably left in Italian and Sicilian ports, en route to the eastern Mediterranean.

It seems possible that, as well as tin, the Phocaeans carried back bronze already made into an alloy by the Tartessians, for the latter had a ready supply of copper in what later became the Rio Tinto mining area. Two passages are of importance in this connection. Pausanias in his account of the sanctuary at Olympia mentions the treasury of the Sicyonians dedicated by Myron.[63] In it were two *thalamoi* which, he was told by the Eleans, were of Tartessian bronze. This, at least, establishes the existence of such a commodity, whatever its value may be for the nature or date of Myron's treasury. The other passage is the well-known account (Her. 4.152) of Colaeus' voyage. It is usually assumed that Colaeus brought back a cargo of silver, but Herodotus does not mention the nature of the cargo at all. He does go on to say that one-tenth of the profits from it were made into a bronze crater and tripod. If the cargo was of silver, it was evidently sold and the tripod and crater commissioned from the proceeds. If it was of bronze, one-tenth of it was converted into the dedication. The latter seems probable from Herodotus' language and the fact that good bronze with a proper tin content must still have been a valuable commodity in the Aegean

[60] Forbes, *op. cit.*, p. 255; whatever the role of the small tin deposits near Byblos in the Bronze Age, they could hardly have been a source by the time of the later Assyrian Empire. Forbes (pp. 239–40) is much less impressed by them than Wainwright (*Antiquity* 17 [1943] 96–98; 18 [1944] 100–02).

[61] Pliny *NH* 7.197 (see also 34.156 ff.). Pliny gives no hint of the time of the voyage nor of Midacritus' origin. Garcia y Bellido (*op. cit.*, I 124–25) considers this a vague tradition of another voyage like that of Colaeus, made about the middle of the seventh century, but it seems preferable to regard it as a voyage made after Tartessus was known to the Greeks, probably in the sixth century (Cary, *JHS* 44 [1924] 169–70) and before passage to the Atlantic was closed to them (see also, P. Bosch-Gimpera, *CQ* 38 [1944] 54). For recent discussion of the Cassiterides see L. Monteagudo, *Emerita* 18 (1950) 1–17 (the west coast and islands of Galicia in this period).

[62] This is the usual reconstruction of the trade (Schulten, *Tartessos* [2d. ed., 1950] 114–16). It is unlikely that the Greeks themselves habitually went to the source of tin in northwestern Spain, since the *Periplus* in Avienus specifies little on the Atlantic coast of Spain but mentions Tartessian voyages to the Oestrymnides (lines 113–14).

[63] Paus. 6.19.2–4. The treasury was dedicated, according to Pausanias, by Myron, tyrant of Sicyon, after his victory in the 33rd. Olympiad. If this can be taken literally and the bronze was really Tartessian, it is evidence that trade in considerable volume had been established by 650, for fifty talents of bronze were used in the *thalamoi*. In the light of other evidence of the voyaging this seems improbable; objections, too, are raised about the date of the treasury.

in the late seventh century. It was the proper material for such great dedications as Herodotus describes. Colaeus' voyage, then, represents the first Greek tapping of the source of supply from Tartessus.

Yet Tartessus was well known as a source of silver. The metal was found in the Sierra Morena behind the town and could be brought down the Guadalquivir. Soon after 600 its reputation was established among the Greeks, but it is significant to note the source. Stesichorus of Himera speaks of the silver-rooted springs of the Tartessus River.[64] Himera and Selinus were the first ports of call in western Sicily for ships en route from Spain and, significantly enough, the first Sicilian towns to coin silver (about the middle of the sixth century). Most of the silver for Sicilian and South Italian coinage is considered to have been brought by Corinth, in the form of Corinthian coins which were to be overstruck.[65] Evidently, however, sufficient came from Tartessus to have made an impression on Stesichorus. It seems unlikely that the Phocaeans brought much Spanish silver back to the Aegean. There, it would have had to compete with Thracian silver carried by Ionian traders, and Phocaea's own coinage was mainly of electrum, designed for local trade with the Lydian area.[66] Probably the long-range trading of Phocaea secured mainly tin and very high quality bronze, which were used in part to provide necessary materials for the Ionian bronze industry. If they made use of the route along the shore of Italy, it is likely that they also brought back some iron from Etruria. While this may accouns for the nature of the cargoes carried eastward, the problem still remains of what was carried west.

The Greek finds of the archaic period in Spain[67] are at first sight rather puzzling in this respect. They are limited in number and extremely varied in character. From Emporion, mostly from the early cemetery, there is a varied assortment of cheap pottery and faience work, one very good lion's head of bronze, and some coins.[68] Obviously the material was brought in for the use of the Greeks of the trading factory there. Its inexpensive character is a mark of the relative unimportance of the factory until the end of the sixth century, and the scarcity of finds in the neighborhood indicates that no very extensive trading was carried on with the natives. The origin of the objects is varied: the earliest vase is Corinthian, and a few other Corinthian objects extend in date to the latter part of the century;[69] there are also Etruscan imitations of Corinthian ware and a few objects of Sicilian manufacture;[70] Naukratite or Rhodian faience work,[71] some pots from Cyprus and some which can better be labeled East Greek than specifically identified have been

[64] Stesichorus 4; Strabo 3.2.11; Avienus 291. Arganthonios, the name of the Tartessian king, is said to have been derived from the Celtic, *argant*, silver: a Greek Eldorado (Carpenter, *AJA* 52 [1948] 480).

[65] Dunbabin, *op. cit.*, pp. 248, 301; Milne, *NumChron* 18 (1938) 36 ff. Corinth probably got most of its silver from Illyria (Will, *Korinthiaka* 535–38) but probably some from Thrace also (below, p. 108).

[66] Head, *HN*² 587–88.

[67] Garcia y Bellido has collected most of the material in *Hispania Graeca*; for the vases in particular see the excellent review by H. R. W. Smith, *AJA* 57 (1953) 35–36.

[68] Garcia y Bellido, *op. cit.*, II 72, 93, 145–68, 231.

[69] *Ibid.*, II 145 ff., No. 6 and Nos. 4–5, 7–8 (perhaps 9–12).

[70] *Ibid.*, II 145 ff., Nos. 1–3, 24 (Smith, *op. cit.*, p. 35).

[71] *Ibid.*, II 145 ff., Nos. 14–15.

found;[72] two Chalcidian vases are also reported.[73] Surprisingly enough, there are three early Athenian shoulder-lekythoi of the middle and third quarter of the sixth century,[74] but Attic takes precedence only *ca.* 500.[75] Until that time the places of origin are mainly Corinth, East Greece, Sicily, and Italy (Etruria). This variation may be accounted for in two ways: first, Emporion was visited by Corinthian, Italian and East Greek traders, which would indicate a general participation in the Spanish trade; second, the ships which visited it carried an assortment of material picked up at different places en route. On the whole the latter seems likely, for the literary evidence emphasizes that the regular trade was in the hands of the Phocaeans, who had to come a long way with many stopping places.[76] A few cheap goods, some oil and perfume, sufficed for the needs of the little sixth-century port at Emporion.

The material from the south of Spain, however, is different in type. The finds were not made on the site of Greek factories but in the native areas and represent the goods of trade. The earliest is a Greek helmet of the seventh century (the Jerez helmet), and there is another of the sixth century (Huelva helmet); most of the finds are good bronze statuettes or fragments of utensils, but again not entirely of East Greek manufacture.[77] To trade fine bronze utensils and art objects in the home of metals was not a matter of bringing coals to Newcastle, for they were of Greek manufacture. The appeal of Greek art in Spain may be seen, of course, in the Iberian crafts which began to produce imitations in the late archaic period. A very interesting exchange was set up from one end of the Mediterranean to the other—the raw materials came from Spain to the workshops of Greece and were returned in the form of manufactured products. Some pottery reported from Villaricos[78] perhaps represents a miscellaneous group of trade objects which supplemented the metal ware, although the circumstances of its discovery are very obscure. There are five pieces: an early sixth century Attic lekanis fragment (the earliest Attic piece in Spain), Etruscan, East Greek and Corinthian vases, which span the whole sixth century in time.

It seems probable that, rather than retrace their steps northward, the Phocaeans, who had loaded with metals in southern Spain, would take the more direct route back through the Balearics and by Sardinia. Obviously, if they did any trading, it was from their cargo of metal rather than with Greek objects. The rarity of the latter in the Balearics is not surprising; from Ibiza, the westernmost island, come a piece of faience and a few Attic lekythoi of the early fifth century.[79] On the other hand, there are some good Greek

[72] *Ibid.*, II 145 ff., Nos. 13, 16–23, 25–27.

[73] *Ibid.*, II 145 ff., Nos. 29–30 (Smith, *op. cit.*, p. 35).

[74] *Ibid.*, II 145 ff., Nos. 31–33 (Smith, *loc. cit.*).

[75] *Ibid.*, II 145 ff., Nos. 34–95; there is also a little good, early red-figure pottery.

[76] The coins give a similar impression (*ibid.*, II 231). Most of those of the archaic period are from the area of Emporion; the Greek states represented are Phocaea, Teos, Miletus, Cyrene (?), anepigraphic of Greek Asia Minor in large quantity (Auriol); Metapontum, Hyele, Taras, Cumae and Syracuse from Magna Graecia. There is only one archaic Corinthian coin reported, and the Athenian pieces date after 480.

[77] Garcia y Bellido, *op. cit.*, I 141–42; II 82 ff., Nos. 1–4, 7–9, 18.

[78] *Ibid.*, II 179.

[79] *Ibid.*, II 191.

statuettes[80] and some interesting Punic terracottas which are very obvious imitations of archaic Greek work.[81] Possibly, as has been suggested, these are a tribute to the Balearic success as pirates[82] or perhaps they were traded for food and water.

The considerable variation in the origin of the goods found in Spain, both pottery and bronzes, might seem to vitiate the evidence of Herodotus that the Spanish trade was almost solely in Phocaean hands. That is not necessarily the case, for Phocaea itself was not an important center of industry. Its traders carried commodities, tin, bronze and silver which were adapted to long-range trading, since they were saleable almost anywhere. The goods obtained in exchange for them would necessarily show considerable variety and reflect the Phocaean contact with the length of the Mediterranean, their own East Greek homeland, Rhodes, Cyprus and Egypt, the Corinthian area of Magna Graecia and Etruria, through which they had to pass. Pareti has argued that Phocaeans brought much of the oriental material found in the Etruscan tombs and founded trading factories on the Italian coast.[83] This is very plausible, although perhaps he starts the trade rather too early, *ca.* 650, and it is likely that Corinth had some share in it. The Phocaean trade came to an end after the battle of Alalia, *ca.* 535, whether abruptly or gradually is a moot question,[84] but certainly by the time of Pindar and Herodotus Greeks were no longer sailing out to Tartessus for its metals.[85] They had to be obtained through the medium of Carthage or Etruria.

IRON

By the end of the eighth century B.C. iron had largely replaced bronze as the ordinary material used for tools and weapons in the Aegean area and Anatolia.[86] The Ionian states, however, were poorly supplied with deposits of iron and all, except perhaps Miletus, had to import it from a distance.[87] There are, in fact, some indications of a scarcity of iron in

[80] *Ibid.*, II 82 ff., Nos. 5, 11–16. Again the places of origin are varied: the Peloponnesus (No. 5); East Greece (No. 11); Greece (No. 12); South Italy (Nos. 14, 16); Athens (No. 15).

[81] *Ibid.*, II 197–201, Nos. 8–12.

[82] *Ibid.*, II 79–81; see, however, Smith's observation that they may have satisfied the needs of certain Punic cults and thus have been deliberately sought after in trade (*AJA* 57 [1953] 35).

[83] Pareti (*op. cit.*, pp. 30, 501 ff.) argues that the Phocaeans obtained metal (iron) from central Italy in exchange for the oriental material. His view of the role of Ionia as an intermediary for this eastern material in the early part of the seventh century is hardly acceptable in the light of our knowledge of Ionia's position in the Near East.

[84] Garcia y Bellido (*op. cit.*, I 193 ff.) considers that the Carthaginian action to take over the Tartessian trade was very prompt, but see Smith, *op. cit.*, p. 33.

[85] Pindar *Nem.* 3.21; 4.69; Her. 3.115. Herodotus knew only that tin came from the *eschate* of Europe.

[86] Przeworski (*Die Metallindustrie Anatoliens* 143 ff.) points out that it is impossible to establish any single center as the original home of iron-working. Its spread was rather a process of experiment over the whole of western Asia Minor, and Anatolia was not ahead of other areas, despite its large deposits of ore; see also Forbes, *Metallurgy in Antiquity* 458 ff.

[87] Above, p. 20. Lydia has been regarded as a center of iron-working, but that is very doubtful, for there are no deposits of importance there, and innovations in the technique of iron-working were made by Ionian craftsmen, not Lydians (Her. 1.25). For what it is worth, Lucian's dialogue between Solon and Croesus indicates the need for importing iron to Lydia (*Charon* 505–06). Lydia, of course, had the means to pay for such imports with its gold, so that it is not surprising to find iron in use in the first part of the seventh century for ordinary purposes (Gyges sent captive Cimmerians to Assurbanipal in iron shackles; Luckenbill, *Ancient Records* II No. 784).

early Ionia. While it is true that a considerable amount was found in the Protogeometric graves at Assarlik in Caria,[88] the Homeric poems do not mention iron mining, but only its smelting. Probably this indicates that iron was imported from elsewhere in trade form and worked in Ionia. Since the metal had its place in the treasuries of the heroes, it cannot have been plentiful.[89] There are also very few iron objects from the Artemision,[90] but iron would not have been very appropriate among the feminine articles of luxury from that shrine. In any case, Ionia probably had difficulties in acquiring iron, for there were no good sources of supply close at hand.

Deposits of magnetite were reported at Magnesia under Sipylos and on Mt. Ida near Andeira. Andeira's association with the legend of the Dactyloi might indicate iron-working at an early date, but probably both these deposits were of little use. Apparently there were technical difficulties in working magnetite ore at this early period, and the literary sources do not praise the deposits. Also iron is scarce at Thermi on Lesbos and at Hissarlik, which might have used them.[91] There were deposits on many of the Aegean islands, including Lesbos, but they were small and probably quickly exhausted in local use.[92] The rest of Asia Minor, however, had important mines in Pontus, Cappadocia, Phrygia, the Cilician Taurus, Armenia and the Caucasus, which supplied the important producing area of Urartu. Most of these were remote from Ionia, although a trading connection did exist with Phrygia and North Syria. Probably small amounts were brought from each with the greater part coming by sea from North Syria.

There, the Cilician Taurus is identified as the site of the Kizzuwadna of the Hittite Empire, described as the King's storehouse for iron, and as the Tabal of the Assyrian Empire, where Tubal Cain is reputed to have worked and which supplied iron to Phoenicia and to Palestine. Its wealth in iron is mentioned in the Assyrian records from the ninth century.[93] Cyprus, too, had deposits, and, at least in the fourth century B.C., was an important center for the manufacture of fine armor.[94] It is likely that this area supplied the Aegean in the Early Iron Age and that Ionia received some of its metal. Greeks, or probably Cypriotes, became identified as carriers of iron in the southeastern Mediterranean, for the annals of Nabonidus record iron being imported to Babylonia from Iamana.[95] Probably, too, the Cypriotes carried it to Egypt as a regular article of trade after the foundation

[88] Przeworski, *op. cit.*, pp. 151–52.

[89] Lorimer, *op. cit.*, pp. 42, 111 ff.; Richardson, *AJA* 38 (1934) 569.

[90] *The Archaic Artemisia* 154.

[91] Magnesia: Pliny *NH* 36.128; Andeira: Blümner, *Technologie* IV, p. 73, n. 4; Thermi: Przeworski, *op. cit.*, pp. 151–52, 155.

[92] Forbes, *op. cit.*, pp. 458 ff., 386; Lesbos: Davies, *Roman Mines* 256.

[93] Forbes, *op. cit.*, pp. 447–48; Wainwright, *Antiquity* 10 (1936) 14–21. See Jeremiah 15.12 (*ca.* 600); Ezekiel 27.12; Przeworski, *op. cit.*, pp. 148–49. Forbes (*op. cit.*, pp. 386, 455) considers that the legends of the Telchines and Dactyloi, the first iron-workers in Greek tradition, were localized to Phrygia and Lydia, but Strabo (14.2.7) reported the movement of Telchines from Crete to Cyprus to Rhodes; the Dactyloi are connected with Mt. Ida in Crete (Strabo 10.3.22), to which iron was probably imported from Cyprus (Lorimer, *op. cit.*, p. 117). Hesiod (frag. 176, Rzach) placed the origin of iron in Crete and of bronze in Scythia. The legends point to the area of Syrian trade as a source of iron rather than to Phrygia.

[94] Forbes, *op. cit.*, p. 385; Plut. *Alex.* 32; *Dem.* 21.

[95] Ezekiel 27.19; *Yale Oriental Series* VI No. 168.

of Naukratis, for Egypt's iron age began, properly speaking, only in the Saite period.[96] In the latter part of the seventh and during the sixth century, however, new sources of supply became available to the Ionians. Perhaps the Phocaeans brought some Etrurian iron from the west, and, after the colonization of the south shore of the Black Sea, Chalybian steel entered the Aegean markets.

Our earliest literary evidence for its export is from the first half of the fifth century, but by that time Χάλυψ was in poetic usage for steel and the Chalybes had become the traditional people of iron-working.[97] Evidently the excellence of their product had been established by considerable experience, and it was prized for certain purposes above local and cheaper supplies. The Chalybes apparently mined and smelted their metal only, exporting it in ingot form to be worked by local smiths in the various areas to which it was carried.[98] This steel must have been distributed mainly by Ionian traders from the time it became available in the mid-sixth century.[99]

COPPER

Copper, too, was lacking in Ionia,[100] and there is evidence for its importation as early as the Late Bronze Age. Nineteen ingots of the typical Cypriote hide form, which is widespread in the Aegean and even in the western Mediterranean, were found in the harbor of Kyme.[101] Evidently at that time the copper mining district in the Troad, near Adramyttion, was not in use. Its opening, like that of the gold mines near Abydos, was probably the result of Greek colonization in the area. The metal was then brought down from the mountains and shipped from the port of Kisthene. It could have supplied Lesbos and Aeolis, but hardly Ionia, for the supply was limited, and by Strabo's time the mines had been exhausted (13.1.51). Probably, too, exploitation of the copper deposits in the Propontis was a product of the Greek colonization. At present several mines are being worked south of

96 Forbes, *op. cit.*, pp. 430–32; Wainwright, *op. cit.*, pp. 22–23. The earliest set of iron tools and armor was found with an Assyrian-type helmet in Thebes and is probably a remnant of Assurbanipal's campaigns (667 and 663). Wainwright notes that A.'s list of booty from Thebes did not include iron; since, by the time of Herodotus, iron tools seem to be common in Egypt (Her. 2.86.3; 125.7), its use was evidently established in the seventh and sixth centuries. At first it was imported in manufactured form, for the earliest evidence of local working is Ptolemaic.

97 Aeschylus *Prometheus* 133, 714–16; *Sept. v. Thebes* 727–33; Apollonius Rhodius *Argonautica* II 1001–08; Sophocles *Trach.* 1260; Euripides *Herakleidae* 161; Pliny *NH* 7.197. For the literary tradition see Blümner, *op. cit.*, pp. 71–72; Xenophon *Anabasis* 5.5.1; Strabo 12.3.19.

98 The emphasis in the sources on mining and smelting seems to indicate that those operations only were carried on by the Chalybes; for the process see Pseudo-Aristotle *De Mir. Ausc.* 48 (833b) and Richardson, *AJA* 38 (1934), p. 566, n. 6.

99 Ps. Aristotle (*De Mir. Ausc.* 48) connects the process with Amisos, and the sources point to Cappadocia (Strabo, Xenophon, above n. 97). Probably it was traded into the Greek colonies with Amisos as the most important center; below, p. 120, n. 27.

100 Above, p. 20.

101 Davies, *BSA* 30 (1928–30) 78–79; Lorimer, *op. cit.*, p. 57; Lorimer suggests that these ingots may have been exported from Ugarit. They are similar in form to many found in Late Minoan contexts in the Aegean and to those from the western Mediterranean, where a large number were found at Sicca Elixi in Sardinia and others at Cannatello, near Girgenti.

Marmora, but it is not certain whether they were known in antiquity, although the deposits on the island of Chalkis near Chalcedon were certainly known.[102] All these mines, however, must have been small. They probably sufficed for local needs and perhaps yielded a little surplus for export, but we cannot judge their importance as a supply for the Ionian states. In any case, they could only have been utilized after colonization and by that time Cyprus had established a strong trading connection with Samos, so that it is probable Ionian supplies continued to be drawn mainly from that source. The name Iamani was connected in the oriental sources with the trade in copper as it was with iron.[103]

The trade in metals must have been one of the main bases of Ionian prosperity from the seventh century. Geography had placed the Ionians beside Lydia, which became the main source of gold in the Aegean. Cypriotes, Rhodians and perhaps Phrygians had supplied them with iron and copper at first, but by the late seventh century the Ionians were in a position to carry much of the metal needed for their own purposes and to partially supply the Aegean and Lydia. They carried Thracian silver to Egypt to pay for the grain needed to feed their growing population. The long Phocaean voyages to Italy and Spain brought tin, a high-grade bronze and perhaps some iron to the Aegean. The colonies on the south shore of the Black Sea provided steel of a quality which fast became traditional. The Ionians were not only able to supply themselves, but acquired valuable trading commodities with which to purchase food and luxury articles.

[102] Forbes, *op. cit.*, p. 303; Theophrastus *De lapid.* 25; Steph. Byz. *s.v.* Chalcitis; Pliny *NH* 37.72.

[103] Forbes, *op. cit.*, p. 363; Forbes implies that the Ionians brought copper directly from western Asia Minor, but surely the reference should be to Cyprus. Since that island had supplied Ugarit in the Late Bronze Age, it is difficult to see why such a trading relation should not have been intensified again in the archaic period.

CHAPTER VII

The Search for Land

Ionian colonial expansion overseas began early in the seventh century. At that time the Ionians were attempting to break into the river valleys which led to Lydia and the interior. Land in Asia Minor, however, was hard won, and any possibility of expansion inland was soon blocked by Gyges' consolidation of Lydia. The Ionians were not even allowed to cultivate their own territory in peace, for Gyges initiated a series of raids on their cities, and from 668 until after 650, the Cimmerian and Trerian invasions further disturbed western Asia Minor. The combination of a growing population and continuous raids on their territory presumably suggested colonization as a means of relief. Accordingly, *ca.* 700 movement out of Ionia began into the nearest areas which were free for Greek settlement, eastern Thrace and the Propontis.

It is likely that by this time they were the only lands in the Aegean open to the Ionians. A recent study of the colonization of the Chalcidice in western Thrace has argued that it was settled by Euboeans in the early eighth century.[1] Thasos and its *peraea* were probably in the process of being settled by the islanders of the northern Cyclades, particularly Parians and Andrians. The Ionians obviously were familiar with this colonial movement from their Cycladic kindred. Similarly, Archilochus was acquainted with the recent developments in Asia Minor, the rise of Gyges and the destruction of Magnesia.[2] It was natural for Ionian attention to be attracted northward to eastern Thrace.

[1] D. W. Bradeen, *AJP* 73 (1952) 356–80.

[2] The range of Archilochus' geographical reference is surprisingly wide and probably represents that of the Cycladic sailors in general. Aside from the references to Gyges (frag. 22) and to the misfortunes of Magnesia (frag. 19) he ranges from Italy to the Black Sea; Siris in Italy: frag. 18, lines 3–4; the Salmydessian wreckers on the Thracian coast of the Black Sea: frag. 79; Thrace: frag. 2 (Ismaros); frag. 6, line 1 (Saioi); frag. 18, lines 1–2 and frag. 19 (Thasos); frags. 28, 51; the Aegean: frag. 3, line 5 (Euboea); frag. 53 (Paros); frag. 56, line 2 (Gyreis); frag. 76 (Lesbos); Asia (Lydia): frag. 23; Phrygia: frag. 28.

THRACE

At first the land must have made a rather grim impression in contrast to Ionia. The coast from Kavalla eastward (Map III) is forbidding, an alternation of steep cliffs and low, marshy deltas backed by hills. Behind the line of hills, however, lie the fertile river valleys with excellent soil for grain and pasture.[3] Perhaps, too, some hope of sharing in the gold of Thasos and its *peraea* was felt. Probably the resources of the land, which later bulked so large in Ionian imagination, were known from pre-colonial trade with the natives. There is no archaeological evidence for this, but the Homeric poems reveal some knowledge of Thrace by the mention of Ismaros, the site of the later Maroneia, of Aenos and of tribal groups like the Kikones and Paeonians. Of more significance from our point of view is a reference to Ismarian wine, which Odysseus acquired from the priest of Apollo there. Archilochus also appreciated the vintage.[4] Another product of Thrace, which received attention in both Homer and the archaic writers, was horses. Mimnermus, for example, referred to Paeonia, renowned for its horses (frag. 14), and, at a much later date, Anacreon addressed a poem to a Thracian colt (frag. 88). Mimnermus may be echoing Homer or putting in epic form an allusion to the Treres, but, on the whole, it seems probable that the Ionians knew of Thracian wine and horses before their colonization began. In the first quarter of the seventh century at the latest the Chians dispatched a colony to Maroneia and, a generation later, the Klazomenians to Abdera.

An *ante quem* date for Maroneia (Map III) is furnished by Archilochus' reference to its quarrel with Thasos over the settlement of Stryme, which apparently marked the frontier between the two colonies.[5] Unfortunately Archilochus' own date is controversial, but most recent treatments favor making him a contemporary of Gyges, thus placing the greater part of his career in the first half of the seventh century.[6] We may conclude that the colony was founded between the time of Homer's notice of the site as in native Thracian hands[7] and Archilochus' reference to it, probably in the early seventh century. Maroneia did not possess a good harbor nor much fertile land, but two passes led through the hills at its back into the rich agricultural land of the Odryssian Thracians. Presumably the Chian motive in placing a colony at this point was to found an agricultural settlement, which could also be used for the procurement of Thracian wine to distribute in Ionia. There, Chios had already been exporting wine to Smyrna in the late eighth century.

The other important Ionian foundation in this region was Abdera (Map III) on the

[3] The area is described by Casson (*Macedonia, Thrace and Illyria*, c. II) who seems to have been rather too conscious of the difficulties experienced by the British in the war of 1914–18, when the anchorage of large ships was a problem which did not exist for the light craft of archaic Greece. Similarly Myres' description of conditions in Thrace (*CAH* III 656) seems too grim. While there is considerable notice of conflict with the natives from the time of Archilochus to that of Thucydides, yet Thracians and Greeks traded profitably, to judge by the large quantity of Thraco-Macedonian silver in the Near East and the place which Thrace occupied in Ionian plans in the late sixth century (below, p. 108).

[4] *Il.* 9.71–72; *Od.* 9.196–98; Archilochus frag. 2; Roebuck, *CP* 45 (1950), p. 246, n. 47.

[5] Harpokration, *s.v.* Stryme; Roebuck, *op. cit.*, p. 246, n. 45; for the site, *AJA* 61 (1957) 285.

[6] Above, p. 91, n. 24.

[7] *Od.* 9.194; Ps.-Skymnos 676–77.

fertile alluvial plain of the Nestos delta. It was founded by Klazomenai (Her. 1.168) *ca.* 650, according to the literary tradition (Solinus 10.10), but the settlement did not prosper, and a refounding was made by the Teans at the time of the Persian conquest of Ionia (Her. 1.168). The authenticity of the earlier foundation seems confirmed by Herodotus' specific reference and an apparent allusion in Pindar.[8] Klazomenian motives of colonization were probably similar to those of Chios, since Abdera was set in a coastal plain with easy access to the interior. Near Abdera was Dikaea, for which there is no record of foundation, but presumably it, too, was Ionian. Herodotus refers to it in connection with Xerxes' march (7.109). Farther to the east was a group of small settlements, Mesembria, Zone and Sale, identified as Samothracian by Herodotus (7.59, 108). Their date of foundation is unknown, and they had no significant development. Thus, Casson's supposition that they were the earliest towns of the area seems incorrect.[9] Since they could serve as ports of call for ships coasting along Thrace, their foundation probably post-dated that of the other colonies and followed upon the establishment of some trade. Further, the Greek colonization of Samothrace, from which the colonists came, took place in the first half of the seventh century.[10]

Another settlement of some importance in eastern Thrace was made at Aenos (Map III), apparently in a pre-existing native town in the delta of the Hebrus River.[11] Aenos was an Aeolian colony, probably of the latter part of the seventh century, for it is said to have been a foundation of Alopekonnesos, itself Aeolian in origin. Later, Aenos was reinforced from Mytilene and Kyme (Her. 7.58; Strabo 7, frag. 52). An *ante quem* date is given for it by a reference in Alcaeus.[12] Although Aenos ultimately became of considerable importance as a port for the upper Hebrus valley, where a strong Thracian kingdom existed, and the terminus of a land route to the Black Sea, it was probably designed in the first place as an agricultural colony of the type of Abdera and Maroneia. It remains to summarize this modest colonial activity on the Thracian foreshore.

The earlier settlements, Maroneia and Abdera, were set near Thasos. Apparently the Ionians were attracted there in the first place by the activity of the islanders, particularly Parians, who made the region known. The possibility of a trade in wine, perhaps in horses and hides, seems to have been a motive in colonization as well as the desire for new homes. Possibly in the case of Klazomenian Abdera the settlers had lost their farms and property in raids by Gyges and the Cimmerians. Abdera was not strong enough to hold out, but Maroneia developed to become a thriving town, serving as a port of call for Chiot and other Ionian ships, which brought goods to Thasos, the chief emporion of the area, to be exchanged for gold and silver.

There is little archaeological evidence from the colonies to supplement this literary record, for Maroneia and Aenos are unexcavated and only late archaic material has been

[8] *Ox. Pap.* v, Paean 2, line 63, schol., p. 85, note.

[9] Casson, *op. cit.*, pp. 92–93.

[10] Lehmann, *Hesperia* 19 (1950) 11; 21 (1952) 35–37.

[11] *Il.* 4.520.

[12] Lobel and Page, *Poetarum Lesbiorum Frag.*, Alcaeus 45 (B13).

found in investigations at Abdera since 1950.[13] Most of our knowledge of archaic Thrace is from Thasos and the region around Kavalla. The material from Bakalakis' excavations there, however, gives an indication of the Greek trade into the region.[14] In Kavalla a temple dedicated to the Maiden Goddess was discovered by chance in a drain-digging operation in 1936. Its votive material included a wide range of imported pottery: Corinthian, Laconian, Attic, Aeolian, Chiot, Cycladic and "Rhodian." The Corinthian belongs to the Early Corinthian style (625–600), the East Greek material is of the same approximate date,[15] while the Attic is of the mid-sixth century and later. The temple itself is Ionic and was built in the latter part of the sixth century. From a cave sacred to the nymphs near Kavalla came a similar assortment of pottery.[16] A small harbor town, probably the ancient Antisara, was excavated at Kalamitsa, seven kilometers west of Kavalla.[17] In addition to local pottery of subgeometric type and Cycladic inspiration, a small amount of Cycladic Orientalizing ware and Attic black-figure of the mid- and late sixth century was found.

The pottery indicates that two currents of trade converged into Thrace, the one, Corinthian and, later, Attic, from the west, the other, Ionian, from the east. By the mid-sixth century Thrace was of considerable importance to Ionia.[18] Teans found Abdera a place of refuge after the Persian conquest, and Histiaeus and Aristagoras planned to found a new Ionia there at the time of the Ionian revolt. Peisistratus, for Athens, stimulated a permanent interest in the region. Herodotus makes the reasons explicit (5.3, 23): Thrace had wood for ship building and oars, silver mines and a large population, both Greek and barbarian. Persia, of course, was sufficiently aware of all this to make it a province. Probably the ship timber was used by the islanders and the colonies in Thrace rather than exported to Asia Minor, for supplies were ample there. Ionians purchased slaves in Thrace from the natives (Her. 5.6.1), among whom was the famous Rhodopis, who passed through several Samian hands to be ultimately freed by Sappho's brother in Naukratis.[19] Thus, for Ionia as the trading connection developed Thrace was a source

[13] *BCH* 79 (1955) 280–81.

[14] *ArchEph*, 1936, 1–32; 1938, 106–54; *Praktika*, 1937, 59–64; 1938, 75–81.

[15] R. M. Cook considers that none of the East Greek material need probably be dated before 600 (*JHS* 66 1946], p. 82, n. 133).

[16] *Praktika*, 1938, 81–97.

[17] *Praktika*, 1935, 29–42; 1936, 74–81.

[18] Roebuck, *op. cit.*, p. 246, n. 47.

[19] The importance of slavery on Chios is often noticed. For example, Theopompus (*FGrHist* 2B, No. 122) states that Chios was the first of the Greek states to use slaves after the Lacedaemonians and Thessalians; these were purchased barbarians, not enslaved natives like the Thessalian and Spartan serfs. The tradition is repeated by Poseidonios of Apamea (*FGrHist* 2A, No. 38), Nikolaos of Damascus (*FGrHist* 2A, No. 95) and Stephanus (*s.v.* Chios). Thucydides observed of the Chians in the late fifth century that they had the most slaves of any Greek state except Sparta (8.40.2); the statement is surprising and questioned by Westermann (*The Slave Systems of Greek and Roman Antiquity* 9), but it should at least indicate an unusually large number of slaves for a state of moderate size like Chios. Presumably the phenomenon is related to the specialized agriculture of the island, oil and wine production, and to the small industrial establishments for metal-working and the like. We know the name of one Chiot slave dealer, Panionius (Her. 8.105), who made a business of buying handsome boys, castrating them and selling them in Sardis and Ephesus. This is akin to the traffic in prostitutes, in which Samians seem to have been active (e.g., the story of Rhodopis, Her. 2.135; Strabo 17.1.33; Sappho 25; Athenaeus 596b, c; see also Douris *FGrHist*

of silver, of wine, of some agricultural products and of slaves. To it probably went textiles and products of Ionian industry for the natives, similar material, pottery, and olive oil for the Greeks.

THE THRACIAN CHERSONESE

Most of the settlements in the Thracian Chersonese (Map III) belonged to a slightly later movement than that into eastern Thrace. They were mainly a product of the expansion of the last quarter of the seventh century and of the developing trade into the Black Sea through the Hellespont and the Propontis. Since there is no pertinent archaeological evidence for the foundation dates or for their early history, we must rely on the literary tradition. It is apparent that the area was settled with the traffic routes rather than agriculture in mind, for the sites are placed mainly in the Hellespont and grouped around the harbors.[20]

Two of the sites, Kardia and Limnae, were sited for trade with Thrace rather than out of the Hellespont. Kardia is situated at the end of the Gulf of Melos and Limnae at its head. Kardia was originally founded by Milesians and Klazomenians[21] but taken over by Athenians under Miltiades I, when he conquered the Chersonese. Probably its foundation was contemporary with that of Aenos in the latter part of the seventh century, but Miltiades developed it to be the anchor point of his long wall across the isthmus (Her. 6.36). Kardia's trading interest is attested by the foundation of Agora inland on the road across the isthmus.[22] Of Limnae we know only that it was also a Milesian foundation of the archaic period.[23] These two sites probably represent a Milesian attempt to participate directly in the trade with Thrace—an expectation which was realized by Miltiades rather than the Milesians.

The other settlements were sited with a view to the profits from traffic proceeding up the Hellespont, tolls and the sale of food. Sestos, of course, had the additional importance of being the chief crossing point into Europe and thus may have served also as a terminus for Thracian trade. Its existence as a Thracian town is attested by Homer (*Il.* 2.836), and we know that it subsequently became a Lesbian colony (Ps.-Skymnos 709–10). Probably Sestos acquired interest in Greek eyes only after the foundation of Abydos across the strait in the reign of Gyges. The Aeolian foundation of Alopekonnesos in Suvla Bay should also be connected with that of Sestos. We know that it was settled earlier than Aenos, and thus an *ante quem* date is provided for it by Alcaeus' reference to Aenos.[24] Most of the other settlement in the region is Aeolian, but, since it is at minor sites farther in the Hellespont,

2A, No. 66, for slaves in Samos). Probably the cities of the Propontis as well as Chios and Samos engaged in the Thracian slave trade, for Cyzicus imposed an indirect tax for exchange of slaves by sale in the sixth century (Ditt. *Syll.*,[3] No. 4), and Hipponax (frag. 39) compared a glutton to a Lampsacene eunuch feasting on tunny fish and pastes.

[20] Casson, *op. cit.*, pp. 210ff.; *ATL* I *Gazeteer*, *s.v.* separate cities; Leaf, *Strabo on the Troad* 119ff.; Bürchner, "Chersonesos," *RE* 3 (1899) 2242ff.

[21] Ps.-Skymnos 698ff.; Strabo 7, frag. 52.

[22] Her. 7.58 (= Chersonesos); *ATL* I 563–64; Ps.-Skylax 67; Hecataeus (*FGrHist* I, No. 163).

[23] Ps.-Skymnos 705; Strabo 7, frag. 52; Steph. Byz. *s.v.*; Hecataeus (*FGrHist* I, No. 164).

[24] Ps.-Skymnos 706; Strabo 7, frag. 52; above, p. 107, n. 12.

it is probably to be dated after the foundations of Sestos and Alopekonnesos.[25] Perhaps the best indication of the importance attained by the region *ca.* 600 is the Athenian foundation of Elaious. Its colonization was evidently a corollary to their attempt on Sigeion across the straits.[26] While the two could scarcely secure the entrance to the Hellespont for Athens as long as Sestos and Abydos were non-Athenian, this Athenian activity does indicate that trade through the Hellespont was of growing importance.

A much more effective bid for control of the area was made by Miltiades I in the time of Peisistratus, when he seized the key harbors of the Chersonese and converted it into a little principality by walling it off and developing its communications and facilities for trade.[27] This complemented the Athenian interest in Thrace, which Peisistratus had selected as the scene of his personal activity. This development of the Chersonese, however, was always secondary to that of the more fertile and hospitable south shore of the straits and of the Propontis, in which Ionians played a major part.

THE PROPONTIS

The problem of the settlement along the south shore of the Hellespont and in the Propontis (Map III) is particularly difficult, since we have little information from other literary sources or from excavations to supplement the traditional (Eusebian) chronology. Recent work on the question has attacked the traditional dating, with the result that serious colonization is regarded as starting only in the early seventh century.[28] In this connection it is useful to review certain general considerations which seem valid and acceptable.

The colonies in this area were divided into three groups, well defined geographically and with some significance for the process of settlement. The westernmost group stretched from Abydos along the south shore of the Hellespont and Propontis to Kios. All the colonies in this area have a tradition of Ionian origin, mainly Milesian, but with a Phocaean intrusion at Lampsacus and an Erythraean (and Parian?) at Parion.[29] The major colonies were Abydos, Lampsacus, Cyzicus, Kios—at least major in their subsequent growth. Beyond this Ionian group and clustering at the east end of the Propontis was the Megarian series of Astakos, Chalcedon, Byzantium and Selymbria. Beyond them on the north shore were the three Samian colonies, Perinthus, Heraion Teichos and Bisanthe. As Myres has pointed out,[30] the natural route through the Propontis in antiquity lay along the south

[25] For Madytos see Ps.-Skymnos 709–10; Her. 7.33.

[26] Ps.-Skymnos 707–08; Wade-Gery, *JHS* 71 (1951), p. 219, n. 37. A cemetery has been partially excavated, yielding some material of the fifth century (*BCH*, 36 [1912] 314–15; 39 [1915] 135–240).

[27] Wade-Gery, *op. cit.*, pp. 218–19; N.G.L. Hammond, *CQ* 49 (1956) 113–29.

[28] Cook, *JHS* 66 (1946) 71 ff.; Carpenter, *AJA* 52 (1948) 1–10; Burn, *JHS* 55 (1935) 132–33. Excavation has been started by Ekrem Akurgal at Cyzicus and at Daskylion. Nothing earlier than late orientalizing pottery (sixth century) has been found at Cyzicus as yet, but at Daskylion Greek pottery of the first half of the seventh century was discovered, Protocorinthian and East Greek Orientalizing with some tile and akroterion fragments. This supports the dating of the start of Greek colonization in the area in the early seventh century (Mellink, *AJA* 59 [1955] 235).

[29] The literary evidence is collected and examined by Bilabel, *Philologus, Supp.* 14 (1920) 43–51.

[30] *CAH* III 657–60.

shore. We would reasonably expect it to be settled first, and tradition does indicate that some of the Ionian colonies were earlier than those of the other groups. Traditionally also, the most important Samian colony, Perinthus, was founded in 603–02, at which time some conflict with Megarians is noticed.[31] The Samian group is traditionally the latest, as might be expected from its occupation of the north shore sites, which are off the main navigation route on a less hospitable and fertile shore, where the natives were hostile and troublesome. This geographical grouping, then, should represent the course of settlement: the Milesians occupied the important sites in the western area; the Megarians found these occupied and proceeded to the east end of the Propontis; the Samians, last on the scene, were forced into the unfavorable sites on the north shore.

As frequently emphasized, the main colonies on the south and east were founded before trade from the Black Sea was a factor in their choice, for otherwise, Byzantium, which could control all the shipping through the Bosporus, would have been founded before the other Megarian colonies. It might be added that, if Miletus had been trading with the Black Sea at the time of its earliest colonization in the Propontis, it should have occupied Byzantium. It is likely that the foundation of Byzantium coincided with a marked development of trade within the Black Sea, that is, with the first penetration in serious fashion, even if occasional ships made their way in at an earlier time. The opportunity to collect tolls and sell provisions and services to the passing crews would have been too profitable not to exploit. As we have noticed, the Samians traditionally arrived *ca.* 600, after the foundation of the Megarian colonies. Since this was their only colonial venture in the north and far from the general direction of Samian trade to south and west, presumably they were attracted by the new development of Black Sea trade. *Ca.* 600 it was reaching valuable proportions. A similar indication is the sudden Athenian attention paid to the Hellespont, apparent in the foundation of Elaious in the Thracian Chersonese and the seizure of Sigeion in the Troad, over which Mytilene and Athens quarreled. Both Samians and Athenians were not wanted in the area *ca.* 600, although Aeolians, Ionians and Megarians seem to have got along without difficulty previously. The new factor in the situation was evidently the profits of trade with the Black Sea. By *ca.* 600 the shores of the Hellespont and of the Propontis were either fully settled or regarded as the preserves of existing colonies. It remains to see whether some upper limit can be found for the colonization.

It is generally held that the Greek settlement of the Troad was Aeolian, probably from Lesbos in the course of the eighth and early seventh centuries. The movement resulted in the foundation of small agricultural settlements for the most part, although Troy may still have had some importance as a trading town.[32] As yet the only important archaeological evidence is from the excavation of Troy itself where the arrival of Greeks in the area should have left some traces among the pottery. To judge from that published, the Aeolian Greeks

[31] Plutarch *Moralia* 303e–304c.

[32] No recent archaeological reconaissance of the Troad has been made, and W. Leaf, *Strabo on the Troad*, remains the most useful study. There is helpful material in the catalogue of the Calvert collection in the Istanbul Museum, and Schefold has noticed some of the Aeolian pottery (*JDAI* 57 [1942] 132 ff.).

probably settled at Troy in the eighth century, and imports began to arrive very quickly. In the preliminary reports a considerable quantity of Protocorinthian and Corinthian pottery is mentioned as well as East Greek of the seventh century.[33] This imported pottery hardly dates the colonies of the Hellespont and of the Propontis, but it should be more or less contemporary with their establishment. Thus, it seems likely that the Milesian colonization is to be placed just after the turn of the century.[34] Since the Eusebian chronology is suspect, we might notice the information to be derived from other sources before considering it.

The most useful item is a notice in Strabo concerning the foundation of Abydos. He states that it was a Milesian colony founded by permission of Gyges.[35] If the obscure reference could be explained satisfactorily, we would have a useful chronological point in the process of colonization, *ca.* 685–52. The phrase "by permission of Gyges" implies either that Gyges was in control of Miletus or of the area around Abydos. The former does not seem correct, but, as we have seen, there is other evidence of Lydian interest in the Troad which may have led to Gyges' sponsoring of a colony. Abydos was the main military crossing point from Europe into Asia, and was probably used by the Thracian Treres who swept into Asia Minor during Gyges' reign and remained to occupy Antandrus in the Troad.[36] To block the Treres, Gyges perhaps installed garrisons at several points, using Ionian and Carian mercenaries, as he did to aid his ally Psammetichos I of Egypt. If so, Abydos may have been originally a colony of Milesian mercenary soldiers. Other indications of this early Lydian interest in the Troad are the Lydian place-name Daskylion near Cyzicus and the obscure notice of a Carian element in the foundation of Kios. The recent discovery at Daskylion of Protocorinthian and East Greek pottery of the first half of the seventh century also helps to support the start of the Greek colonization in the area in the early seventh century.[37]

The other pertinent scrap of information concerns Proconnesus. In some fashion and on some evidence which Herodotus found in Proconnesus adjacent to Cyzicus, he calculated that Aristeas, the Shaman, had disappeared two hundred and forty years previously. Since the calculation was made while Herodotus was in Italy, in the mid-fifth century, Aristeas' *floruit* may be set *ca.* 690.[38] The group of harbor towns and settlements around

[33] The Geometric pottery at Troy is identified as local rather than imported (Hanfmann, *AJA* 52 [1948], p. 144, n. 37; Schefold, *op. cit.*, pp. 136–38). Hanfmann considers that Troy was non-Greek in the eighth century, but Schefold apparently thinks that Greeks had taken over the settlement. According to the preliminary reports, importation of Greek orientalizing wares began in the eighth century, and even some of the Geometric was imported (*AJA* 41 [1937] 30; 43 [1939] 223). The considerable amount of imported pottery, Corinthian, Aeolian and East Greek, indicates that the town still had some importance as a trading center, but a detailed picture necessarily waits on publication.

[34] For discussion see Cook, *JHS* 66 (1946) 71, 77; Burn, *JHS* 55 (1935) 132 ff.; Carpenter *AJA* 52 (1948) 1–10.

[35] Strabo 13.1.22; R. M. Cook (*op. cit.*, p. 71, n. 41) suggests that the apparent connection with Gyges may have originated in the presence of Cape Gygas in the vicinity.

[36] Above, p. 53, n. 59.

[37] Daskylos was the father of Gyges (Hasluck, *Cyzicus* 56; Her. 1.6); Kios: *Schol. Apoll. Rhod.*, I, 1177 (from Aristotle); for the pottery see above, note 28; cf. also p. 51, n. 51.

[38] Her. 4.14–15.

Cyzicus, Artake and Proconnesus, was closely connected with the life of Aristeas and thus may have been founded *ca.* 700. Cyzicus was traditionally the earliest of the colonies, and, while there is reason to reject its earliest foundation date (756) on several grounds, there is no reason to doubt that it was the earliest colony of Miletus in the area. Unlike the other colonies a wealth of tradition hangs about it and its native predecessors, whose legends are Hellenized.[39] It should not be surprising that it was founded before Abydos. As Myres points out, Cyzicus was at the end of the run up the Hellespont and along the south shore of the Propontis. Its site was admirable, and the selection justified by its later growth and importance. Abydos, of course, only had some importance after traffic began to use the Hellespont regularly and cross from Europe to Asia. There was little reason for it to be the first, but it might well have been the second colony.

If the traditional chronology is at least correct in the relative dating of the other major Ionian colonies, Cyzicus and Abydos were followed by the Erythraean foundation of Parion, by the Phocaean colony at Lampsacus and finally by Kios. The dates (709, 654, 627) should probably be scaled down in accordance with the foundations of Cyzicus and Abydos in the first and second quarter of the seventh century. Burn's scale sets Parion *ca.* 657, Lampsacus in 615, Kios in 595.[40] This seems very reasonable for the Phocaean activity, of which we scarcely hear until the late seventh century, and the colony of Lampsacus may well reflect a Phocaean interest in the development of the Black Sea trade. It is likely, too, if political considerations have some validity, that the Erythraean settlement at Parion was properly third in order and made at least as early as *ca.* 650. Since Erythrae and Miletus seem to have been hostile in the seventh century,[41] the former's colonial activity in a strongly Milesian area should be placed before that area had developed to any great degree. The Parian element in the colonization rests on rather slight evidence, but may be correct, since the name is difficult to explain otherwise.[42] Perhaps a small settlement was made by the islanders in the eighth century to be reinforced later by Erythrae. Kios would fall into line as a Milesian foundation at the time of the development of the Black Sea trade *ca.* 600, usefully filling in the gap between Cyzicus and the westernmost Megarian colony at Astakos.[43]

In the case of most of these Ionian colonies the tradition indicates that the Milesians occupied pre-existing native settlements. The primary colonies were obviously well sited with an eye to harbors and sailing routes, but also with good agricultural hinterlands, for in each case the Ionians eventually moved inland to expand their agricultural areas and established secondary towns along the coast. Abydos was the center of an area including Astyra, Arisbe and perhaps Priapos; Cyzicus of an area comprising Apollonia on the Rhyndacus, Miletopolis, Artake and Proconnesus; Lampsacus of Kolonae, Paisos, Abarnis

[39] For a discussion of the literary traditions see Bilabel, *Philologus*, *Supp.* 14 (1920) 46–47. In the Eusebian chronology (Eusebius 2.81; Syncellus 213 B) the foundation of Cyzicus I is placed in 756 B.C., of Cyzicus II (Eusebius 2.87) *ca.* 675.

[40] Cook, *op. cit.*, p. 77 (table).

[41] Above, pp. 72–73.

[42] Strabo 13.1.14; Bilabel, *op. cit.*, p. 49.

[43] Bilabel, *op. cit.*, pp. 43–44.

and Kallipolis across the straits; Parion of Pitya.[44] We have noticed that Abydos may have been founded in the first instance as a military colony. In the case of Cyzicus perhaps trade was the predominant motive, not that with the Black Sea, but in the Propontis itself. The siting of the primary colonies is in itself sufficient indication that the area was already known when serious colonization began and the subsequent expansion inland a result of their growth. The articles of this early trade were probably the small agricultural surplus of the area and the fish of the Propontis, where the schools of tunny made their way along its south shore.

The Megarian group of colonies, Astakos, Chalcedon, Selymbria and Byzantium was a little later than the primary Milesian colonies.[45] Their traditional dates are later and help to confirm the implication of their siting at the east end of the Propontis. It seems probable, on the whole, that Chalcedon was the earliest colony. According to the Eusebian chronology Astakos was the earliest (711), but Charon of Lampsacus (*FGrHist* 3A, No. 6) considered it a foundation from Chalcedon, which may, of course, only indicate a Chalcedonian reinforcement. In any case, the whole group should probably be placed in the third quarter of the seventh century to accord with the earlier foundation of the Milesian colonies and of the Samian Perinthus *ca.* 600. The choice of Chalcedon in preference to Byzantium is probably to be explained by the later establishment of trade with the Black Sea, but another factor may have operated as well. On the island of Chalkis, which, it is probable, was the site of the original foundation rather than the mainland, were deposits of copper, which should soon have become known to the settlers, if they did not provide the motive for settlement. Chalcedon's date of foundation, 685 in the traditional chronology, is scaled down to 639 by Burn.[46] The founding of Byzantium is set by Herodotus (4.144) seventeen years later, which Cook rightly observes seems to be a traditional half-generation. This, however, sets the foundation rather late (*ca.* 620) in the light of evidence of trade into the Black Sea. A date shortly after the middle of the seventh century seems more reasonable.[47] Selymbria may have been founded shortly before that time (Ps.-Skymnos 715–16). The motive for Chalcedon may have been copper, for Byzantium, trade; the purpose of Astakos and Selymbria was probably similar to that of the Milesian colonies. They were desirable places to settle for the purpose of making a living by local trading and agriculture.

In the general process of colonization in the Hellespont and Propontis there seem to be two waves of colonization. First, Ionians and then Megarians settled to find new

[44] Astyra: Leaf, *op. cit.*, pp. 133–35; Arisbe: Leaf, *op. cit.*, pp. 109–10 (Strabo 14.1.6); Bilabel, *op. cit.*, p. 51; Priapos: perhaps Priapos was Cyzicene rather than founded from Abydos (Strabo 13.1.12; Leaf, *op. cit.*, pp. 73 ff.; Hasluck, *Cyzicus*, pp. 97–98); Apollonia: Hasluck, *op. cit.*, pp. 68 ff.; Miletopolis: Hasluck, *op. cit.*, pp. 74 ff.; Artake: Her. 4.14.2; Hasluck, *op. cit.*, pp. 16–21; Proconnesus: there is some difficulty about the identification (*ATL* I 542–43); Hasluck, *op. cit.*, pp. 30–35; Kolonai: Strabo 13.1.19; Leaf, *op. cit.*, pp. 101–102; Paisos: Strabo 13.1.19; Leaf, *op. cit.*, pp. 98–100; Abarnis: Leaf, *op. cit.*, pp. 93–94; Kallipolis: Strabo 13.1.18; Pitya: Leaf, *op. cit.*, pp. 87–88.

[45] See the table in Cook, *op. cit.*, p. 77.

[46] Cook, *op. cit.*, p. 77; for the copper, above pp. 103–04.

[47] Cook, *op. cit.*, p. 71, n. 42; the discovery of a Late Protocorinthian aryballos at Byzantium helps to support this suggestion (and the Eusebian chronology), *AJA* 60 (1956) 383.

homes and a way of life in a generally hospitable area with possibilities of local trade and agriculture. From the middle of the seventh century a new factor entered the situation with the growth of the Black Sea trade, although it hardly reached substantial proportions until the end of the century after the foundation of colonies there. This is reflected first in the foundation of Byzantium, then in the entry of Samos, Athens and Phocaea to the Propontis. Their colonies did not necessarily have to participate in the new trade themselves, but they offered harborage and provisions to the ships passing between the Black Sea and the Aegean.

CHAPTER VIII

The Search for Food

EARLY CONTACTS WITH THE BLACK SEA

Information about the first Greek contacts with the Black Sea (Map IV) is wrapped in almost as complete a fog as those which rendered navigation perilous there at certain seasons of the year. The attempt to draw conclusions from the very scanty evidence is likely to produce some scholarly shipwrecks, as excavation of the sites proceeds and the material from the Russian excavations on the north coast becomes better known.[1] It was obviously, however, a region of particular interest to the Ionians, whose enterprise was to make it one of the chief sources of food for the Aegean region.

It is clear from the Greek literary tradition and such archaeological evidence as we possess that Greek knowledge of the Black Sea and its coasts was derived primarily from contacts by sea. The story of its first penetration, the legend of the Argonauts, is probably typical. Long voyages were made from the Aegean and a body of information gradually built up about the coast line and native peoples as contacts multiplied and the clusters of colonies began to grow. We have the accumulated experience of the archaic period in the fourth book of Herodotus, but it is curiously lacking in the foundation data for these colonies which is found in later sources. Perhaps this is a hint that the colonies were of a somewhat different nature than most other Greek foundations.

For their exploration of the Black Sea the Ionian Greeks probably had no stock of traditional knowledge, upon which they could draw. The possibility of Mycenean voyaging through the Bosporus can hardly be excluded in the light of their very considerable interest in Troy, but the tangible evidence is slight. A figurine with Linear A (?) characters inscribed on it is reported from Samsun. Its provenance, however, is doubtful, and at

[1] Summaries of the work on the sites in South Russia, some publication of material and special studies of Greek colonization have appeared in *Vestnik Drevnei Istorii* and *Sovetskaia Arkheologiia*. I have used these and such other Russian publications as have been available. Specific references are in the footnotes.

present it seems to be known only through a drawing.[2] Artifacts of Mycenean type have been found in some tumuli in Georgia, but there are no identifiable imports.[3] The voyage of the Argonauts lies in the realm of myth and saga.[4] Its origin is evidently in Minyan Thessaly, and some of its heroes belong to the generation before the Trojan War. The ship Argo and some other details of the story are familiar to Homer,[5] but the first known mention of Colchis as the destination of the heroes is apparently in Eumelus of Corinth, whose date is in the late eighth century.[6] The legend's geographical detail of the Black Sea region has usually been regarded as a product of Ionian voyaging there rather than as a part of the original story. Probably little information about the Black Sea came to the western coast of Asia Minor through Phrygia and Lydia.[7] The Greeks of the Propontis colonies, however, would hear of the Danube and the west coast of the Euxine from their Thracian neighbors and try to get through the Bosporus.[8] The earliest colonies in the Propontis were founded in the first half of the seventh century, and, as frequently assumed,[9] the exploration of the Euxine should follow chronologically and logically as the next step.

Many historians, notably Minns and Rostovtzeff,[10] have considered that the Ionian ventures into the Black Sea were synchronous with the advent of the Iron Age, *ca.* 1000. It is suggested that first Carians, then Ionian traders from Miletus sailed into the Black Sea and made their way along the south coast to its southeast corner. The goal was the iron and gold of the Caucasus, the Argonaut legend a Carian tale of this enterprise, Sinope and Trapezos the earliest colonies of the Ionians. This activity is placed in the tenth and ninth centuries; in the eighth, it is suggested, a northern route and the important colonies of the north shore were developed to open up the fishing and grain-producing regions of South Russia. This theory of the distribution of Caucasian gold and iron by a Black Sea water route has little tangible support. The Carian part in the enterprise rests mainly on the mention of a Carian thalassocracy in Eusebius' list of thalassocracies[11] and on some

[2] H. Bossert, *Altanatolien*, p. 18, fig. 6.

[3] C. F. A. Schaeffer, *Antiquity* 17 (1943) 183–87.

[4] Roscher, I 510 ff.

[5] *Od.* 12.69 ff.

[6] Roscher, I 530–31; below, note 14.

[7] Above, p. 47.

[8] R. Carpenter, *AJA* 52 (1948) 1–10; Carpenter concludes from the development of Greek ships that Greek navigation through the Bosporus was only possible by oared ships and not by sail. Thus, penetration into the Black Sea was delayed until the use of penteconters became established in the early seventh century. His calculations are based on too many variables to be convincing; for example, prolonged southerly gales can produce a change in the direction of the surface current in the Bosporus (*Mediterranean Pilot* IV [1941] 18), so that it flows into the Black Sea. B. W. Labaree has argued from a study of wind and current conditions that passage through the Bosporus was possible by sail, although a wait for favorable conditions might have been necessary (*AJA* 61 [1957] 29–33).

[9] Beloch, *GG* I², 2, 231–35; R. M. Cook, *JHS* 66 (1946) 77 ff.

[10] Minns, *Scythians and Greeks* 436–39; Rostovtzeff, *Iranians and Greeks* c. IV. This theory of a double colonization, in the tenth and again in the eighth century, has been standard, but is effectively criticized by R. M. Cook, *op. cit.*, pp. 72–73.

[11] J. L. Myres, *JHS* 26 (1906) 107–09; 27 (1907) 87, 123–30; A. R. Burn, *JHS* 47 (1927) 165–77. The list is frequently ignored or rejected in historical reconstructions; if it is used, considerable modification is needed (Cook, *op. cit.*, pp. 69–70).

Carian place-names in the Black Sea like Kallatis. If this entry in the list has any validity, it belongs in time to the eighth and seventh centuries and in place to the southeastern Aegean. The Carian names are probably to be accounted for by the fact that the Milesians were part Carian and that Carians may well have participated in Ionian sea-faring, as they joined in military service as mercenaries. The view that the Iron Age was the result of a dissemination of products and techniques of iron-working from a single center in Asia Minor is no longer held.[12] The early foundation dates of Sinope and Trapezos rest on dubious data, of which Herodotus says nothing, and on an exaggerated estimate of the early importance of the Ionian cities. At the time of the presumed colonization they were small towns, intent on enlarging their land frontiers at the expense of their native neighbors and one another rather than leading trading or colonial ventures into the Black Sea. Probably no permanent Greek settlement was made there until the last quarter of the seventh century, but trade and information about it had been increasing for the two previous generations.

There are several indications that trade with the Black Sea began in the second quarter of the seventh century: Archilochus (frag. 79) mentions the danger to sailors of navigation along the Salmydessian coast, where wreckers were active (cf. Xen. *Anab.* 7.5.12); in the excavation of Old Smyrna a sherd inscribed with the name of Istrokles was found. As the excavators observe, it may indicate an acquaintance with the Ister in the early second quarter of the century, to which it is dated.[13] Like other such names its use by Greeks perhaps coincides with the first flush of knowledge of a new region. Although Eumelus of Corinth, as well as mentioning Colchis, seems to have referred to Borysthenis and Sinope, both the ascription of the references to Eumelus and the date of Eumelus are doubtful.[14] For this early period of the seventh century there is only one dubious confirmation provided by archaeology. A subgeometric vase, obtained by purchase, is said to have been found on Berezan island near Olbia. While its provenance is doubtful, it is difficult to see why such a vase would be brought into Russia from elsewhere for sale; it was presumably found in South Russia and appeared, significantly enough, at the time of the Berezan excavations.[15] Archaeology offers rather more in the period from 650 to 625, a group of Rhodian vases from near Nemirov,[16] two hundred miles inland up the Bug River from Olbia, and an oinochoe from Temir Gora near Kertch.[17] Both are dated *ca.* 630 and should be regarded as the products of pre-colonization trade, since they were found far inland from the site of a Greek colony. A Transitional style Corinthian vase (*ca.* 640–625) is also reported from South Russia.[18] This evidence seems to indicate that

[12] Above, p. 101, n. 86.

[13] *ILN*, Feb. 28, 1953, p. 328. R. M. Cook, however, has pointed out to me that the reference may be to the island, Istros, in the Dodecanese; note, however, the use of such names as Psammetichos by the tyrant of Corinth.

[14] On Eumelus and his references to the Black Sea see E. Will, *Korinthiaka* 124–28. Will discusses the difficulties involved in accepting this evidence as valid for the eighth century.

[15] *AA* 25 (1910), p. 227, fig. 27; Cook, *op. cit.*, p. 76, n. 90.

[16] *AA* 26 (1911), p. 235, fig. 42; 27 (1912), p. 378, fig. 70.

[17] Kinch, *Vroulia*, p. 220, fig. 107; see also von Stern, *Klio* 9 (1909) 141.

[18] Payne, *Necrocorinthia*, p. 271, No. 30a; Payne's No. 230, pl. 17, 1–2 from *Olbia* is Transitional or Early Corinthian.

a few Greeks were sailing up the west coast and along the north shore of the Euxine in the second and third quarters of the seventh century. Probably they were Ionians who sailed from their home ports to the new colonies in the Propontis or men from the colonies themselves. In any case information was acquired which led to the planting of colonies in the Black Sea in the next generation. It is probable, too, that ships went along the south shore. Curiosity should have supplied the motive, and perhaps the evidence is to be seen in Mimnermus' familiarity with the legend of the Argonauts.[19] Archaeology, too, has produced a little confirmatory evidence, for the earliest Greek material from Sinope dates from *ca.* 600. Like that from the north shore it may have come from Greek traders operating along the coast, but it possibly dates the foundation of the colony.[20] Presumably by the third quarter of the century the trade was reaching sufficient proportions to make it desirable to establish a port at which ships could lie before and after running through the Bosporus. Byzantium was probably founded soon after 650.

COLONIZATION

It can hardly be said that we have a traditional chronology for the Black Sea colonies. In fact, it is very likely that one never existed, but that a few correlations and synchronisms were made in the Hellenistic period. How valid these were is a further problem. There is no organized information for the colonies in Herodotus, such as Thucydides supplies for those of Sicily and Southern Italy. Despite his long account of the Scythians and Greeks of the Black Sea, we are told only that one foundation (Borysthenis) was Milesian.[21] Later sources have much to say about Milesian activity in the Black Sea, but the Eusebian chronology, presumably constructed out of this material, gives dates for only a few foundations: Istria (657) and Olbia (647) on the west and north shores, Trapezos (756) and Sinope II (631) on the south.[22] This is a surprisingly small number of foundation dates to have been preserved from Miletus' reputed ninety colonies and from Ionia, the home of the early logographers. Yet, one of the chief sources for Black Sea geography, Pseudo-Skymnos, made quite a different and more extensive series of synchronisms.[23] They are in general terms and are all related to events of Median and Persian history. The source of Pseudo-Skymnos is probably Demetrius of Kallatis, a writer of the late third century B.C. He should have been familiar with such records of Black Sea chronology as existed, particularly if he is correctly credited by Stephanus of Byzantium with a history of Odessa. Demetrius, however, found it necessary to date the foundations by general synchronizations with Median and Persian history. How he worked them out is unknown, but they accord

[19] Mimnermus frag. 11; since Aia, not Colchis, is given as Jason's destination, it is possible that the legend was not localized to the southeast corner of the Black Sea in Mimnermus' time.

[20] Below, n. 27.

[21] Her. 4.78.3; reported with a note of doubt.

[22] The dates of Istria, Olbia and Sinope are from J. K. Fotheringham's edition of Hieronymus, Trapezos from Eusebius. Eusebius' date for Trapezos implies that Sinope I was even earlier, since it was the traditional founder of Trapezos (Xenophon *Anabasis* 4.8.22).

[23] C. Müller, *GGM* I 196–237; A. R. Burn, *JHS* 55 (1935) 133–36.

with the archaeological evidence. Burn has stressed the importance of this variant chronology and it is worth reporting by way of contrast to that of Eusebius:

Apollonia (lines 730–33) is dated about 50 years before Cyrus (= *ca.* 610–600).

Chersonesus (lines 822–34) was founded by Heraclea (lines 972–75), itself founded when Cyrus conquered the Medes (= 560–50).

Istria (lines 767–72) was founded when the Scythian armies crossed into Asia in pursuit of the Cimmerians (in the reign of Ardys of Lydia; Her. 1.15, 106).

Kallatis (lines 761–64) was founded from Heraclea when Amyntas held rule over the Macedonians (*ca.* 520, the time of Darius' Scythian expedition).

Olbia (lines 809 ff.), at the time of the Median Empire (presumably 625–560).

Amisos (line 917) was founded four years before Heraclea (= *ca.* 560).

Sinope (lines 940 ff.): I, pre-Cimmerian (saga);[24] II, post-Cimmerian (presumably after the Cimmerians had been driven out of Phrygia by Alyattes in the early sixth century).

Odessa (lines 748–50) was founded when Astyages ruled Media (= 585–50).

The dates given by Pseudo-Skymnos for Istria and Olbia are shortly before and in the last quarter of the seventh century rather than near its middle where Eusebius had placed them.[25] This is in general agreement with the archaeological evidence of the pottery from those sites, and to them Apollonia should probably be added.[26] From Sinope pottery of the late seventh and early sixth century is now reported, and in Ak Alan, a native site inland about twenty miles from Amisos, some Greek sherds of *ca.* 600 have been found.[27] Chersonesus has been revealed as mainly a fifth century site,[28] and the case of Odessa is ambiguous. Some archaic material is reported from Kyalnetsky Bay, but that from the

[24] Ps.-Skymnos has a cautious δοκεῖ for this legend (line 948).

[25] Burn, *op. cit.*, p. 134.

[26] Cook, *op. cit.*, pp. 71–72, 76, n. 90; Aelian (*Var. Hist.* 3.17) states that Anaximander (born *ca.* 610) was the oekist of the colony at Apollonia. Hanfmann prefers an earlier date (*ca.* 650) for Istria as a result of his study of the "Ionian" cups (*The Aegean and the Near East*, p. 171, n. 19).

[27] Ak Alan, above, p. 47, n. 31; Sinope: the tradition of its foundation is very confused (Bilabel, *Philologus Supp.* 14 [1920] 30–40), but Herodotus (4.12.2) implies that its foundation as a Greek colony was after the Cimmerian invasion. Probably it had previously existed as a native town taken over by some Cimmerians in the seventh century. Then Milesian colonists settled towards the end of the century. For discussion of the date see Burn, *op. cit.*, p. 136; Cook, *op. cit.*, p. 72. Some excavation has been done recently and Corinthian pottery of the late seventh and early sixth century discovered. This is from a cemetery and possibly represents the earliest graves of the Greek colony (Akurgal and Budde, *Turk Tarih Kurumu Yayinlarindan* V, No. 14 [1956]). Amisos: The site of Amisos was also apparently occupied by a pre-Greek town (Eustathios schol. on *Il.* 2.852: Enete = Amisos). Its early history is confused, for Strabo, on the authority of Theopompus, states (12.3.14) that it was first colonized by Milesians, then was under Cappadocians and finally was colonized by Athenians, but there is a lacuna in his text. Ps.-Skymnos (917), however, states that it was a colony of the Phocaeans. He dates the foundation four years before Heraclea which, he says, was founded at the time of Cyrus' conquest of Media, *ca.* 560–550. According to this tradition, then, Amisos was founded *ca.* 560. Perhaps a solution for this state of the evidence is to assume that Amisos was a Phocaean foundation of *ca.* 600, which was refounded by Milesian colonists *ca.* 560.

[28] A. I. Tioumeneff, *Vestnik*, 1938, 2, 246–64. There is some material earlier than the mid-fifth century, which is considered to be the product of pre-colonization trade, but the earliest cemetery is said to have graves of the late fifth and fourth centuries; among them are graves of the Tauric population which the Greeks found in the area.

site proper is of the fifth century and later.[29] The only site seriously out of line is Amisos, but in the literary tradition of its founding there is some indication of a reinforcement in the course of the sixth century. Thus, on the basis of the evidence of Pseudo-Skymnos and of archaeology it seems likely that the beginning of colonization on some scale should be placed in the last quarter of the seventh century.

Archaeological evidence from some sites not mentioned by Pseudo-Skymnos helps to fill out the record. Settlement of the Cimmerian Bosporus probably started in the first half of the sixth century. Pottery of that period has been found on the acropolis of Panticapaeum. Theodosia has produced an Attic black-figured pot of *ca.* 560. Tiritake and Mirmake near Panticapaeum were probably a little later, since material from their excavation is dated 550–500. Phanagoria and Nymphaeum probably should be placed about the middle of the sixth century, along with Cercinitis on the Tauric peninsula.[30] The latter is mentioned by Hecataeus and Herodotus (*FGrHist* I, No. 184; Her. 4.55). In the archaic period there seem to have been three waves of colonization into the Black Sea. The earliest came in the last quarter of the seventh century and resulted in the establishment of Apollonia, Istria, Olbia, Sinope and, perhaps, Amisos. The second, in the first half of the sixth century, was directed mainly to the Cimmerian Bosporus in the area near Panticapaeum, but resulted also in the foundation of Heraclea and probably Odessa (Tyras). The colonies of the third wave in the latter half of the century were scattered: Kallatis, Cercinitis, Nymphaeum, Chersonesus, Mesembria, Phanagoria and probably Hermonassa. Evidently the sixth century was one of continuous settlement and development of the Euxine.

The earliest settlements, which demonstrate an excellent selection of key sites (Map IV), seem to have been very small in size and were evidently founded with fishing and trade in view. Apollonia,[31] near the modern Sozapol on the Bulgarian coast, was situated on the island of St. Cyriac, one of a group which closes off the harbor. Sozapol is an important modern fishing town with mackerel being the chief catch; on the adjacent mainland the fertile soil produces grain and vines. Since there does not seem to have been a native site on the island, it was presumably selected as offering safety to a small community. Istria,[32] at the edge of the Danube delta, was also on an island with no native town. It, too, was

[29] *Vestnik*, 1939, 2, 140–42. The record of the pottery found in 1924 at Kyalnetsky Bay, suggested as the site of the first trading factory, is not very definite. It speaks of early Ionian (seventh century) pottery and an archaic amphora from a tumulus.

[30] Panticapaeum: E. Diehl, "Pantikapaion," *RE* 18^3 (1949) 820–21; Tioumeneff, *Vestnik*, 1938, 2, 260; B. D. Blavatsky reports Greek pottery of the first half of the sixth century from the acropolis, *Vestnik*, 1946, 2, 158–59; Theodosia: A. Herrmann, "Theodosia," *RE* 5A (1934) 1921–22; the black-figured vase is by the painter of Acropolis 606 (Beazley, *The Development of Attic Black-Figure* 40); Tiritake and Mirmake: V. C. Gajdoukevitch, *Vestnik*, 1937, 1, 216 ff.; *ibid.*, 1939, 2, 129–34; see also E. Diehl, *op. cit.*, p. 784; Phanagoria: E. Diehl, "Phanagoreia," *RE* 19 (1938) 1751–57; *RE* 18^3 (1949) 785; Bilabel, *op. cit.*, p. 197; M. M. Kobylina, *Vestnik*, 1938, 2, 336–49; the earliest material found in the excavation was late archaic, *AJA* 49 (1945) 103; Nymphaeum: M. M. Khudiak, *Sov. Ark.* 16 (1952) 232–58; E. Diehl, "Nymphaion," *RE* 17 (1936) 1600–03; Cercinitis: Minns, *op. cit.*, p. 490.

[31] For the siting see Short, *LAAA* 24 (1937) 142–45.

[32] For the siting see Short, *op. cit.*, pp. 148–50.

in a good fishing district with access by water to the delta region and, to judge by the remains of shells, near mussel beds. While a considerable amount of archaic pottery has been found on the site, it came from unstratified deposits. Unfortunately it was not possible to make out a plan nor trace the town's growth, for excavation was hindered by Byzantine walls. The sites of Berezan and Olbia were on the estuaries of the Bug and Dnieper Rivers, which facilitated communication with the interior, in this case the grain-producing area of South Russia, to which Herodotus devoted a very laudatory account (4.53, 82). At present Berezan[33] is an island but was probably made so by the action of the rivers, and the original settlement was on the tip of a peninsula. Since there was no preceding native town, the settlers had security. The settlement was small, and it probably served only as a fishing factory until the inhabitants moved over to Olbia in the second quarter of the fifth century. Olbia[34] seems to have been founded about the same time as Berezan but remained relatively unimportant until the middle of the century. The Greeks found the natives hostile at first, for its fortification wall was built soon after the foundation. Since, however, native burials of the mid-sixth century are found in the cemetery to the northeast of the town, trade relations and fusion probably started fairly soon. The town was set partly on the river bank, partly on the cliff above and grew at first in irregular fashion, for its Hippodamian plan was not introduced until *ca.* 500. Early Sinope and Amisos are almost unknown archaeologically as yet, so that we must rely on general considerations to explain their function. Leaf has done so admirably for Sinope.[35] It had the only good harbor on the south coast, and from it the shortest crossing to the north side could be made. Like Thasos it was admirably situated to become an emporion for its area, founding small dependent colonies which offered access to the interior. Its best known export was ultimately Cappadocian miltos, but probably in the first instance the fishing was the chief attraction for settlement. Amisos may not have been founded until *ca.* 560, but it soon began to develop trade relations with the natives, which led to the export of the famed Chalybian steel.[36] All the earliest colonies were traditionally Milesian in origin, except Apollonia, for which there is a notice of Rhodian participation,[37] and perhaps Amisos. They were trading factories, which took root and developed because of favorable natural facilities and a demand for their products in the Aegean. Evidently this character was retained well into the fifth century, since Herodotus refers to them collectively as emporia.[38] We can hardly expect to tie their foundation and growth to any particular occasion in Milesian history. The inital exploration of the Black Sea was a corollary to the movement into eastern Thrace and the Propontis, which resulted from over-population

[33] Von Stern, *Klio* 9 (1909) 142–44; Pharmakovsky, *AA* 21–28 (1904–10), excavation reports; Minns, *op. cit.*, pp. 338–39, 451–53; Slavin, *Olbia* I 8; Cook, *JHS* 66 (1946) 75–76.

[34] Excavation reports in *AA* from 1897 to 1914; Minns, *op. cit.*, pp. 453 ff.; E. Diehl, "Olbia," *RE* 17 (1936) 2405–23; *idem, Gnomon* 8 (1932) 545–48; Slavin, *Olbia* I; Cook, *op. cit.*, p. 76, n. 90; Tioumeneff, *Vestnik*, 1938, 2, 259. A plan of the excavations is published by E. H. Minns, *JHS* 65 (1945) 109–12.

[35] Leaf, *JHS* 36 (1916) 1–15.

[36] Above, p. 103.

[37] Steph. Byz. *s.v.*

[38] Her. 4.17.1, 20.1, 24, 108. For Herodotus' use of the term see Roebuck, *CP* 46 (1951), p. 219, n. 22.

and the difficulties caused by Lydian and Cimmerian raids in Ionia. Settlement and the development of trade presumably were a response to the need of imported food in Ionia and the Aegean. Perhaps the initial movement received direction and encouragement from Thrasyboulos of Miletus with whose tyranny it coincided, but we can hardly assume that Miletus' discontented aristocrats sailed off to the Black Sea to trade and found colonies.[39] The vigorous development of the sixth century is a part of the general economic growth of Ionia and Greece as a whole.

In the first half of the sixth century the second wave of colonization opened up the important district of the Cimmerian Bosporus. The pot from Temir Gora near Kertch indicates that it had been known from *ca.* 630, but intensive settlement resulted only after the establishment of the primary colonies. In some respects this region had the most interesting development of any of the colonies, for out of it grew the Bosporan Kingdom in the fifth century from the fusion of Greek and native elements.[40] The claim of Panticapaeum, the center of the later Kingdom, to be the mother-city of the whole region seems justified by the archaeological evidence, but Theodosia, which ultimately became the chief port for the Kingdom, must also have been early.[41] Despite its poor harbor, it was near good wheat land. It is likely that the motives of Greek settlement were purposes of trade, since the Greeks settled in a heavily populated district. There were initial difficulties, as the early fortifications of Panticapaeum indicate, but, to judge from the sequel, a speedy and strong fusion resulted as in Olbia. Here again the colonization was traditionally Milesian, but with some other elements[42] perhaps to be associated with the settlement of Heraclea in the same period.

The foundation of Heraclea[43] (Eregli in Bithynia) represents an intrusion into the generally Ionian area of the Black Sea. Its colonists came from Megara and Boeotia, and the choice of site was probably predetermined by the existence of the Ionian areas of trade at the west end of the Black Sea, at the mouths of the Danube, Bug, Dniester and Dnieper, and at Sinope. The colonists chose a harbor site on the south coast, which would provide a stopping place on the run to Sinope and which was visited by the tunny fish. Perhaps, too, the availability of timber in Bithynia was an attraction. It was very scarce on the north shore of the Euxine (Her. 4.61.1) and must have been in demand by the growing colonies. The town grew rapidly, for by the end of the sixth century secondary colonies were planted at Kallatis and Chersonesus.[44]

The third wave of colonization filled in the existing clusters of settlements: Kallatis[45] (Mangalia) in the Dobrudja, Mesembria (Nesebin) across the bay from Apollonia, Cer-

[39] They remained at home to create difficulties in the early part of the sixth century: Her. 5.28–29; Phocylides frags. 5, 7, 12 (Bergk).

[40] Rostovtzeff, *Skythen und der Bosporus.*

[41] Minns, *op. cit.*, pp. 555–56.

[42] Bilabel, *op. cit.*, pp. 26–27.

[43] Bilabel, *op. cit.*, p. 153.

[44] Minns, *op. cit.*, pp. 493 ff.

[45] Kallatis: Bilabel, *op. cit.*, pp. 17–18; T. Sauciuc-Saveanu, *Dacia* (1924) 109–10; Short, *op. cit.*, pp. 146–48.

cinitis in the Tauric peninsula near Eupatoria, Chersonesus near Sevastopol, Phanagoria and Hermonassa in the Taman peninsula across from Panticapaeum. These are all in varying degrees second choice sites and reflect the growth of Greek population in the Euxine and of a trade which was reaching out to fringe areas and poorer anchorages. Kallatis, for example, a secondary foundation from Heraclea, was on a completely exposed coast but did have access to good agricultural land. Mesembria,[46] while enjoying the same advantages in general as Apollonia, had an inferior site. Cercinitis[47] was also in an exposed position but had a good plain. The latter two are traditionally Milesian, but Phanagoria and Hermonassa[48] were Tean colonies, planted in strong native districts. Perhaps their settlers were refugees from Teos after the Persian conquest *ca.* 540, and the choice of sites reflects the fact that good localities were becoming scarce. The selection of Chersonesus probably indicates the knitting together of the Euxine colonies in the latter part of the century, for it was a useful port of call on crossings to Olbia from the south shore or from Olbia to the towns in the Cimmerian Bosporus.

On the whole, it seems that motives of trade were the chief factor in the selection of settlements throughout the sixth century. In the Greek tradition we hear a considerable amount about the rigors of life and the difficulties of navigation on the Black Sea.[49] The Greeks evidently found it uncongenial and did not get into its pleasanter areas, the warm valleys of the Crimea. Instead, the colonies were on islands, on peninsulas and at river mouths, where fog and cold winds are frequent. The incentive to settle lay evidently in the hope of profits from trading the raw products of the area, which were needed to feed the growing population of Greece. New land for large scale settlement was not available, since the native population was large. Apparently it was also feared, if we may judge from the legends of Medea and Iphigenia and the relegation of Prometheus to a peak in the Caucasus. Yet, the colonies helped to solve the problems of overpopulation and unemployment by providing a new supply of food and a market for Greek manufactured goods, as well as an enlargement of the shipping to carry them.

TRADE

It is not possible in the present state of publication of the archaic pottery from the sites to make a detailed analysis of the various fabrics and of their distribution. For example, the East Greek pottery from Istria has been well published in a monograph by Lambrino,[50] but the Corinthian and Attic from the site are mentioned in general terms only. Much material from the old excavations at Berezan, Olbia and Panticapaeum is published but identified by out-moded classifications and often not illustrated. Material from the Soviet excavations is frequently published in brief summary only and poorly illustrated. Perhaps

[46] Short, *op. cit.*, pp. 145–46.

[47] Minns, *op. cit.*, pp. 490–91; *ATL* I 496–97.

[48] Phanagoria: above, note 30; Hermonassa: Steph. Byz. *s.v.*; M. M. Kobylina *op. cit.*, pp. 336–49.

[49] Strabo 7.3.18; 2.1.16; Aristotle *Prob.* 25.6; Minns, *op. cit.*, pp. 5 ff.

[50] M. Lambrino, *Les vases archaiques d'Histria*; some adjustment of the dating is made by R. M. Cook in his review *JHS* 59 (1939) 148–49; see also *JHS* 66 (1946) 76 and *BSA* 44 (1949) 160–61.

the pottery from Istria is indicative of the situation as a whole. There, no local ware seems to have been made at first by the Greek settlers, so that the pottery used by the colony for its various purposes was imported. It was mainly East Greek from various Ionian centers. Probably traders from Miletus, the mother-city, carried a considerable amount of pottery from other towns and redistributed the Black Sea products on their homeward voyage.[51] The various fabrics identified at Istria are: Rhodian in moderate quantity and a variety of shapes (amphoras, dinoi, oinochoai, cups, plates and a fragment of a relief pithos); a considerable amount of Chiot ware in its usual shapes of the sixth century; a few pieces of Aeolian have been tentatively identified, and there is some Fikellura of the mid-sixth century. If these fine wares are a guide to the coarser fabrics, the southern East Greek states, Miletus, Samos and Rhodes, had most of the trade in their hands. Chios is the only northern state definitely represented, although some bucchero was found which may come from Lesbos. This East Greek material was both the earliest at Istria and continued in large volume to the end of the sixth century. The amount of Corinthian is said to have been relatively small, and the time of its coverage is not clear; its most common shape is apparently the aryballos. The Attic black-figure on the other hand is relatively abundant, but only for the last half of the sixth century as elsewhere. Its importation started with some cup fragments of *ca.* 570, and cups continued to be very popular. A few lekythoi are also mentioned, but Lambrino reports that few unguent vases were found. Probably the chief source of oil and perfume for the Istrians was the East Greek area.

The pottery from Berezan and Olbia gives the same impression as that of Istria.[52] The identifiable East Greek fabrics are "Rhodian" in large quantity, Chiot in good quality and fair quantity, some Fikellura and a mass of the ordinary products of the East Greek *koine*. There is a little Attic black-figure before 550, but it grew rapidly in volume only after that date, reaching substantial proportions in the last quarter of the century. As it grew the Corinthian faded out: there is a fair amount of Early Corinthian, Middle Corinthian and some Late Corinthian I and II, but by 550 it had obviously lost its popularity. In general, Corinthian was found on the sites as early as the East Greek material and was as widely distributed but in much smaller volume. It is reported from Istria, Olbia, Berezan, Panticapaeum, Tiritake and Sinope.[53] Alabastra and aryballoi are the most common shapes. There seems to be enough pottery to attest that Corinthian ships traded in the Black Sea from the date of its opening until the middle of the sixth century, as might be expected

[51] Some potters' kilns which manufactured amphoras for the sanctuary at Nymphaeum (*ca.* 550–500) have been excavated (*Sov. Ark.* 16 [1952] 249 ff.; for the type see Hanfmann, *op. cit.*, pp. 178–80). For the pottery from Istria: Lambrino, *op. cit.*, pp. 20 ff.; for the Chiot see R. M. Cook, *BSA* 44 (1949) 160–61. Cook has informed me in a letter of the Attic black-figure cups.

[52] See the pottery bibliography given by Diehl, "Olbia," *RE* 17 (1936) 2418–19.

[53] Istria: Lambrino, *op. cit.*, pp. 22 ff.; there is no Protocorinthian and relatively little Corinthian; Olbia: Slavin, *Olbia* I, p. 106, Nos. 870, 2690, pl. X, 8; Payne, *op. cit.*, Nos. 230, 338, 373 (Early Corinthian); Payne lists a number of other Corinthian pieces from Olbia or South Russia: Nos. 788, 842A, 843, 867, 872, 918, 1079A are Middle Corinthian; Nos. 1206, 1215, 1264A, 1294, 1367–69, 1397, 1466 are Late Corinthian I; No. 1519 is Late Corinthian II; Berezan: the unsatisfactory condition of the pottery for study is noted by Cook, *JHS* 66 (1946) 75–76; Panticapaeum: *AA* 18 (1903) 83; Tiritake: *Vestnik*, 1939, 2, 129–34; Sinope: above, note 27.

from the considerable amount of Corinthian pottery found in Aeolis and the Troad.[54] Certainly, the opening of this new area was reflected in Corinthian tradition by the story of Medea and the various references attributed to Eumelus.

Pottery, then, was evidently an article of trade in considerable volume, imported to take care of the ordinary and luxury needs of the Greek colonists and, as its presence in native burials indicates, traded also with the natives nearby and far inland from the colonies. It also packaged the oil and wine needed in the early years of the colonies and some unguents and perfumes. The greater part of this trade throughout the whole of the sixth century was in East Greek hands, probably those of Miletus and Chios, with Samos, Phocaea and Lesbos having a smaller share. From the inception of the trade until the mid-sixth century Corinth participated. After that date it was probably replaced by Aeginetan and Attic traders, who found their full opportunity in the fifth century after the Ionian Revolt.

The trade between the Aegean and the Black Sea has usually been represented as an exchange of the products of Greek specialized agriculture, wine and oil, and of industry for the natural products of the Black Sea area, particularly fish and grain.[55] In this exchange the Greek colonies are pictured as both markets for and distributing centers of the Greek goods to the native population. This picture seems substantially correct, although some qualifications on the score of date and volume should be made for the archaic period. It is salutary to remember that most of our literary evidence for the grain trade is from the fourth century B.C., when the Athenian organization of the trade is known in some detail. The first explicit mention of the articles of trade from the Black Sea is by Polybius (4.38):

"For as regards necessities it is an undisputed point that the most plentiful supplies and best qualities of cattle and slaves reach us from the countries lying round the Pontus, while among luxuries the same countries furnish us with an abundance of honey, wax and preserved fish, while of the superfluous produce of our countries they take olive oil and every kind of wine. As for grain there is a give-and-take, they sometimes supplying us when we require it and sometimes importing it from us."

This, of course, is the pattern of trade in the second century B.C., after the organization of the native peoples around the Sea into centralized states and the development of local industry.

In the archaic period the situation differed considerably. Herodotus' description of Darius' march though Thrace indicates that eastern Thrace was completely unurbanized and its people lived in semi-nomadic, tribal organizations. Presumably those who dwelt on the coast were anything but hospitable, if Archilochus' picture of their wrecking activities is correct. The Greeks could trade with them only in considerable danger from piracy and seizure of their goods. In Scythia proper, from the mouth of the Danube eastward, the Scythian invaders had probably organized centralized kingdoms by the sixth

[54] Above, pp. 78, 112.

[55] Rostovtzeff, *Iranians and Greeks*, c. IV; Myres, *CAH* III 664–66; Bilabel, *op. cit.*, pp. 60–66; Minns, *op. cit.*, pp. 440–44; J. Röhlig, *Der Handel von Milet*; M. Dunham, *History of Miletus*; Cook, *op. cit.*, pp. 82, 85.

century and were in a position to exploit the agricultural labor of the native people whom they had conquered.[56] The northeastern and Caucasian shores of the Sea were in the possession of mountain tribes. The centers of the Phrygian kingdom, under Lydian control after *ca.* 600, were far inland, and presumably their chief connections with the Greek world lay through Lydia and the river valleys rather than through the Black Sea. Any trade in volume was with the Scythians rather than with the other people of the coast. Of the main products of the area, fish, grain and cattle, the latter two could only be supplied by the river valleys of Scythia, while the fish were in the sea for the taking. Accordingly, it seems probable that the first object of trade from the Black Sea was its fish. The fish had to be exported in some preserved form, dried, salted or in a sauce, and the preparation and packing entailed some organization of the export trade in shore stations.[57]

The impression made by the choice of location and character of the earliest Greek settlements is that they were chosen with this end in view. The favorite type of site is an island as at Apollonia or a peninsula tip like Sinope and Berezan. The settlements were in areas where the fishing grounds are best. In the case of Apollonia the modern town is the chief center for Bulgarian fishing in the Black Sea; the other archaic settlements of this coast are at the Danube estuary (Istria) and in the northwest corner (Odessa), where good fishing waters exist. Herodotus comments on the supply of fish in the Borysthenis and Strabo on the tunny run at Sinope.[58] The runs of fish from the Black Sea into the Propontis evidently caught the attention of the Greek colonists there, and the initial push into the Black Sea was probably an attempt to find good fishing grounds. This specialized fishing industry seems to have developed in the seventh century, for Hesiod mentions pickled fish, perhaps indicating the Bosporus as a source of supply. In the writers of the sixth century like Hipponax these special fish products are a commonplace of luxurious eating.[59] The supply of fresh fish was local and a non-luxury product, which the abundantly stocked waters of the west coast of Asia Minor could supply. If, then, export of preserved fish was a luxury trade, we should be careful not to ascribe any great volume to it. Its products could be carried in relatively few ships and might have a rather wide distribution, but it served the comparatively small, wealthy group who, like the Lampsacene eunuch of Hipponax, could afford such luxuries, the rich man regularly, the poor man only very occasionally.

Probably, so far as the Black Sea stations were concerned, the first fishing was seasonal. The Greek crews would catch and preserve the fish at convenient points and depart at the end of the season; as the demand grew, it would seem advantageous to establish a permanent factory for the storage of gear and its preparation to await the boats at the start of the next year's navigation season, thus making possible the carriage of heavier cargoes. A relatively small number of Greeks could man such stations, and, while their number might grow, a rise in population and the choice of sites for other types of trading

[56] Rostovtzeff, *op. cit.*, pp. 41 ff.

[57] S. Séménov-Zouser, *Vestnik*, 1947, 2, pp. 237–46.

[58] Her. 4.53; Strabo 12.3.11; 7.6.2; Minns, *op. cit.*, pp. 6–7.

[59] Athenaeus 116a (Hesiod); Hipponax frag. 39.

might wait for some time. In the Black Sea we find a period of very slight trading activity from *ca.* 675 to 625, then apparently the establishment of regular factories and the development of a more complex trade in the last quarter of the seventh and throughout the sixth centuries.

This trade in preserved fish was largely a Greek operation and hardly involved an exchange of goods with the native population. If we may judge by their more modern counterparts, life in such fishing factories was not comfortable. Perhaps Berezan island offers a hint in this respect. That fishing was its main *raison d'être* seems confirmed by the fishing gear, hooks, and the "fish" currency found in its late archaic graves. The pottery from Berezan does not include any fine pieces and is average or poor in quality. Significantly, too, the Berezan graves, in contrast to those of Olbia, do not have any jewelry and metal *objets d'art*.[60] If the fish trade enriched any one, it was not the fishermen and workers in the stations but the owners of the boats who engaged in the trade, the Ionians and some of the citizens from the Propontis colonies. It provided a living for a few men and their families in the stations. The case, however, was different for the other products of the Black Sea area, the agricultural produce and metals.

By the end of the archaic period the export of grain from the Black Sea had reached substantial proportions and was regularly supplying some cities of mainland Greece as well as of Ionia. In his account of Xerxes' expedition Herodotus tells an anecdote (7.147) about Xerxes watching ships loaded with grain proceeding down the Hellespont to their destinations in Aegina and the Peloponnesus. When asked why he did not stop them, Xerxes replied that they were carrying his own provisions, since he expected to conquer the regions for which they were bound. While we may legitimately question the anecdote, there is no reason to doubt the circumstances that provoked it, the Persians had evidently made no attempt to cut off the export of grain from the Black Sea to Greece during the Persian Wars. It is hardly surprising that Xerxes did not stop the traffic, for conceptions of economic warfare were undeveloped. Throughout the years of Athenian-Persian rivalry in the fifth century Athenian goods entered Al Mina, and Athenian silver purchased Egyptian wheat in Naukratis.[61] There is no valid reason to deny that the Black Sea area was supplying grain to Greece in the early fifth century. The carriers for Aegina and the Peloponnesus were probably Aeginetan ships, which had taken the place of Corinthian about the middle of the century. To judge from the quantity of Athenian pottery on the sites, Athens presumably carried the grain which she purchased in Athenian bottoms after 525. The need for foreign grain in Greece in this period is apparent from the terms of Gelon's conditional acceptance of the Greek alliance (Her. 7.158), in which he offered to supply the Greek forces with Sicilian grain. So far as East Greece is concerned, we do not have such explicit evidence, but it is to be remembered that Histiaeus made a practice of stopping Ionian merchantmen as they came out of the Black Sea during the latter years of the Ionian Revolt (Her. 6.5.3; 26.1). At this time the mainland of Asia Minor was largely in Persian hands, and the Greek cities had to supply themselves from elsewhere.

[60] Minns, *op. cit.*, pp. 415–16.
[61] Sutherland, *AJP* 64 (1943) 140 ff.

Perhaps Herodotus also indicates the beginning of the grain trade. When Alyattes was besieging Miletus in yearly raids in the late seventh century, destroying the crops and trees in the countryside, the Milesians are said to have lived in part on imported grain.[62] This coincides with the foundations of Naukratis and Olbia.

It is very probable that the main center of the grain trade in the archaic period was Olbia,[63] for the archaeological evidence indicates that the development of this area preceded that of the Cimmerian Bosporus, which was so important to Athens in the fourth century. For the grain trade a different organization was necessary than for the fishing industry. The grain exported was the surplus of Scythian agriculture carried on in the river valleys and their tributaries.[64] It had to be collected and brought down the rivers, stored and loaded on the ships. In this activity, as for the other agricultural produce (cattle, hides, honey and wax), the Greek colonists were presumably the middlemen and in a position to make what profit they could from the business. They would approach the Scythian chieftains for permission to trade and organize the transport for their purchases. The trade was a barter transaction, in which they exchanged imported Greek goods for the produce. Eventually these were placed in the tumuli of the Scythian kings. As the Scythians developed a taste for such imported objects, Greek workmen might find a market for their skills, as the stonework in some of the tombs indicates.[65] The development of Olbia and the date of the imports in the earliest tumuli should indicate the time when this trade began to develop considerable proportions. By the middle of the sixth century Olbia had grown to an appreciable size and wealth, to judge from its city wall, the houses and the amount of pottery from the site; *ca.* 500 it was reorganized on a new plan and extended considerably. We might conclude that the grain trade began in the first half of the century and was reaching sizable proportions at its end. The earliest Greek metal objects found in the Scythian tombs date from that time,[66] while the range of Greek trade had extended up the rivers into the interior. Most of the objects traded were of Ionian (and Iranian) origin, as might be expected. Athenian and Corinthian payment to the colonists is apparent in the quantity of pottery found, but the case of Aegina is not clear. Perhaps the Aeginetans found their opportunity in the Black Sea mainly in the early fifth century.

After the Ionian Revolt Miletus and Chios in particular were temporarily crippled, and Athens preoccupied with the threat of further war against the Persians as well as a struggle with Aegina in its own waters. Perhaps in this hostility there is a reflection of Athenian-Aeginetan trade rivalry in the Black Sea. To the colonies in the Black Sea the slackening of Ionian and Athenian trade meant the loss of imports necessary for their own livelihood and for trading with the Scythians. Aegina with its extensive trade in the Aegean was in a position to supply them, particularly with needed metals. Probably the Aeginetans had

[62] Her. 1.17–22; Roebuck, *CP* 45 (1950), p. 245, n. 36. The grain may have come from other Ionian states or from Egypt.

[63] Her. 4.53; this applies primarily to the fifth century.

[64] Minns, *op. cit.*, 1 ff; Her. 4.16–18, 24.

[65] Rostovtzeff, *op. cit.*, pp. 75 ff.

[66] Minns, *op. cit.*, pp. 150, 375–77 (bronzes); 205 ff., 236 ff. (gold).

already brought metals to trade from the outset, since they had no pottery fabric or industry of their own. In any case, the Ionian Revolt ended the dominating position which the Ionians had enjoyed in the Black Sea from the time of its opening.

The trade which they had established was evidently of great value to them and to Greece as a whole. The Ionians were enabled to augment their own grain supply, probably at cheaper cost than in Egypt where silver had to be exchanged, while in the Black Sea their own industrial products, pottery, olive oil and wine could find a market. As well as for their own use they probably carried fish and grain to other Greek states in the Aegean and controlled the export of Chalybian steel and Sinopic miltos.

CHAPTER IX

The Pattern of Trade

In the course of the archaic period the Ionian Greeks successfully solved the economic problems with which they had been confronted, the shortage of metals and of food for their growing population; in addition they fed the appetite for luxuries which increasing wealth stimulated. Their success is attested by the high level of population and material prosperity in the latter part of the sixth century. The prosperity was not only a subject for criticism in literature but has left impressive material remains. In Ionia were three of the most grandiose shrines of archaic Greece, the Heraion of Samos, the temple of Artemis at Ephesus and the shrine at Branchidae. This prosperity rested mainly on the network of trade and colonization which we have traced in some detail. It remains to summarize its growth and to evaluate its significance in more general historical terms.

Modern historians of Greece until recently had tended to describe its early economic development in terms of a more or less explicit analogy with that of modern Europe.[1] Their language was the quasi-political vocabulary of mercantile imperialism, and they spoke of monopolies and closed areas of trade, of intrusions into these, of the exchange of the raw materials from colonies for manufactured goods of mother-cities. Deliberate policies of colonial development and the economic motivation of political alignments and actions were emphasized. A generation ago, Johannes Hasebroek, in his book entitled *Staat und Handel im Alten Griechenland* sharply criticised such reconstruction and proposed a drastic revision of archaic Greek development.[2] The presumed political interest

[1] Such views are exemplified by books like G. Glotz, *Ancient Greece at Work*, P. N. Ure, *The Origin of Tyranny* and most of the text books and histories currently in use. They are criticized in particular by J. Hasebroek, *Trade and Politics in Ancient Greece* (translated by L. M. Fraser and D. C. MacGregor) 44ff., and less explicitly by F. M. Heichelheim in his general study of ancient economic history, *Das Wirtschaftsgeschichte des Altertums* I; see also M. I. Finkelstein, *CP* 30 (1935) 320, 332–36 (on the organization of trade) and E. Will, *Korinthiaka*, *passim*.

[2] Hasebroek, *Staat und Handel im Alten Griechenland* (*Trade and Politics* 44–71); see also his *Griechische Wirtschafts- und Gesellschafts-Geschichte bis zur Perserzeit*.

of Greek states in mercantile imperialism was denied or reduced to a slight exchange of luxury goods, and the importation of grain on a large scale considered a development of Athenian imperialism in the fifth century. The first revision, strictly speaking, seems to be largely correct; the network of archaic Greek trade was woven by the individual efforts of Greek traders, not by deliberate policies of their governments to establish markets and use economic tools in diplomacy and warfare. Yet, we have noticed that in the seventh century the lines of trade in the Aegean seemed to follow the lines of political alignment among states. Probably, however, that merely reflected the fact that, in a period when the dividing line between trade and piracy was thin, ships could find haven in the harbors of their captain's "guest-friends" or their state's *proxenoi*, if the latter institution was established. These trading ties dissolved in the sixth century, when trading had become much more general. But certain areas were established as markets like that of Corinth in Sicily or of Ionia in the Black Sea. The dominating position of these states was lost, if not by action of the Athenian government, at least by the work of Athenian craftsmen and traders which brought prosperity to their state in its turn. Certainly, to separate the trader from his city-state and place trade and crafts in the hands of metics, non-citizens, as Hasebroek did,[3] is unrealistic, particularly in the archaic period. Colaeus recorded his gratitude for a safe return from Spain to his native Samian goddess, the Greeks at Naukratis established ancestral shrines in their new town, and Herodotus seems to associate the growth of the new commercial group in Lydia (and Ionia) with the use of coinage. Trade and industry on a small scale became a new source of livelihood for many citizens in certain Greek city-states, not an activity carried on for them by foreigners.

Hasebroek's minimization of the volume of archaic trade and the characterization of its goods as almost entirely luxuries are equally faulty. Reviewers have pointed out his misconception of the organization of the pottery industry, the failure to appreciate its mass production and his omission of the evidence of coinage.[4] A consideration of the surviving articles of trade by themselves, however, does give an impression of an exchange of objects which are luxuries by their intrinsic value or by their nature: some goods of precious metal, the bric à brac of faience, terracotta figurines and the like. Aside from the pottery there is scarcely evidence of a volume of trade—and a large amount of pottery could be packed in even a small Greek ship. Unless the existence of a volume trade in essential commodities can be established, it is hardly possible to argue that this new activity was a potent factor in the social development of the city-state.

From a review of Ionian trade its characterization should fall between these two extremes. If our population figures are approximately correct, the Ionians needed to import food; their activity in the Black Sea and in Egypt can scarcely be explained except as a search for food, since the trading factories were small and drained off only a small amount of the surplus population. We know from the literary evidence that by the early fifth century both the Black Sea area and Egypt were regarded in a matter-of-fact way as

[3] Hasebroek, *Trade and Politics*, pp. 22 ff., 64.

[4] C. H. V. Sutherland, *AJP* 64 (1943) 129–31; see also A. W. Gomme, *Essays in Greek History and Literature* 42–66.

producing grain to feed Greece.[5] It seems clear that the Ionians should be credited with the development of importation of grain in volume in the course of the sixth century. Perhaps Corinth had used Sicilian grain in the seventh for the same purpose.

Ionian exploitation of the sources of metal for the Greek states was also of fundamental importance. This did not require any great volume of shipping, since a small, highly priced commodity was concerned, but it provided a very valuable trading asset as well as taking care of their own needs. Close at hand was Lydia with its supply of electrum. Phocaeans apparently carried tin and high-grade bronze from Spain; Chios brought silver from the Thraco-Macedonian mines and Ionian colonies tapped the area of production of Chalybian steel.

Another valuable item of Ionian trade was pottery, although the distribution tended to be local or among the Ionian trading factories. Unlike Corinthian and, in its turn, Attic, Ionian wares did not serve the general needs of Greece and large foreign areas. Little has been found, for example, in the Aegean and mainland Greece. It was not an important article of trade with Egyptians, Phoenicians, Syrians or Cypriotes, but the mass of Ionian pottery from the Black Sea sites, particularly Istria, and the scarcity of local wares indicate that Ionia provided the fine and ordinary china for the trading factories there. The same is true of Naukratis. In these instances we do seem to have a clear-cut example of the industrial production of a mother-city being absorbed by its colonies. Further, although this demands a separate treatment, Ionian ware had considerable popularity in southern Italy in the sixth century, where it was plainly a significant article of trade with foreign states.[6]

In addition, the Ionians traded the special commodities of their own agriculture and workshops. From the dedications of Chiot merchants in Aegina we may suspect that Chian wine was exported to that island, and Chiot amphoras have been found in Corinthian wells of the sixth century.[7] Wine and probably olive oil were sent to Naukratis and the other colonies. These and other perishable commodities like unguents and textiles have left only a slight trace in the archaeological and literary evidence. Ionian access to metals stimulated the growth of metal-working crafts, which supplemented the largely domestic industry of textile weaving. Probably the latter moved from the household to the small factory in the sixth century. The metal work, at least, has left some trace in the literary allusions to innovations by Ionian craftsmen and in the finds in sanctuaries and graves.

We should hardly speak of closed trading areas and monopolies or of deliberate economic policy in the acquisition and distribution of these articles of trade, nor does their absence indicate an addiction to the principles of free trade. The economic activity of archaic Greece marked a vigorous transition from the primitive forms of Homeric society

[5] Her. 7.147; 6.5.3, 26. 1(Black Sea); Bacchylides frag. 20, lines 9–11 (Egypt).

[6] For Ionian trade with Sicily and South Italy see Dunbabin, *The Western Greeks*, 225–58 and *passim*. In the seventh century it seems to have been almost entirely in Rhodian hands; in the sixth Phocaea, Miletus and Samos were the chief Ionian states represented—Phocaeans en route to Spain, Miletus by its Sybarite connection and Samos with its influence on the art of the southern Italian colonies and by the pottery exported to them.

[7] *Hesperia* 7 (1938), p. 608, No. 219; above, p. 84, n. 55.

to the commercial imperialism of the Athenian Empire, but it provoked only moral speculations about the individual's place in the process, not that of his society. Certain areas of the Mediterranean were exploited mainly by Ionians: eastern Thrace, the Propontis, the Black Sea, Egypt and Spain, but other states, like Aegina, Corinth, Rhodes and Athens had a share in them. Also, certain Ionian cities played a more predominant part than others, like Phocaea in Spain, Miletus in the Propontis and the Black Sea, Chios in Thrace and Naukratis. Unlike the major trading cities of mainland Greece, the trading of the Ionians seems to have been a more collective enterprise of its sea-going states than one confined to a particular city. The varied Ionian pottery from Istria and Naukratis indicates that characteristic. It is not simply that we are unable to classify the pottery as specifically as would be desirable, but there existed in Ionia a closer cultural and political union among the states of its League than between any political units in mainland Greece. While it was not strong enough to weld the cities into a single state, which might have used the economic tools which their citizens forged, yet, in solving the problem of food supply by long distance importation, in the carriage of metals and in establishing joint trading factories, the Ionians were pointing the way to political and large-scale use of economic resources. Their organization of trade occupied an interesting transitional phase between the purely personal enterprises in single ships of the eighth and seventh centuries and the deliberate policies of the Athenian Empire. Histiaeus, engaged in stopping Ionian traffic through the Hellespont, was half-pirate and half-politician, but Athens' control of the distribution of trade goods in the late fifth century was wholly political:

"If one may descend to more trifling particulars, it is to this same lordship of the sea that the Athenians owe the discovery, in the first place, of many of the luxuries of life through intercourse with many countries. Thus it is that the choice things of Sicily and Italy, of Cyprus and Egypt and Lydia, of Pontus and Peloponnesus, or wherever else it may be, are all swept, as it were, into one center, and all owing, as I say, to their maritime empire...

"They alone are able to possess the wealth of Greek and Barbarian. If any city is wealthy in ship timber, where will it dispose of its product, unless it persuades the ruler of the seas? What other course for the city rich in iron, bronze or linen?"[8]

The best example of the typical Ionian trading factory is Naukratis, about which we know something from both the literary and archaeological evidence.[9] Regular Greek contacts with Egypt were apparently established about the middle of the seventh century, when Psammetichos I began the reconsolidation of the Delta region. Previously there had perhaps been sporadic trading, varied by piracy when the opportunity offered. Odysseus, on one occasion, spun a finely elaborated story representing himself as a Cretan pirate

[8] Ps.-Xen. *Ath. Pol.* 2.7, 11.

[9] This section is drawn from my articles in *CP* 45 (1950) 236–47 and 46 (1951) 212–20. Al Mina can hardly be used as an example, for it was Cycladic, Rhodian and Cypriote. Archaic Olbia and Emporion are known by pottery rather than by their topography or organization, for Olbia's reconstruction on a Hippodamian plan dates from *ca.* 500; about that time, too, Emporion moved from its peninsula to the adjacent shore (Olbia: E. Diehl, "Olbia," *RE* 17 [1937] 2413–17, 2422; Emporion: above, p. 95, n. 49).

making descents on Egypt and bargains with a Phoenician merchant. Regular trading in some volume would only be possible after the foundation of Naukratis, when merchants found it worth their while to settle and build warehouses. The archaeological evidence indicates that the town was established in the last quarter of the seventh century.[10] It was perhaps in the first instance a settlement of Milesian mercenary soldiers used by Psammetichos I, but very soon after its foundation other Greeks began to come. They were allowed to settle on land granted by the King and to erect shrines to their native deities.

A study of the pottery, however, which was dedicated in the shrines indicates that at an early date they were used in common by Greeks of various origins. This feeling of unity evidently grew quickly among the residents, as the common problems of life in a new community presented themselves. Perhaps in the time of Amasis, in the second quarter of the sixth century, a common sanctuary, the Hellenion, was founded. Herodotus tells us that it was established by Chios, Teos, Phocaea, Klazomenai, Rhodes, Cnidus, Halicarnassus, Phaselis and Mytilene. Outside this organization Miletus, Samos and Aegina retained their own sanctuaries, and later arrivals, such as Athenians, were excluded. The Hellenion seems to have served as the core for the political organization of the community; probably the qualification for citizenship was descent from an original member. The city was apparently administered by its own officials, the *prostatai*, selected by the members of the Hellenion, *i.e.*, the citizens of Naukratis. The nationals of the states which remained outside the civic organization had either to seek entrance to it as individuals or remain content with the terms of the Egyptian charter—they were welcomed by Egypt as resident aliens, but were metics in the eyes of the Greek community of Naukratis. We cannot trace the growth of the city step by step, but it was complete by the time of Herodotus. Such an organization is neither in the pattern usually given a Greek state nor that of its colony—the replica in miniature of the mother-city. It might be explained by the particular circumstances of Naukratis in Egypt, but among the East Greeks and Ionians, in particular, there had been more experience of unity than in mainland Greece. Ionian cities, at the outset, seem to have been linked in an ethnic organization under a chief king. In the process of growth they had absorbed other Greeks and natives into their citizen bodies and had created a clearly marked cultural *koine*. The joint trading factory was a natural expression of such experience. Although there is not sufficient evidence to discuss the Black Sea emporia from this point of view, the evidence of joint trading by various Ionian states perhaps indicates that they initially had a similar organization.

[10] *Od.* 14.257ff. Diodorus (1.66.8) observed that Psammetichos (I) used to provide cargoes for the merchants, particularly for Phoenicians and Greeks. Whatever the precise value of this observation, the earliest Greek pottery found at Naukratis is dated in the last quarter of the seventh century, and there is little Egyptian material found in Greece to be placed before 600 (Pendlebury, *Aegyptiaca* 19 and *passim*; *Perachora* I, 142–43, 76–77, 118–19). A subgeometric sherd is reported to have been found in Memphis (Ch. Clairmont, *Berytus* 11 [1955], p. 100, No. 8, pl. XX, 6), but the remaining Greek pottery from there is after 550. Probably this sherd is Cycladic and another example of the islanders' activity in the Near East in the ninth and eighth centuries; above, pp. 61–62.

In the trade which was established in these Ionian areas, however, each state by the energy of its own merchants worked out a little nexus of trade for itself, utilizing its own resources, those of the new region opened up and of other Greek states. Perhaps Chios furnishes the clearest example. The island had developed a specialized agriculture by the late eighth century, when it began to export wine locally to Old Smyrna. The foundation of Maroneia in Thrace added the vineyards of Ismaros, and, when the time was ripe, offered access to the Thraco-Macedonian silver mines. In the seventh century Chios also forged a link of trade across the Aegean with Aegina. Chios took advantage of the Egyptian trade to use the Thracian silver for the purchase of Egyptian grain and linen but at the same time sold its wine and oil to the Greek residents of Naukratis. As the trade with the Black Sea developed, Chiot traders participated in that also using their pottery, wine and manufactured goods in exchange for grain and fish. Thus Chiot prosperity rested on this intricate system of trade rather than on colonization *per se*. The same is evidently true of Phocaea. It served as a port for Lydia and acquired the metals of Spain by the exchange of various Greek and Italian goods picked up on long voyages. Similarly the trading of Miletus and Samos could be traced from local activity in the seventh century to a general participation in the key trading areas of the Mediterranean in the sixth. The volume of trade was in grain, oil, wine and fish for food, in pottery, of which the mass as well as the fine art products cannot be ignored, in metals and slaves, rather than in the luxury products of Greek, Egyptian or Syrian workshops.

In the course of the study it has been suggested that the economic growth of Ionia was marked by three main dividing lines: the first *ca.* 700, when Ionian trade and colonization began to break out of its local area; the second in the last quarter of the seventh century, when the great overseas expansion and long distance voyaging began in earnest; the third at the time of the Ionian Revolt, when the Ionian cities began to sink into a provincial status in the enlarged world of Classical Greece and the Persian Empire. The initial conquest of Ionia by Persia *ca.* 546–40 did retard the activity of certain states like Phocaea and Teos but stimulated others to greater activity like Miletus and Samos. It had the general effect of immediately turning Ionian trading to Italy and Thrace more intensively and of ultimately bringing Ionia and the Aegean into a closer relationship with Anatolia and the Near East.

By the first quarter of the seventh century the Ionian cities seem to have expanded to the limits of their local territory, to have solved the problems of adjustment with the natives and to have become urbanized. We know little of the major Ionian cities of this early period, but in general their horizon seems to have extended to the Cyclades and Rhodes and inland to Phrygia and Lydia. The delicate balance between food supply and population had been reached. The example of their Cycladic neighbors and the existing ties with the Aegean were sufficiently strong to suggest sea-faring as a solution to their growing difficulties, and soon after 700 the process of colonization in Thrace and the Propontis started. This was stimulated by the difficulties created by Cimmerian raids and Lydian razzias. All this activity is sufficient to explain the limited range of Ionian trading throughout the first half of the seventh century. The traders apparently ventured little beyond the west coast of Asia Minor from Rhodes to the Hellespont and across the Aegean to Delos.

Throughout most of the seventh century Lydia must have occupied the foreground of Ionian attention, partly as an enemy who raided their cities and destroyed their crops from time to time, but increasingly as a partner in economic relations. Gradually the intimate interconnection developed which resulted in the issuance of coinage as a medium for the exchange of goods and services. The stimulus of closer relations with the Aegean also contributed its share to this growing market. Ionians apparently began to participate in the trade with the North Syrian area after 650, as objects from the Samian Heraion, from Old Smyrna and elsewhere indicate. Lines of trade were forged across the Aegean to Corinth and Aegina as well as with the Cyclades and Rhodes. In general, however, this was the century of Corinth and Rhodes.

The great period of Ionian expansion opened in the last quarter of the seventh century, when Africa, Spain and the Black Sea were brought into its orbit. The way was prepared by long individual voyages such as that of Colaeus to Spain *ca.* 638. In each case there is evidence of some pre-colonization trade: in Spain, from Colaeus' own voyage and possibly the Jerez helmet; in southern France, from the seventh-century pottery found on the Riviera; in Egypt, at least of the activity of mercenaries and perhaps of sporadic traders; in the Black Sea, from the pottery found inland at Nemirov and perhaps in the name of Istrokles inscribed on the sherd from Old Smyrna. Migration to the colonies followed on these preliminary voyages, and Ionians also found a steady market for their services as mercenaries in Egypt, Babylonia and closer to home in Lydia.[11] The new factories and migration solved one Ionian economic problem, but they brought a social and political crisis to Ionia.

A new class grew in the society of the Ionian cities to carry on the extensive trade of the sixth century—sailors, merchants, shipowners, traders, the owners of small industrial establishments and of vineyards and olive groves. The time of its emergence was probably in the last quarter of the seventh century, when coinage came into general usage in the Lydian-Ionian area. Its leaven in the society of the cities began to work rapidly, as the record of tyrants, law-givers and stasis in Ionia of the sixth century indicates. This phenomenon in Ionia seems to have sprung from similar causes and to have run the same course as in the cities of the Aegean and mainland Greece, but that is another story.

[11] Parke, *Greek Mercenary Soldiers* 4–6.

Select Bibliography[1]

This is a list of the works most used; they are cited by author and short title or author and publication reference in the notes. The system of abbreviations used there is that suggested in "Notes for Contributors," *American Journal of Archaeology* 54 (1950) 268–72.

Åkerström, A. *Architektonische Terrakottaplatten in Stockholm. Skrifter utgivna av Svenska Institutet i Athen*, 1951, Series 1.

Akurgal, E. *Späthettitische Bildkunst.* Ankara, 1949.

— — "Bayrakli. Erster vorläufiger Bericht über die Ausgrabungen in Alt-Smyrna," *Zeitschrift der philologischen Fakultät Universität Ankara* 8 (1950) 52–97.

— — *Phrygische Kunst.* Ankara, 1955.

Albright, W. F. "Some Oriental Glosses on the Homeric Problem," *American Journal of Archaeology* 54 (1950) 162–76.

Anderson, J. K. "Excavation on the Kofina Ridge, Chios," *The Annual of the British School at Athens* 49 (1954) 123–82.

Bailey, B. L. "The Export of Attic Black-Figure Ware," *Journal of Hellenic Studies* 60 (1940) 60–70.

Bakalakis, G. "Νεάπολις, Χριστούπολις, Καβάλα," *Archaiologike Ephemeris*, 1936, 1–48.

— — "Ἐκ τοῦ Ἱεροῦ τῆς Παρθένου ἐν Νεαπόλι," *ibid.*, 1938, 106–54.

— — "Ἀνασκαφὴ ἐν Καλαμίτσᾳ Καβάλας," *Praktika tes en Athenais Archaiologikes Hetairias*, 1935, 29–42; *ibid.*, 1936, 74–81; *ibid.*, 1937, 59–67.

— — "Ἀνασκαφὴ ἐν Καβάλᾳ καὶ τοῖς πέριξ," *ibid.*, 1938, 75–102.

Barnett, R. D. "Explorations in Cilicia: The Greek Pottery," *Liverpool Annals of Archaeology and Anthropology* 26 (1939) 98–130.

— — "Early Greek and Oriental Ivories," *Journal of Hellenic Studies* 68 (1948) 1–25.

— — "The Excavations of the British Museum at Toprak Kale near Van," *Iraq* 12 (1950) 1–43.

Beazley, J. D. and Payne, H. "Attic Black-figured Fragments from Naukratis," *Journal of Hellenic Studies* 49 (1929) 253–72.

Beloch, K. J. *Griechische Geschichte.* Vols. I and II. 2ᵈ ed. Berlin, 1912–14.

Bengtson, H. "Φιλόξενος ὁ Μακεδών," *Philologus* 92 (1937) 126–55.

Bilabel, Fr. "Die ionische Kolonisation. Untersuchungen über die Gründungen der Ionien, deren staatliche und kultliche Organisation und Beziehungen zu den Mutterstädten," *Philologus Supplementband* 14 (1920) 1–260.

Bittel, K. *Grundzüge der vor- und frühgeschichte Kleinasiens.* 2ᵈ ed. Tübingen, 1950.

Blinkenberg, C. *Fibules grecques et orientales.* Copenhagen, 1926.

— — and Kinch, K. F. *Lindos*, Vol. I. Berlin, 1931.

Blümner, H. *Technologie und Terminologie der Gewerbe und Künste der Griechen und Römer.* Vols. I^2, II–IV. Berlin, 1879–1912.

Boehlau, J. *Aus ionischen und italischen Nekropolen.* Leipzig, 1898.

Bolkestein, H. "Zur Entstehung der 'ionischen' Phylen," *Klio* 13 (1913) 424–50.

[1] Unfortunately F. Cassola, *La Ionia nel mondo miceneo* (1957) and Michel B. Sakellariou, *La Migration Grecque en Ionie* (1958) coincided too closely in publication date with this study to be used.

Bosch-Gimpera, P. "The Phokaians in the Far West, An Historical Reconstruction," *Classical Quarterly* 38 (1944) 53–59.
Bossert, W. *Altanatolien*. Berlin, 1942.
Bowra, C. M. "Xenophanes, fragment 3," *Classical Quarterly* 35 (1941) 119–26.
Bradeen, D. W. "The Chalcidians in Thrace," *American Journal of Philology* 73 (1952) 356–80.
— — "The Lelantine War and Pheidon of Argos," *Transactions of the American Philological Association* 78 (1947) 223–41.
Brock, J. K. and Young, G. M. "Excavations in Siphnos," *The Annual of the British School at Athens* 44 (1949) 1–92.
Broughton, T. R. S. *Asia Minor. Economic Survey of Rome*, Vol. IV. Baltimore, 1938.
Burn, A. R. "The So-called Trade Leagues in Early Greek History and the Lelantine War," *Journal of Hellenic Studies* 49 (1929) 14–37.
— — "Dates in Early Greek History," *ibid.*, 55 (1935) 130–46.
Buschor, E. "Heraion von Samos. Frühe Bauten," *Athenische Mitteilungen* 55 (1930).
Busolt, G. *Griechische Geschichte*. 3 vols. Gotha, 1893–1904.
Butler, H. C. *Sardis*, Vol. I. Leiden, 1922.
Cambridge Ancient History. Edited by J. B. Bury, S. A. Cook, F. E. Adcock, M. P. Charlesworth. Vols. II and III. Cambridge, 1924, 1925.
Carpenter, R. *The Greeks in Spain*. New York, 1925.
— — "The Greek Penetration of the Black Sea," *American Journal of Archaeology* 52 (1948) 1–10.
Caspari (Cary), M. "The Ionian Confederacy," *Journal of Hellenic Studies* 35 (1915) 173–88.
— — "The Ionian Confederacy – Addendum," *ibid.*, 36 (1916) 102.
— — "The Greeks and Ancient Trade with the Atlantic," *ibid.*, 44 (1924) 166–79.
— — "The Sources of Silver for the Greek World," *Mélanges Glotz*, Vol. I. Paris, 1928.
— — *The Geographic Background of Greek and Roman History*. Oxford, 1949.
Casson, S. *Macedonia, Thrace and Illyria*. Oxford, 1926.
Chamoux, F. *Cyrène sous la monarchie des Battiades*. Paris, 1953.
Clairmont, Ch. "Greek Pottery from the Near East," *Berytus* 11 (1955) 85–141.
Cook, J. M. "The Palai-Names," *Historia* 4 (1955) 39–45.
Cook, R. M. "Fikellura Pottery," *The Annual of the British School at Athens* 34 (1933–34) 1–98.
— — "Amasis and the Greeks in Egypt," *Journal of Hellenic Studies* 57 (1937) 227–37.
— — "Ionia and Greece in the 8th and 7th Centuries B.C.," *ibid.*, 66 (1946) 67–98.
— — "The Distribution of Chiot Pottery," *The Annual of the British School at Athens* 44 (1949) 154–61.
— — "A List of Clazomenian Pottery," *ibid.*, 47 (1952) 123–52.
— — and Woodhead, A. G. "Painted Inscriptions on Chiot Pottery," *ibid.*, 47 (1952) 159–70.
Davies, O. "Ancient Mines in Southern Macedonia," *Journal of the Royal Anthropological Institute* 62 (1933) 145–62.
— — "Bronze Age Mining Round the Aegean," *Nature* 130 (1932) 985–87.
Davison, J. A. "The First Greek Triremes," *Classical Quarterly* 41 (1947) 18–24.
Délos, Vol. X. *Les vases de l'Héraion*. By C. Dugas. Paris, 1928.
Délos, *Vol. XV*. *Les vases préhelleniques et géometriques*. By C. Dugas and C. Rhomaios. Paris, 1934.
Délos, Vol. XVII. *Les vases orientalisants de style non Mélien*. By C. Dugas. Paris, 1935.
Démargne, P. *La Crète dédalique*. Paris, 1947.
Desborough, V. *Protogeometric Pottery*. Oxford, 1952.
Dragendorff, H. *Thera*, Vol. II. Berlin, 1903.
Dressel, H. and Regling, K. "Zwei ägyptische Funde altgriechischer Silbermünzen," *Zeitschrift für Numismatik* 37 (1927) 1–138.
Dunbabin, T. J. *The Western Greeks*. Oxford, 1948.
Dunham, A. G. *History of Miletus*. London, 1915.
Edgar, C. "The Inscribed and Painted Pottery (Naukratis)," *The Annual of the British School at Athens* 5 (1898) 57 ff.
Eilmann, R. "Frühe griechische Keramik im samischen Heraion," *Athenische Mitteilungen* 58 (1933) 47–145.
Finkelstein (Finley), M. I. "Ἔμπορος, ναύκλαρος and κάπηλος," *Classical Philology* 30 (1935) 320–36.
— — *The World of Odysseus*. New York, 1951.
Forbes, R. J. *Metallurgy in Antiquity*. Leiden, 1950.
Forrer, E. "Eine unbekannte griechische Kolonie des sechsten Jahrhunderts v. Chr. in Phönikien," *Bericht über den VI Internationalen Kongress für Archäologie* 360–65. Berlin, 1940.
Garcia y Bellido, A. *Hispania Graeca*. 2 vols. Barcelona, 1948.
Gardner, P. "The Financial History of Ancient Chios," *Journal of Hellenic Studies* 40 (1920) 160–73.
Garstang, J. *Prehistoric Mersin, Yümcik Tepe in Southern Turkey*. Oxford, 1952.
Georgiades, A. "Antike Minenwerke in Macedonia und Epirus," *Archaiologike Ephemeris*, 1915, 88–93.
von Gerkan, A. "Zur Lage des archaischen Milet," *Bericht über den VI Internationalen Kongress für Archäologie* 323–25. Berlin, 1940.

Gjerstad, E. "Studies in Archaic Greek Chronology, I. Naukratis," *Liverpool Annals of Archaeology and Anthropology* 21 (1934) 67–84.
— — "II. Ephesus," *ibid.*, 24 (1937) 15–34.
— — *The Swedish Cyprus Expedition*, Vol. IV. Lund, 1948.
Glotz, G. *Ancient Greece at Work*. New York, 1926.
— — and Cohen, R. *Histoire grecque*. Vol. I. Paris, 1948.
Gowland, W. "Silver in Roman and Earlier Times: I. Prehistoric and Proto-Historic Times," *Archaeologica* 69 (1918) 121–60.
Gray, D. H. F. "Metal-Working in Homer," *Journal of Hellenic Studies* 74 (1954) 1–15.
Hanfmann, G. M. A. "Horsemen from Sardis," *American Journal of Archaeology* 49 (1945) 570–81.
— — "Archaeology in Homeric Asia Minor," *ibid.*, 52 (1948) 135–55.
— — "Ionia, Leader or Follower?," *Harvard Studies in Classical Philology* 61 (1953) 1–37.
— — "The Prehistoric Pottery from Sardis," *Studies Presented to D. M. Robinson*, Vol. I 160ff. St. Louis, 1953.
— — "On Some Eastern Greek Wares Found at Tarsus," *The Aegean and the Near East* (ed. S. Weinberg) 165–84.
Hasebroek, J. *Staat und Handel im Alten Griechenland*. Tübingen ,1928.
— — *Griechische Wirtschafts- und Gesellschafts-Geschichte bis zur Perserzeit*. Tübingen, 1931.
— — *Trade and Politics in Ancient Greece*. Translated by L. M. Fraser and D. C. MacGregor. London, 1933.
Hasluck, F. W. *Cyzicus*. London, 1910.
Haspels, C. H. Émilie. *La Cité de Midas, Céramique et Trouvailles diverses. Phrygie*, Vol. III. Paris, 1953.
Head, B. *Historia Numorum*. 2d ed. Oxford, 1911.
Heichelheim, F. M. *Wirtschaftsgeschichte des Altertums*, Vol. I. Leiden, 1938.
Hogarth, D. G. *Ionia and the East*. Oxford, 1909.
— — *Excavations at Ephesus, The Archaic Artemisia*. London, 1908.
— — "Naukratis, 1903," *Journal of Hellenic Studies* 25 (1905) 105–36.
Holland, L. B. "Colophon," *Hesperia* 13 (1944) 91–171.
Hunt, D. W. S. "An Archaeological Survey of the Classical Antiquities of Chios, 1938," *The Annual of the British School at Athens* 41 (1940–45) 29–52.
— — "Feudal Survivals in Ionia," *Journal of Hellenic Studies* 67 (1947) 68–76.
Jacobsthal, P. "The Date of the Ephesian Foundation-Deposit," *Journal of Hellenic Studies* 71 (1951) 85–95.
Jacoby, F. *Die Fragmente der griechischen Historiker*. Oxford, 1923–57.
— — "The Date of Archilochos," *Classical Quarterly* 35 (1941) 97–109.
Johansen, K. F. *Les vases Sicyoniennes*. Copenhagen, 1923.
Judeich, W. "Zur ionischen Wanderung," *Rheinisches Museum* 82 (1933) 307–14.
Karo, G. "Orient und Hellas in archaischer Zeit," *Athenische Mitteilungen* 45 (1920) 106–56.
Keil, J. "Forschungen in der Erythrai I," *Jahreshefte des österreichischen archäologischen Instituts* 13 (1910) *Beiblatt* 5–74.
— — "12 vorl. Bericht über die Ausgrabungen in Ephesos," *ibid.*, 23 (1926) *Beiblatt* 247–56.
Kinch, K. F. *Fouilles de Vroulia*. Copenhagen, 1914.
Kirk, G. S. "Ships on Geometric Vases," *The Annual of the British School at Athens* 44 (1949) 93–153.
Körte, G. and A. "Gordion," *Archäologisches Jahrbuch, Ergänzungsheft* 5, 1904.
Köster, A. "Studien zur Geschichte des antiken Seewesens," *Klio, Beiheft* 32 (1934).
Kourouniotes, K. "Ἀνασκαφαὶ καὶ ἔρευναι ἐν Χίῳ," *Deltion* 1 (1915) 64–93; *ibid.*, 2 (1916) 190–215.
Kunze, E. "Ionische Kleinmeister," *Athenische Mitteilungen* 59 (1934) 81–122.
— — *Kretische Bronzereliefs*. Stuttgart, 1931.
— — "Orientalische Schnitzereien aus Kreta," *Athenische Mitteilungen* 60–61 (1935–36) 218–33.
Lamb, W. "Antissa," *The Annual of the British School at Athens* 32 (1932) 41–67.
— — "Excavations at Kato Phana in Chios," *ibid.*, 35 (1934–35) 138–64.
Lambrino, M. *Les vases archaiques d'Histria*. Bucarest, 1938.
Lane, E. A. "Lakonian Vase Painting," *The Annual of the British School at Athens* 34 (1933–34) 99–189.
Larisa am Hermos. Die Ergebnisse der Ausgrabungen 1902–34. 3 vols. Stockholm, 1940–42.
Leaf, W. "The Commerce of Sinope," *Journal of Hellenic Studies* 36 (1916) 1–15.
— — *Strabo on the Troad*. Cambridge, 1923.
Lehmann, K. "Samothrace: Third Preliminary Report," *Hesperia* 19 (1950) 1–20.
— — "Samothrace: Fifth Preliminary Report," *ibid.*, 21 (1952) 19–43.
Lenschau, T. "Zur Geschichte Ioniens," *Klio* 13 (1913) 175–83.
— — "Die Gründung Ioniens und der Bund am Panionion," *Klio* 36 (1944) 201–37.
Lorimer, H. L. "The Hoplite Phalanx with Special Reference to the Poems of Archilochus and Tyrtaeus," *The Annual of the British School at Athens* 42 (1947) 76–138.
— — *Homer and the Monuments*. London, 1950.

Luckenbill, D. D. *Ancient Records of Assyria and Babylonia.* 2 vols. Chicago, 1927.

Macridy-Bey, Th. "Une citadelle archaique du Pont," *Mitteilungen der vorderasiatischen Gesellschaft* 12 (1907) 167–75.

Magie, D. *Roman Rule in Asia Minor.* 2 vols. Princeton, 1950.

Mallet, G. "Les Premiers établissements des Grecs en Egypte," *Memoirs de la Mission archéologique française au Caire* 12 (1897), 1, 277–364.

Mazzarino, Santo. "Per la Storia di Lesbo nel VI° Secolo a. C.," *Athenaeum* 21 (1943) 38–78.

— — *Fra Oriente e Occidente.* Florence, 1947.

Mellink, M. "Karatepe," *Bibliotheca Orientalis* 7 (1950) 141–50.

— — "Archaeology in Asia Minor," *American Journal of Archaeology* 59 (1955) 231–40 (and annual reports).

Meritt, B., Wade-Gery, H. T. and MacGregor, M. *The Tribute Lists*, Vol. I. Cambridge, Mass., 1936.

Milne, J. G. "Trade Between Greece and Egypt Before Alexander the Great," *Journal of Egyptian Archaeology* 25 (1939) 177–83.

— — "The Economic Policy of Solon," *Hesperia* 14 (1945) 230–45.

— — "Herodotus 1.94, νόμισμα," *Classical Review* 73 (1949) 85–87.

Minns, E. *Scythians and Greeks in South Russia.* Cambridge, 1913.

Miltner, F. and H. "Forschungen in Alt-Smyrna," *Jahreshefte des österreichischen archäologischen Instituts* 27 (1931) *Beiblatt* 125–88.

Müller, C. *Geographi Graeci Minores*, Vol. I. Paris, 1855.

Munro, J. A. R. "Pelasgians and Ionians," *Journal of Hellenic Studies* 54 (1934) 109–28.

Myres, J. L. "On the List of Thalassocracies in Eusebius," *Journal of Hellenic Studies* 26 (1906) 84–130; *ibid.*, 27 (1907) 123–30.

Naster, P. *L'Asie Mineure et l'Assyrie aux VIIIe et VIIe siècles av. J. C.* Louvain, 1938.

Nilsson, M. P. *Cults, Myths, Oracles and Politics in Ancient Greece. Skrifter utgivna av Svenska Institutet i Athen*, 1951, Series 2, 1–180.

— — "Political Propaganda in Sixth Century Athens," *Studies Presented to D. M. Robinson*, Vol II 743–48. St. Louis, 1953.

Noe, S. "A Bibliography of Greek Coin Hoards," *Numismatic Notes and Monographs* 78 (1937).

Ohly, D. "Frühe Ton-Figurigen aus dem Heraion von Samos, I," *Athenische Mitteilungen* 65 (1940) 57–102.

Poulsen, F. *Der Orient und die frühgriechische Kunst.* Leipzig, 1912.

Pauly, A. F.; Wissowa, G; Kroll, W. *Real-Encyclopädie der classischen Altertumswissenschaft.* Stuttgart, in progress. Articles: Chersonesos, Erythrai, Kelenderis, Kimmerier, Lydia, Myos, Nagidos, Naukratis, Nymphaion, Olbia, Pantikapaion, Phanagoreia, Phaselis, Phokaia, Soloi, Teos, Theodosia.

Payne, H. *Necrocorinthia.* Oxford, 1931.

— — *Perachora*, Vol I. Oxford, 1940.

Pendlebury, J. D. S. *Aegyptiaca.* Cambridge, 1930.

Petrie, W. M. F. and Gardner, E. A. *Naukratis.* 2 vols. London, 1886–88.

Pfuhl, E. "Der archaische Friedhof am Stadtberge von Thera," *Athenische Mitteilungen* 28 (1903) 1–288.

Price, E. "Pottery from Naukratis," *Journal of Hellenic Studies* 44 (1924) 180–222.

Prinze, H. "Funde aus Naukratis," *Klio, Beiheft* 7 (1908).

Przeworski, S. *Die Metallindustrie Anatoliens in der Zeit von 1500–700 vor Chr. Rohstoffe, Technik, Produktion. Internationales Archiv für Ethnographie XXXVI Supplement.* Leiden, 1939.

Radet, G. *La Lydie et la monde grecque.* Paris, 1893.

Reichel, W. *Griechische Goldrelief.* Berlin, 1942.

Richardson, H. C. "Iron, Prehistoric and Ancient," *American Journal of Archaeology* 38 (1934) 555–83.

Robertson M. "The Excavation at Al Mina, Suedia, IV. The Early Greek Vases," *Journal of Hellenic Studies* 60 (1940), 2–21.

Robinson, E. S. G. "Coins from the Ephesian Artemision Reconsidered," *Journal of Hellenic Studies* 71 (1951) 156–67.

Roebuck, C. "The Grain Trade Between Greece and Egypt," *Classical Philology* 45 (1950) 236–47.

— — "The Organization of Naukratis," *ibid.*, 46 (1951) 212–20.

— — "The Economic Development of Ionia," *ibid.*, 48 (1953) 9–16.

— — "The Early Ionian League," *ibid.*, 50 (1955) 26–40.

Röhlig, J. *Der Handel von Milet.* Hamburg, 1933.

Rostovtzeff, M. *Iranians and Greeks in South Russia.* Oxford, 1922.

— — *Skythen und der Bosporus.* Berlin, 1931.

Rumpf, A. "Zu den klazomenischen Denkmälern," *Jahrbuch des deutschen archäologischen Instituts* 48 (1933) 55–83.

— — "Lydische Salbgefäße," *Athenische Mitteilungen* 45 (1920) 163–70.

Schefold, K. "Knidische Vasen und Verwandtes," *Jahrbuch des deutschen archäologischen Instituts* 57 (1942) 124–42.

— — "Die Tonfriese von Pazarli," *Istanbuler Forschungen* 17 (1950) 137–48.

Schmidt, H. *Heinrich Schliemann's Sammlung trojanischer Altertümer.* Berlin, 1902.
Schulten, A. *Tartessos.* 2d ed. Hamburg, 1950.
Schwabacher, W. "Geldumlauf und Münzprägung in Syrien im vi. und v. Jahrhundert v. Chr.," *Skrifter utgivna av Svenska Institutet i Rom* 15 (1950) 139–49.
Short, G. A. "The Siting of Greek Colonies on the Black Sea Coast of Bulgaria and Romania," *Liverpool Annals of Archaeology and Anthropology* 24 (1937) 141–55.
Slavin, O. *Olbia.* Kiev, 1938.
Smith, E. M. *Naukratis.* Dissertation. Bryn Mawr, Pa., 1924.
Smith, H. R. W. "The Hearst Hydria," *University of California Publications in Classical Archaeology* 1 (1944) 240–90.
Smith, S. "The Greek Trade at Al Mina," *Antiquaries Journal* 22 (1942) 87–112.
von Stern, E. "Die griechische Kolonisation am Nordgestade des Schwarzen Meeres," *Klio* 9 (1909) 139–52.
—— "Die politische und soziale Struktur der Griechencolonien am Nordufer des Schwarzmeergebietes," *Hermes* 50 (1915) 161–224.
Sutherland, C. H. V. "Overstrikes and Hoards," *Numismatic Chronicle* 2 (1942) 1–18.
—— "Corn and Coin: A Note on Greek Commercial Monopolies," *American Journal of Philology* 64 (1943) 140 ff.
Technau, W. "Griechische Keramik im samischen Heraion," *Athenische Mitteilungen* 54 (1929) 6–64.
Tioumeneff, A. "Études de la Chersonèse," *Vestnik Drevnei Istorii,* 1938, 2, 245–75 (in Russian).
Ure, P. N. *The Origin of Tyranny.* Cambridge, 1922.
Wade-Gery, H. T. "Miltiades," *Journal of Hellenic Studies* 71 (1951) 212–21.
—— *The Poet of the Iliad.* Cambridge, 1952.
Wainwright, G. A. "The Coming of Iron," *Antiquity* 10 (1936) 5–24.
Weber, G. "Zur Topographie der ionischen Küste," *Athenische Mitteilungen* 29 (1904) 222–36.
Weinberg, Saul S. (ed.). *The Aegean and the Near East. Studies Presented to Hetty Goldman.* Locust Valley, New York, 1956.
Wiegand, T. and Schrader, H. *Priene.* Berlin, 1904.
Wiegand, T. (ed.). *Milet. Ergebnisse der Ausgrabungen und Untersuchungen seit dem Jahre 1899.* Berlin, 1906–36.
von Wilamowitz-Moellendorff, U. "Über die ionische Wanderung," *Kleineschriften* V, 1, 152 ff. (*SB: Berlin,* 1906, 59–79).
—— "Panionion," *Kleineschriften* V, 1, 128 ff. (*SB:Berlin,* 1906, 38–57).
Will, E. *Korinthiaka.* Paris, 1955.
Woolley, C. "Excavations at Al Mina, Suedia, I," *Journal of Hellenic Studies* 58 (1938) 1–30; "II" 133–70.
Young, R. "Gordion: Preliminary Report, 1953," *American Journal of Archaeology* 59 (1955) 1–18; "1954" *ibid.,* 60 (1956) 249–66; see also the preliminary reports in *University of Pennsylvania Museum Bulletin* 16 (1951), 1, 3 ff.; 17 (1953), 4, 3–39.

Index